The Larousse

Spiders

Dick Jones

Larousse and Co. Inc.
New York

Acknowledgements

I should like to express my thanks to Kodak Ltd, London for the award of a Photographic Bursary which helped to finance the earlier years of the photography for this guide; and also to Pentax UK Ltd for their generosity in supplying special equipment used for some of the photographs.

To the Forestry Commission, Ministry of Defence, Nature Conservancy Council, David Billet of the Hants and Isle of Wight Naturalists' Trust and the wardens of Kenfig Local Nature Reserve, Mid-Glamorgan (Steve Moon and Wilf Nelson) for permission to look for spiders on their land, I extend many thanks.

I especially thank fellow members of the British Arachnological Society who very kindly helped me in supplying locations, identifications, or sent rare spiders which had eluded me: Dr J.A.L. Cooke, J. Crocker, Dr J. Dalingwater, Dr E. Duffey, M. Fulton, T. Kronestedt, G. H. Locket, Dr P. Merrett, G. O'Neill, J. Parker, and A. Thornhill. Through the kindness of F. Wanless and P. Hillyard of the British Museum (Natural History) I had access to specimens and literature in the Arachnida section; Drs P. van Helsdingen, R. Bosmans and R. Jocqué very kindly supplied me with many helpful details of spiders in Holland and Belgium, and my thanks are due to Professor J. Martens and J. H. P. Sankey for their help concerning the harvestmen.

Special thanks go to Ray and Jill Fry for reading the preliminary drafts and making many useful suggestions, and to John and Frances Murphy for their help at every stage of the book, particularly in reading the later drafts and supplying numerous locations, identifications, and literature, and in discussions on all the aspects of arachnid behaviour. To Frances Murphy, in particular, for allowing me to use her photographs of *Euscorpius flavicaudis*, *Philodromus rufus*, *Thanatus formicinus*, and *Tetragnatha striata*, I offer many thanks.

Dick Jones, Hampshire 1983

First published in Great Britain by Newnes Books,
a Division of The Hamlyn Publishing Group Limited,
84-88, The Centre, Feltham, Middlesex, England

Published in the United States by
Larousse & Co., Inc.
572 Fifth Avenue
New York, N.Y. 10036

ISBN 0-88332-324-9
Library of Congress Catalog No. 83-81216

First published 1983

Printed in Spain
by Artes Gráficas Toledo, S.A.

D.L.: TO.1146-1983

Contents

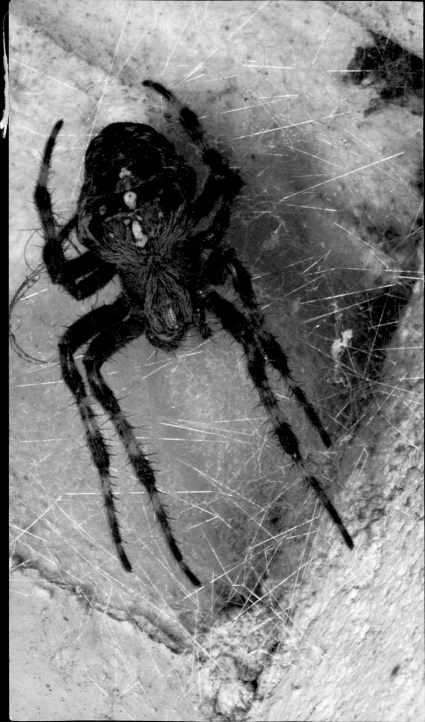

Spiders and their allies

In the middle of the eighteenth century, Clerck and Linnaeus used a binomial system to describe living organisms, giving each two names. The first name indicates the genus, the second the species. Each species consists of a group of living organisms with slight individual differences but many features in common and in a combination which is not found in any other species. The members of the species are capable of interbreeding and producing offspring which have the same features and capabilities. When this system was first used, Latin was the lingua franca among scientists, and it was in Latin that each species was described and named. Once established, the species name becomes an international shorthand way of describing the species, so that *Araneus diadematus* will mean the same spider to arachnologists all over the world, and especially to those in the northern hemisphere who will be familiar with it. This common spider might otherwise be known in France as *Epeire diadème, Epeire des jardins*, or *Araignée porte-croix*; in Germany as *die Kreuzspinne*, and in Britain as the cross spider or garden spider. After the species' name it is customary to include the name of the first worker to describe the species, viz. *Araneus diadematus* Clerck. Where the genus or species has been given a new name to conform with later ideas of taxonomy, the author's name is placed in brackets.

The species are grouped into a genus (plural genera) to include a number of species with some features in common; the genera are collected into families or subfamilies. The family names are derived from those of the genera and are suffixed –idae; subfamilies –inae. These are contained in orders which together make up a class; the classes form a phylum, and the phyla constitute a kingdom. Systematics are a rather subjective exercise and, at each stage of classification, there will always be some organisms which do not fit easily into any particular scheme. The long evolution of spiders, and the scarcity of fossil remains, make them a difficult group to classify, and there have been no less than eighteen different systems proposed this century. It would be preferable to list the families in ascending order of development but different orders are used by workers in different countries. The one used here is based on that given in *British Spiders* by G. H. Locket, A. F. Millidge, and P. Merrett. The most recent revisions have been adopted as detailed on page 40. Therefore, you will find differences from the classification used in *British Spiders*.

For the moment, spiders belong to the Animal kingdom, subkingdom Metazoa, class Arachnida.

The class Arachnida

Eighty per cent of all the animals described so far belong to the phylum Arthropoda – one-and-a-quarter million species. An arthropod has an external skeleton (exoskeleton) and three or more pairs of tubular legs which possess a number of joints. Indeed, the word Arthropoda is derived from the Greek and means 'jointed foot'. The earliest known arthropod was the trilobite, an extinct marine animal which was at its peak when the first arachnid, an ancestor of the scorpion, first left its footprints on the land about 500 million years ago. Some 200 million years later the insects began to make their impact. Today, there are more than a million species of insects, with many more to be described. The arachnids have had a more conservative evolutionary trend and now number about 50 000 species.

Many insects are vegetarian but most arachnids are predatory, feeding mainly on insects. Unlike insects, arachnids have four pairs of walking legs, do not possess antennae or wings, and have simple, rather than compound eyes. The body of an arachnid is divided into two clear regions, except in the mites and harvestmen, where it appears to be in one piece. The front or anterior section is the prosoma to which the fours pairs of legs, the chelicerae, and the pedipalps are attached. The number of eyes in arachnids varies from none to as many as twelve in some scorpions, but arachnid sight is poor and most of them are nocturnal. Many have long sensory hairs (setae) on their limbs with which to detect prey, and most have pincer-like devices on their pedipalps or chelicerae. Pedipalps are analogous to human hands, while the chelicerae have the function of jaws or teeth. The abdomen, which is segmented in most orders of arachnids, but not in the spiders or mites and only very weakly in the harvestmen, is known as the opisthosoma. The reproductive organs, in contrast to those of insects, are situated on the ventral side of the abdomen at the anterior end nearest the prosoma. The reproductive behaviour is bizarre in many groups with prolonged and complex courtship; care of the young is the rule.

In spiders, silk is produced from abdominal glands but in mites from the mouth region, and in pseudoscorpions from the chelicerae. Poison is produced by the spiders from the chelicerae, by scorpions from the terminal point of the tail or telson, and by the pseudoscorpions from the pincers of the pedipalp. The poison is used to subdue prey or to deter predators from attacking them. None of the other arachnid orders produces either silk or poison.

Apart from some Acari (mites) and the water spider (*Argyroneta aquatica*), most arachnids are terrestrial, some orders being typical animals of hot, dry places. However, the ancestors of the scorpions, the extinct sea scorpions (Eurypterida) and *Limulus*, the horseshoe crab (which is sometimes grouped with the arachnids and bears a superficial resemblance to the fossil trilobites) are marine animals.

The sea scorpions, at 3 metres long, were the largest arthropods ever known. The Pycnogonida, or sea spiders are odd creatures with four pairs of legs attached to a thin, tubular trunk; the abdomen is vestigial. It is now considered that they are not closely related to the arachnids.

There are eleven orders of arachnids, of which five have representatives within northern Europe. The tropics are the home of the remaining orders. Solifugae or wind scorpions (also known as sun spiders). These have a segmented abdomen without a telson, enormous chelicerae, and use their front legs and long, heavy palps to probe the ground, while using three pairs of legs for running 'like the wind'. They have two median eyes and will feed on small lizards as well as on insects. The orders Uropygi, Palpigradi, and Schizomida are rather similar in general form but members of these groups have tails or telsons of varying length. These three orders total less than 200 species.

Tailless whip scorpions, or Amblypygi, are flattened animals with long legs and powerful, toothed pedipalps. The first pair of legs are antennae-like in form. About fifty species have been described. The order Ricinulei comprises twenty-five species. They measure up to 15 millimetres long, without eyes, and with a hood covering the mouth parts. The males have copulatory organs on the extremities of the third pair of legs, and the young have only three pairs of legs. The first described species were fossil forms and were thought originally to be primitive beetles.

The remaining orders, scorpions, pseudoscorpions, mites and ticks, spiders, and harvestmen are found within the limits of northern Europe.

Scorpions

Scorpions are quite large animals ranging in size from 40 to 170 millimetres. The long telson has a 'sting' at its extremity. They do not possess silk glands. Each of them has a pair of median eyes set in the middle of the head or carapace. Two rows of lateral eyes are present in many species, and these vary from two to five set in a line at the sides of the head. Their sight is poor and most are nocturnal spending the day under stones. Although scorpions are typical of hot, dry climates, *Euscorpius flavicaudis* (Degeer) has been found in Kent, England for over 100 years. Its body is dark brown to black while the legs and sting are yellow-brown. It occurs at Sheerness and has been seen in daylight, possibly in response to the climate which is cooler than it experiences in the Mediterranean region which is its home. It occurs sporadically in central France but this is probably the most northerly record. It is about 40 millimetres long but unaggressive and its poison has no effect on humans.

Scorpion courtship consists of a pas de deux by the two scorpions which lasts for hours or even days. The male produces a spermato-

Euscorpius flavicaudis c. 40 mm including telson

phore which is a complex structure that holds the sperm and releases it when the spermatophore becomes attached to the female's genital operculum. Once the sperm are transferred to the female, the two animals part. The fertilized eggs develop within the female and live young are born which climb on to their mother's abdomen and are carried about until they have their first moult and disperse.

Pseudoscorpions

The pseudoscorpions are a small group, with just twenty-five species occurring in Britain. Few are larger than 5 millimetres and the characters used for determining the species are not visible in the field. A pseudoscorpion has a segmented abdomen, four pairs of short, pale legs, and long pedipalps with terminal pincers that are held out in front as it walks. This makes them resemble slightly their larger relatives, the scorpions. The animal has one or two pairs of eyes on the sides of the carapace but these are little more than silvery patches below the surface of the head, and there is no lens, as such. The body and appendages are sparsely covered with long tactile setae with which they detect prey and avoid predators. They are found in moss, leaf litter, and the top layers of the soil, as well as under stones.

Prey is caught in the pincer and injected with poison prior to eating. The small chelicerae produce silk which is used for making chambers for moulting, overwintering, and brooding the young. The courtship is similar to that of the scorpions, the pair hold each other by the pedipalps and walk to and fro. The male produces a spermatophore on the substrate and guides the female over it. The eggs remain in a small sac held below the abdomen of the female. The larvae remain in the sac to be nourished by a milk-like secretion from the mother's ovaries. When they leave the sac, the young attach themselves to the sides of the mother's abdomen.

Some species disperse by clinging to the legs of passing flies and other animals; they may be carried for considerable distances without damaging the host, unlike the mites. This is known as phoresy. In terms of numbers found, they are the fourth largest arachnid group of the region, but you will come across far fewer pseudoscorpions, than harvestmen and spiders. Two species, *Chelifer cancroides* (Linnaeus) and *Cheiridium museorum* (Leach), occur in houses. The first is one of the larger species (at 4 millimetres) while the second is one of the smaller and is only 1·3 millimetres long. Both feed on unwelcome guests like carpet beetle larvae, book lice, and bed bugs. *Neobisium muscorum* (Leach) is fairly common in moss and litter; the pedipalps are reddish brown. *Chthonius tenuis* L. Koch is distinguished by the dark palpal 'hand' – it occurs in much the same place as *N. muscorum*.

Mites and ticks

The Acari are the largest group found in the region but nearly all of them are very small and impossible to identify in the field except to

Neobisium muscorum c. 2·5 mm

Chthonius tenuis 1·5–2 mm

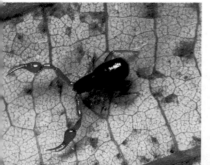

Ixodes ricinus 1–11 mm depending on feeding

Trombidium holosericeum c. 4 mm

suborder level. Unlike the other arachnids, they have numerous members which are parasitic on plants and animals, and a few which are exclusively aquatic. Many are very damaging to humans and their activities. The mites cause damage to crops and stored produce. The ticks are blood-suckers which can spread diseases, and are pests of livestock. *Ixodes ricinus*, the castor bean tick, is damaging to cattle and sheep, while another acarine causes Isle of Wight disease in bees by infesting their tracheal tubes. The larvae of *Ixodes* and other hard ticks have only three pairs of legs.

The harvest mite, *Trombicula autumnalis*, can reach a size of 4 millimetres but, in its smaller stages, it can be one of the hazards facing the arachnologist. In summer and autumn this mite is abundant in low vegetation and can produce unpleasant itches if it becomes trapped by tight clothing. Velvet or trombidiform mites can grow to a similar size but they are predatory on small insects and other mites. Oribatid mites are small, almost spherical acari which live in moss and leaf litter, feeding on fungal hyphae. Some have a habit of heaping debris on top of themselves. Some mites indulge in phoresy, like the pseudoscorpions, and some at least may feed from their host while being transported.

Spiders

Unlike the prosoma of other arachnids, that of a spider is not broadly joined to the opisthosoma but is connected by a narrow pedicel. In most species there are eight eyes in two or three rows on the front of the prosoma. Some species have six eyes while others may have four, two, or none at all. The pedipalps or palps are never armed with pincers, although a small claw is frequently present. The palps of the males are enlarged into copulatory organs, and the courtship is extremely varied, even among the species within a small region such as Europe. The legs vary greatly in the individual lengths on the spider and among the spiders of different families, but the final segment is never divided further except in the Pholcidae (page 68).

The chelicerae have ducts from a poison gland opening near the extremity but, of the 50 000 described species, perhaps half-a-dozen are known to be poisonous to humans, and only one of these is described as aggressive.

They exhibit the greatest variety of shape, colour, and behaviour of all the arachnids. They all produce silk, but some are free-living hunters and only use their silk to construct retreats or cells in which they spend either night or day, or to make egg sacs. Silk is trailed after the animal and can be used as a safety line to drop out of sight of predators, or as a means of travel through the air or vegetation. Most spiders make webs which occur in a wide variety of designs and are used passively to catch the aerial plankton of insects. The silk sometimes takes part in the courtship and mating rituals, and it is used extensively as a protection for the eggs. Egg sacs are made from several varieties of silk and in many different shapes and colours. The young are tiny versions of their parents, rather plump little creatures with short legs. Most spiders are solitary, but a few species from diverse families are social, sharing webs and prey. They are all predatory and will eat one another; some will also scavenge. Spiders are very numerous and probably play a useful, but not vital, role in keeping insects in check.

In most cases the families are easy to distinguish in the field by the disposition and number of the eyes, the overall shape, length of legs, and form of the spinners. There are about 700 species in northern Europe, about half of which can be identified in the field with a lens. The small, black money spiders of the family Linyphiidae are numerous in species and sometimes individuals, but no attempt has been made to describe more than a few of them because they must be collected and examined using a microscope. Nevertheless, they are sometimes of greater interest than their larger relatives, and the heads of the males are produced into many varied and strange forms.

Harvestmen

The harvestmen or Opiliones are characterized by the small body, with prosoma and opisthosoma broadly united, and with two large eyes set on a tubercle. The legs are usually very long and thin, the second pair being longest and used to probe the ground ahead. Some species, which live in litter, have short legs and reduced eyes. Unlike other arachnids, there is no courtship and insemination is direct through the male's penis. The fertilized eggs are laid by means of an ovipositor, and abandoned, as in some insects. Twenty-seven species are found in northern Europe, most of which are identifiable in the field.

The anatomy of spiders

A spider's body is composed of two distinct sections: a **prosoma** (head) to which six pairs of limbs are attached; and the **opisthosoma**, where the characteristic organs of the order, the **spinners**, are situated. There is a narrow connecting tube, the **pedicel**, through which the main artery, the gut, and various nerves pass. The surface of the spider bearing the eyes and carapace etc is called **dorsal** while the other side where the sternum is visible is called **ventral**.

The prosoma, or **cephalothorax** is covered dorsally by a sclerotized plate called the **carapace**. The eyes are situated on the front margin or, more rarely, in the anterior half. The majority of the spiders in the region have eight eyes, but nine spiders occur which have six. The eyes are simple and usually have convex lenses; they are pearly (sometimes called nocturnal) or dark (diurnal). The disposition of the eyes and their formation into two or three rows are of great value in determining the families. The eyes are usually protected by a number of bristles in the **ocular region**. In many spiders the front portion of the carapace is raised from the posterior region and is called the **head**. The region behind and at the sides is known as the **thorax**. Immediately behind the head there is a depression or simply a dark mark, the **fovea**. This forms a rudimentary internal skeleton to which the muscles of the sucking stomach are attached. The region below the eyes, which is often very narrow, is the **clypeus**. The front aspect of the prosoma is known as the **facies**.

On the ventral side of the prosoma is the **sternum**, a broad plate with scalloped edges where the legs are inserted. On the anterior margin is a small plate,the **labium**, which may be fused to the sternum in a few families, but is usually hinged by a cuticular membrane. At the sides of the labium is a pair of **maxillae** or **endites**, furnished thickly with fine hairs on their inner sides and functioning as a filter for the mouth which lies beneath the labium. The maxillae are outgrowths of the basal segments of the **pedipalps** or **palps**. These limbs have six divisions: the first, basal, segment which forms the maxilla is the **coxa**; the following segments are **trochanter**, **femur**, **patella**, **tibia**, and **tarsus**. The tarsus is sometimes provided with a small claw. In adult male spiders, the palps are transformed into copulatory organs, a feature which is found in no other arthropods. The palpal organs are generally conspicuous and allow males and females to be distinguished with ease even in the smallest species. In the female, the palp is slender resembling a small leg.

In front of the mouth region lies a pair of **chelicerae**. Each is composed of two segments, a robust basal part surmounted by a movable tooth, known as the **fang**. The basal segment is provided with fixed teeth in many species. Within the basal segment of each chelicera and inside the head is a muscle-controlled sac which con-

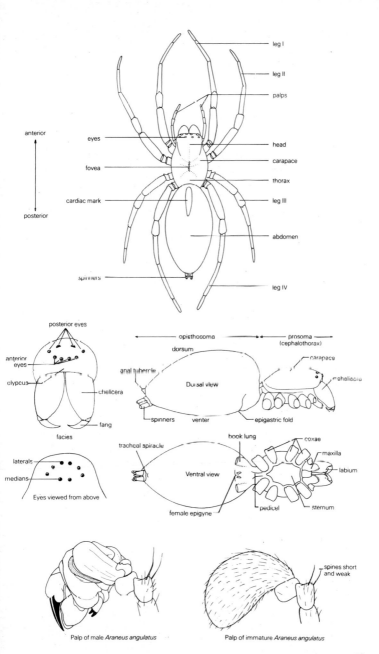

anterior

posterior

leg I

leg II

palps

eyes

head

fovea

carapace

thorax

cardiac mark

leg III

abdomen

spinners

leg IV

posterior eyes

anterior eyes

clypeus

chelicera

fang

facies

laterals

medians

Eyes viewed from above

opisthosoma

prosoma (cephalothorax)

dorsum

anal tubercle

carapace

chelicera

spinners   venter

epigastric fold

Dorsal view

tracheal spiracle

book lung

coxae

maxilla

labium

Ventral view

female epigyne

pedicel

sternum

Palp of male *Araneus angulatus*

spines short and weak

Palp of immature *Araneus angulatus*

13

tains poison. A duct leads from the poison gland to a small aperture near the tip of the fang, through which the poison is injected into the prey. Spiders which have cheliceral teeth use them to grind up their prey, making the remains totally unrecognizable. Those that lack such teeth, such as the crab spiders (Thomisidae), leave the empty carcasses of their prey in apparently perfect condition. Two spiders in the family Uloboridae are the only ones in the region which lack poison glands. Most spiders, however, are timid creatures, preferring to run or to sham death rather than fight a large opponent. Provided they are handled with consideration and care, spiders will never bite. In any case, the chelicerae of the vast majority found in the region are too small and weak to penetrate human skin. In warmer climates, however, there are a very few spiders whose poison is known to be dangerous to humans. Two spiders, *Herpyllus blackwalli* and *Leptorhoptrum robustum*, have been reported to bite people, although the latter linyphiid spider required provocation. Spiders are attuned to feeding on insects of various kinds, principally in response to their movements; these signals are lacking when they are handled so that human skin is merely a substrate for them.

The legs

By convention, the legs are numbered from the front of the animal as I, II, III, and IV. The first and fourth legs are usually longer than the others which are subequal (more or less equal) in length. The thomisids are distinctive in having legs I and II very long and robust, while III and IV are short and thin. *Episinus*, a theridiid spider, is notable in having legs I and IV of subequal lengths, while leg II is unusually short and barely longer than III.

Each leg is composed of seven segments. The most basal segment is the elbowed **coxa** (plural coxae) with a limited degree of movement. A short, ring-like segment follows, the **trochanter**, which precedes the largest segment of the leg, the **femur** (femora). This can articulate in the vertical plane and, to a limited extent, in the horizontal as well. The **patella** (-ae) is short and equipped with a vertical hinge which allows the following segments to move in the horizontal plane. The **tibia** (-ae) is a thinner member but usually it is nearly equal in

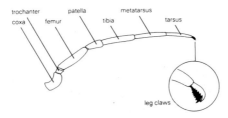

length to the femur. The **metatarsus** (-si) is shorter and thinner and is articulated with the final or apical segment, the **tarsus** (-si). This is the most delicate segment of the leg and is furnished at its extremity with two or three claws. The hunting spiders have two claws whereas the weavers are provided with a third, median claw. The claws can be moved by the action of muscles and are armed with small ventral teeth, like a comb.

The legs are usually armed with combinations of spines, bristles, and hairs. The word, armed, does not imply any offensive quality, and it is known that the majority of this 'armament' is of a sensory nature. The leg setae all have nerves attached (as indeed do all the setae on the spider's body), are sensitive to touch, and, in some instances, to chemical stimuli.

The setae may be of different types. **Spines** are the stoutest setae and arise from a prominence on the cuticle. In some spiders, araneids and oxyopids, for example, the spines are stiff and arise at right-angles from the surfaces of the legs. In the liocranids, the legs have ventral spines which are prone and occur in two rows. **Bristles** are smaller and thinner than spines and are often very short. In fact, there is no clear dividing line between the two terms, except where a differentiation needs to be made in a particular, single example. **Hairs** are much finer and softer, for example, the covering of the carapace in araneids and clubionids. In the Salticidae, many species have flattened, squamose hairs which have a finely structured surface, giving rise to iridescent reflections. The philodromids and some members of the Agelenidae have plumose hairs which are shaped like small feathers, with many distinct side branches, but these are only visible under the microscope.

Finer than any hair, and arising from a socket is the **trichobothrium**, a receptor sensitive to air currents and low-frequency air vibrations. These are usually too fine to be seen with a hand-lens, but they are of great value in separating the many species of money spiders (Linyphiidae) because they occur in different positions on the metatarsi of different genera.

Many of the hunting spiders have a dense 'brush' of short hairs on the metatarsi and tarsi of their legs. These fine hairs are split at their ends into many thousands of extensions. These **scopulae** allow the spiders to walk on smooth surfaces such as leaves, or even clean glass, provided there is a tiny film of water to give a capillary effect. In some species the scopulae cover the claws, although these are always present.

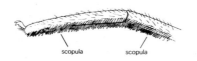

scopula   scopula

The opisthosoma (abdomen)

The abdomen is extremely varied in its shape, from being tubular in *Harpactea*, *Tibellus*, and *Tetragnatha* to spherical in many of the Theridiidae. In this family and others there are sometimes conical tubercles on the front, sides, or rear of the abdomen. In the majority of species, the abdomen is relatively soft and extensible; in the thomisids, for example, it is often wrinkled at the sides. The dorsal surface or dorsum frequently displays small pits which are the attachment points for the muscles within. The number and arrangement of these are diagnostic for some families or genera. In the mid-line anteriorly is a lanceolate mark which may be lighter or darker than the surroundings. Just below the cuticle at this point lies the heart and, in some species, the vessel can be seen to beat. In large spiders the rate is about thirty beats per minute but it can be more than 100 beats for small species. When the spider exerts itself, this rate can rise dramatically. The size of the **cardiac mark** is useful for distinguishing some species.

The pattern found on the abdomen of many spiders is either composed of coloured hairs or of pigmentation of the cuticle itself. In the first case, the pattern will be altered if the hairs are rubbed off, as is sometimes the case in old specimens. Such specimens are very difficult to identify in the field. Where the cuticle is coloured, the darker marks are usually found within the cuticle and the lighter parts of the pattern are below it and move in sympathy with the heart beat. It is this which gives the metallic appearance to tetragnathids and other spiders.

In the spiders of the Theridiidae and Araneidae, the dorsum is outlined with a dark band, or has a broad area with the characteristic colour and pattern of the species. Because of the leaf-life shape of this, it is known as the **folium**. In these families, and especially in the latter, there is considerable variation of colour in many species.

Unlike most other animals, spiders are often marked with transverse bars which are flexed forwards at their mid-point. These **chevrons** usually follow behind the cardiac mark. Only in the Oxyopidae do these chevrons run in the forward direction.

In the males of some species, and rarely in the females, the abdomen has one or more sclerotized plates, called scuta. Many male gnaphosids have a small dorsal scutum which covers the cardiac area; the male *Atypus* is similarly adorned. In the male of both species of *Phrurolithus* the entire dorsum is covered by scuta; in the theridiid spider, *Pholcomma*, the male has scuta on both the dorsal and ventral sides of the abdomen.

At the rear of the abdomen is the single excretory pore, the **anus**. In some species a small prominence, the **anal tubercle** is present. Below this, either on the ventral side of the abdomen or at the terminal point, are the **spinners**, sometimes called spinnerets. In the most primitive spiders known (*Liphistius*, which is found in the Far East), the spinners are found in the middle of the venter, and it is thought that they have migrated to a more terminal position in the more advanced species. Their primitive situation has given rise to the terminology: the most ventral pair are called anterior; while those in the most dorsal position are posterior. The smaller medians are often covered by the other two pairs. In the majority of spiders, the anterior and posterior spinners are of two segments, but this is difficult to discern except in the agelenids where several genera have long, clearly two-segmented posterior spinners. In the genus *Atypus*, the posterior spinners are extremely long and composed of three or even four segments. The spinners are supplied with muscles which give them some mobility but, in families like the Araneidae whose members spin the most 'designed' webs, the spinners are small, inconspicuous, and held tightly against the abdomen when not in use.

Behind the spinners, in the base of the abdomen, are the silk glands. Silk is produced as a liquid and stored within the glands. It is emitted through tiny **spigots** on the ends or ventral sides of the spinners, but quickly becomes solidified when stretched. Six different types of silk glands have been described, all of which are found in the orb weavers. Hunting spiders have four types of gland, two of which are responsible for the attachment discs and drag lines. An attachment disc is made on the substrate and, as the spider moves off, the drag line is extended from the spinners. This is the equivalent of a climber's safety rope and supports the spider if it needs to take evasive action and fall safely from a twig or even from its web. The third gland makes the silk used for wrapping prey, the outer wall of the egg sac, and, in males, the sperm web. The fourth gland produces the silk which forms the inner part of the sac. The orb weavers have two additional glands which produce the viscous liquid that coats the spirals, and the spiral thread itself.

In some families there is a small, probably vestigial, tubercle between the anterior spinners, called the **colulus**. In cribellate spiders,

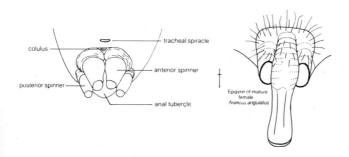

colulus

posterior spinner

tracheal spiracle

anterior spinner

anal tubercle

Epigyne of mature female
Araneus angulatus

the anterior spinners are separated, and this region has a broad flat plate, sometimes divided into two, or even four in one genus. This is the **cribellum**. The surface of the plate is densely covered with spigots. These cribellate spiders also have a row of small, curved bristles on the dorsal side of the metatarsus of leg IV. This **calamistrum** combs out the very fine strands from the cribellum to form the characteristic, bluish silk of the cribellates.

Just in front of the spinners, on the venter, is a short transverse groove, the **tracheal spiracle** which, like the spiracles of insects, conveys oxygen to the interior. In *Anyphaena*, the tracheal spiracle is found near the middle of the abdomen, while in *Dysdera* there is a pair of spiracles immediately behind the openings to the book lungs.

The **book lungs** are situated on the sides of the abdomen immediately behind the pedicel. In many spiders they are visible as pale squares beneath the cuticle. They are composed of many fine leaves (hence the term 'book') and allow the blood which flows through them to absorb oxygen. The **branchial opercula** (the openings of the lungs) are capable of being closed and opened. The mygalomorph spiders have two pairs of book lungs but no trachea. The efficiency of the book lungs may be judged by the fact that the fastest-moving spiders lack them but have four tracheal spiracles instead. Even the large and unreasonably feared European house spider, *Tegenaria*, can be reduced to a state of collapse by forcing it to run for more than half-a-minute.

The female genital pore, the **epigyne** is situated between the book lungs on the anterior edge of the **epigastric fold**. In the females of the entelegyne families, the epigyne is an external structure which confirms the maturity of the specimen. It is a sclerotized, reddish-brown area which is sometimes rather flat (occasionally very prominent) and which varies in shape for every species, just as the male palp can confirm the species when viewed under the microscope. The genitalia form the best guide to the species in these families, and particularly in the Linyphiidae which are too small and superficially too similar to determine with any accuracy in the field with a low-power lens. The haplogyne females have no external genital structure and the corresponding males have palpal organs of a simple type, consisting of little more than a pear-shaped bulb protruding from the ventral side of the palpal tarsus. The haplogyne families in the region are the Oonopidae, Dysderidae, Segestriidae, and Scytodidae. On the venter of some of the male theridiids and the male of the linyphiid *Linyphia (Neriene) emphana*, the anterior region between the book lungs, the pedicel and the branchial opercula (known as the **epigastric region**) is elongated and distinctly swollen.

The life history of spiders

Egg sacs and eggs

Spider eggs are approximately spherical, and about 1 millimetre in diameter; they are laid in a compact mass and covered to a greater or lesser extent with silk, forming a sac. The eggs are variously coloured – pale yellow or brown, pink, or, in the case of *Micrommata*, bright green. The number of eggs laid depends on the size of the female – larger spiders lay more and sometimes larger eggs. Underfed females produce fewer eggs but the size of the eggs depends on the species. Some species produce more than one sac, and subsequent sacs tend to hold fewer eggs. *Dolomedes*, a large hunting spider, has been recorded to lay more than 2000 eggs in four sacs, whereas *Oonops*, a tiny six-eyed species, lays just two eggs in each sac; the total number of sacs may not exceed half-a-dozen. Neither spider is common, and it is probable that both species manage to maintain their numbers from year to year in spite of the enormous difference in fertility.

Egg sacs are very distinctive and, in many cases, the design is unique to the family or even to the species. The clubionids and some of the salticids lay their eggs directly in the retreat (a bag-like structure made of tough silk, and placed under stones, logs, or in higher vegetation). The mother remains enclosed in the sac guarding her eggs until they hatch. The gnaphosids are similar but enclose the eggs in a sac within the retreat; *Atypus* and *Fresus* make sacs which are kept within the tubular webs, the latter actually moving the sac so that a constant temperature is maintained. Some spiders from diverse families keep the sac in the web retreat; these include *Nuctenea cornuta*, *Dictyna* species, some agelenids, and some theridiids. *Theridion sisyphium* (named after the Corinthian king, Sisyphus who was condemned to push to the top of a hill a stone which constantly rolled down again) can be found fussing over its green egg sac in the

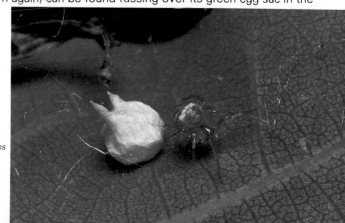

Theridion pallens and sac under oak leaf

summer. *Agelena labyrinthica* takes its specific name from the labyrinth-like sac where the eggs are laid in an inner chamber, supported by columns of silk to an outer envelope.

Tegenaria spiders also keep their sacs within the confines of the web but use whatever they can find in the way of soil, small pieces of wood, or prey debris, to cover the sac, weaving a further layer of silk to keep the additions in place. *Zodarion* species also fix pieces of plant debris to their sacs.

There are comparatively few spiders which abandon their sacs although there are several families in which the females die before their offspring emerge but guard the sac until their own deaths. *Araneus diadematus* does this in the autumn, and the extra time gained by the presence of the mother perhaps prevents parasites from interfering with the eggs. Female thomisids and philodromids also guard their single sacs during the summer but the eggs may still be parasitized. Abandoned sacs tend to be composed of fluffy silk or to have large spaces within them which prevent parasitic insects from reaching the eggs. Sacs which contain eggs that hatch quickly, like lycosid and pisaurid sacs, are smooth and tight. These spiders run about so that the eggs are less likely to be attacked by parasitic wasps and the like, but, in the south of England, *Pisaura mirabilis* is frequently the target for an ichneumonid wasp, *Trychosis tristator* (Tschek).

Normally, *Agroeca* spiders are ground dwelling, but they climb up into heather to attach their sacs by a stalk to the upper twigs. The sacs are made from white silk and shaped like inverted wine glasses. Occasionally, they are found in this state, probably as a consequence of the spider being interrupted, because the finished sac is completely covered in particles of soil which the spider must painstakingly carry in its chelicerae (a few grains at a time) while continually climbing up and down the vegetation. The camouflage is kneaded into the silk using the chelicerae and further silked over to keep it in place.

Some spiders make sacs which are self-camouflaged because of their colour or resemblance to vegetable material. *Agalanatea redii* makes a fluffy, khaki-coloured silk sac which is often found exposed on the upper parts of heather and other plants. *Tetragnatha*, the lanky orb weaver of lake-sides and marshes, makes a sac that looks remarkably like a fungus and is attached to the leaves of reeds and other low vegetation.

Like the lacewings of the insect world, some spiders (from diverse families) place their egg sacs on stalks, a stratagem which makes them less easy to find by wandering predators. *Meta menardi*, a cave and cellar dweller, makes an exceptionally large sac with a moderately short stalk. The tiny orb weaver, *Theridiosoma gemmosum*, makes a tiny pear-shaped sac, similar in shape to that of *Meta* but suspended from a thin stalk which is many times longer than the egg bundle.

Pirata hygrophilus and family

Some spiders, like *Agroeca* and *Agelena*, make their sacs with a chamber incorporated in the structure, so that the spiderlings can escape and begin their development.

Spiderlings

The eggs are smooth at first but, within a week or so before hatching, the form of the spiderling can be seen on the surface. Generally, the legs can be seen as parallel grooves, the smoother area indicating where the abdomen is being formed. The egg has an outer 'shell' (the chorion) which is ruptured by an 'egg tooth' on the base of each palp of the prelarva. This tiny, hairless, and blind creature must wait a few days to moult into a more advanced stage, the larva, which has rudimentary eyes and a few hairs but lacks poison and the ability to spin silk. Both of these stages are unable to feed, and subsist on the yolk present within them. After a short period, the larva moults into a nymph or spiderling which resembles the adult in general form. At this stage, some cannibalism may take place within the sac, and those spiderlings which are disadvantaged in any way are often destined to be a meal for their brothers and sisters.

Several species in the region adopt a limited type of social behaviour. *Theridion sisyphium* and several closely allied species, including the theridiid *Achaearanea riparia* regurgitate a liquid for the spiderlings, which cluster around the mouth of their mother to imbibe. As the spiderlings grow by this method of feeding, the females then resort to catching prey and summoning the young to come to feed on it. This technique is adopted by *Coelotes* spiders which carry maternal feeding a stage further – when the mother dies the spiderlings cluster around and feed on her.

An apparently similar but really quite different phenomenon can be seen in the cluster of minute spiderlings on the abdomen of lycosid spiders. The female carries her sac attached to her spinners; curiously, the spider is usually well camouflaged but the bundle of eggs is quite conspicuous, at least to human eyes.

Periodically, the mother removes the sac from the spinners and touches it with her legs. No doubt she can feel the movement of the larvae within and, when the young are ready to emerge, the female tears open the sac at the seam, releasing the imprisoned young. Once free, they immediately climb up the mother's legs and on to her abdomen although, in a large clutch, they will spill over her carapace as well. The spiderlings are carried about for a week or so before they disperse.

In matters of hygiene, spiders are quite particular (except, apparently, in the dusty *Tegenaria* spiders which occur indoors) and *Pirata* and *Xerolycosa* spiders which carry their white sacs about in the manner of *Pardosa*, have been seen to remove their sacs to excrete. The sac is held below in the rear legs and then replaced after the spider takes a few seconds to secure the ball of eggs to the spinners. Incidentally this demonstrates the spider's ability to control the emission of its silk.

Dispersal of the spiderlings

As soon as the nymphs of most species are capable of feeding, they leave the sac, minimizing any cannibalistic tendencies and so maintaining the numbers of the new generation. Some spiderlings, such as some web makers, move a short distance from the sac, and construct their own tiny webs in which they can soon catch their own food, while others disperse by air.

Ballooning

Spiders are not able actually to fly but they are very light in weight and the pull of the slightest breeze on a short line of silk is enough to lift them aloft and carry them considerable distances. Aerial dispersal or ballooning is most noticeable in the autumn and the word 'gossamer' is possibly a corruption of 'goose summer' describing

Pardosa immature ballooning from fence

those mild and still days of October when 'goose down' is seen drifting through the air. When large numbers of spiders balloon, their silk threads tend to drift together and form patches which are readily noticed. This phenomenon was known to the Greeks and, in recent times, it has been mistakenly associated with chemical warfare during World War 2 and with visitors from outer space by UFO-watchers, who charmingly called it 'angel hair'.

In the autumn, the majority of ballooners are adult linyphiid spiders but, in the early summer, these aeronauts are more likely to be immature spiders on their way to invade new areas. Many perish in the attempt as the wind takes them to unfavourable environments, such as lakes and the sea where they will drown or be eaten by fishes. Darwin reported large numbers of spiders which he took to be all one species, the gossamer spider, covering the rigging of HMS *Beagle* as it lay 100 kilometres off the mouth of the River Plate.

A spider intent on ballooning climbs to a high point and turns to face into the wind (fences are often used and are most convenient from an observer's point of view because the creatures can be seen most easily). Several strands of silk are expelled and these are carried into the air. The aeronaut then stands on 'tiptoe' and, when the force of the air currents is sufficient, the leg claws release their grip and the tiny traveller is airborne. *Lepthyphantes tenuis* has been observed to use a different method. The spider drops from its perch on a silk strand, letting out further 'sail' strands. Then it severs the retaining lines and drifts into the sky. Quite large but immature spiders, such as thomisids and lycosids (nearly always *Pardosa* species), use the 'tiptoe' method and are capable of drifting very long distances in favourable conditions.

Hunting and feeding methods

If the spider lands in a suitable place, it must set about finding food. All spiders are carnivorous and most are stimulated only by living and moving prey. The hunters are divided into the day shift and the night workers. Diurnal species tend to have reasonably good eyesight (for arachnids) and dark eyes. Some spiders feed at all times of the day and night, but jumping spiders (Salticidae) wrap themselves in silk at the onset of darkness, and most of them are diurnal. *Sitticus pubescens* has been observed near midnight out on walls in different localities but this is the exception to the rule. All spiders are well equipped with tactile sensory hairs on their bodies and legs, and these inform them of the presence and nature (via chemosensitive hairs) of nearby prey. Their lightning reflexes enable them to hunt just as efficiently by this method as by sight.

The nocturnal hunters are safe from most flying enemies during their nightly forays but spiders will, and frequently do, eat other spiders. Most hunters will attack prey which is smaller than they are, and run from insects which are larger. The immatures of some families occupy slightly different habitats from the larger stages, so that they are kept apart and the risk of the adults or larger immatures feeding on the spiderlings is minimized. This also has the effect of making different types and sizes of prey available to the different stages so that there is less competition between them. Typically, *Pardosa* spiders use this strategy because they occur at different degrees of growth (instars) at similar times of year. They achieve this because several batches of eggs are laid throughout the summer; by the autumn the older spiderlings are almost as big as the adults whereas the younger ones are still little more than babies.

The smaller spiders can, in general, only cope with small prey. *Linyphia triangularis* females, which occupy bushes and trees, lay their eggs at ground-level, and the emerging spiderlings also make their early webs at low levels, climbing higher as they increase in size and ability to deal with the larger and stronger insects which occupy these zones. Other members of this genus live permanently in low vegetation, although they are not much smaller than *L. triangularis*. Among the orb weavers, the smallest species such as *Singa* and *Cercidia*, make their webs a few centimetres above the ground. All these species are, therefore, predators of ground-layer insects. Curiously, the spiderlings of *Araneus diadematus* are found in much the same sort of places as the adults; they catch smaller prey to begin with but, within several weeks, they are capable of catching insects which are much bigger than they are. Even as immatures, the weavers are able to tackle quite large creatures without losing them, because it is the web, rather than the spider, which initially catches and holds the prey which is then immobilized by being wrapped in silk. The first webs are often neater than those of the adults although the young spiders are not trained in the complex procedure. The ability is completely inherited as is the manner of dealing with the prey. They are active by day and night, at least in the earlier instars,

Araneus diadematus with small white butterfly.

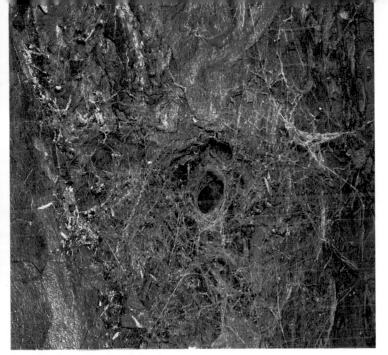

Amaurobius fenestralis web on pine trunk

but they are not able to catch moths so easily because these insects are able to shed their wing-scales and do not become stuck to the web.

The orb web is designed principally to catch insects in flight, whereas the webs of *Segestria* and *Amaurobius*, which adhere to the substrate, will catch crawling insects. *Segestria* depends on speed for success, but the cribellates are sometimes rather lethargic creatures, certain in the knowledge that their cribellate silk will hold fast the largest insects. The webs of some theridiids, such as *Steatoda*, will catch both types of prey; the random maze of threads above will stop fliers in their tracks, while the viscid feet of the web will haul the crawlers off the ground ready for the spider to wrap in further viscid silk.

Digestion is external in spiders. They cannot ingest solid food, so that the digestive juices must be introduced to the immobilized prey. The hunting spiders bite and inject poison for this effect (except *Scytodes* which 'wraps' its prey at a distance) while the web makers tend to wrap their prey first and bite for added efficiency. The families which do not have cheliceral teeth, Thomisidae and Theridiidae, must introduce the digestive juices through the aperture made by their chelicerae and suck out the resulting soup through the same hole.

Consequently, their prey is left externally undamaged. Araneids have cheliceral teeth and tear their food while pouring the digestive fluids over it; the remains are then a totally unrecognizable ball of inedible parts. Feeding is slow, and a large fly can take up to twelve hours to be consumed by *Pholcus*, for example.

Most spiders will take a variety of prey, and this will vary according to the seasonal availability, the size of the spider, and its method of prey capture. Some spiders specialize in one kind of prey although it is known in some cases that they will feed on alternative diets. *Dysdera* is one of the few spiders which will eat isopods (woodlice); *Steatoda bipunctata* has been seen eating woodlice, flies, other spiders, and harvestmen. Several spiders willingly eat ants although many others will not tolerate them at all. *Callilepis* and *Zodarion* apparently feed on little else but *Xysticus* spiders and some theridiids can be found eating workers and sexual winged ants. *Achaearanea riparia* has a diet which includes a large proportion of ants.

Several species of spiders are known to associate with ants; *Evansia merens* and the unpronounceable *Acartauchenius scurrilis* are linyphiids which are always found with them. A number of cell-making spiders, such as gnaphosids and salticids, may be found under stones which also harbour ants, but this is probably coincidence and merely shows a preference for similar habitats; it also shows the effectiveness and strength of silk in repelling boarders. When they run, *Micaria* spiders greatly resemble ants, and several salticids are also good ant mimics. The precise advantage to the spider is not understood, especially when these mimics are found in northern Europe, where ants are not so conspicuous as they are in warmer climates. Ants are avoided by many carnivores which might otherwise eat spiders, however, and the few eggs produced by *Synageles* for example, show that they have few enemies. Many of the small black linyphiids resemble ants when they are found running and these, too, are often left unmolested by other spiders. *Sitticus pubescens* has been seen to take an *Erigone*, however, and *Tetragnatha* immatures will catch large numbers of this family when they are ballooning.

Warning colours in insects may well deter birds, but orb weavers have poor eyesight and it is not uncommon, especially in the late summer and autumn, to see *Araneus diadematus* feeding on bees, wasps, and even ladybirds, all of which have strong warning colours.

Moulting

As the soft cuticle of a spider's abdomen becomes stretched by the intake of food, a point is reached where no further enlargement is possible. None of the harder, sclerotized parts is capable of increasing in size because the skeleton is on the outside (exoskeleton). The spider grows by a series of moults in which the old cuticle is shed

Linyphia triangularis moulting from the sheet of the web

leaving a temporarily soft outer covering which can be expanded until it hardens. The nymphs moult every few days and, at this stage, there is also some slight increase in size of the prosoma in the intermoult period, but this never occurs in the more advanced stages. The interval between moults lengthens as the spider ages. Small species have fewer moults, perhaps about five or less, while larger, more long-lived spiders require up to double this number.

Spiders about to moult stop eating and take no interest in prey for a period ranging from a day or so up to a fortnight before they shed their skins. Some spiders seal themselves up in a moulting chamber and wait there until moulting is completed: those families which habitually make cells, the gnaphosids, clubionids, and salticids, belong to this group. Web makers mostly moult from an upper line in their web although *Argiope* moults at the hub of its web. These spiders hang inverted by a silk thread at the moment of moulting (ecdysis). First, the carapace lifts from the front and then the sides of the abdomen split. The legs and sternum are still attached at this point and the leg claws cling to the silk line, although the silk thread is still attached and holds the spider to its perch. As the sternum becomes freed, the difficult job of extracting the legs and palps is undertaken. The new cuticle is soft and a fluid is produced which lubricates the process of removal. Thus, parts, such as the adult male palp, can be removed from an old cuticle which is smaller than the member will be after it has hardened. Spiders frequently die in the moulting stage, however, or one or more appendages may remain stuck in the old skin. Sometimes this leads to their death but the limbs can be autotomized, and the spider can break its own leg or palp at the point between the coxae and trochanter by means of a sharp tug. Spiders are very often found with a leg or two missing, the larger species nearly always at this point on the leg, but linyphiids are also often found with the leg ending at the patella. Both of these points have

27

weaker joints than the others and are more likely to break. The coxa-trochanter joint is specially designed to break with the minimum of bleeding.

Legs or palps which are lost in moulting or within the first quarter of an instar (the intermoult period) can be regenerated at the following moult. A new limb is formed within the coxa. This becomes free when the spider next moults and manifests itself as a shorter, thinner member, often with fewer spines and lacking other organs. The leg regenerated in this way is not as mobile as the existing limbs and may not be used to the same extent but, in subsequent moults, it can become indistinguishable from the other legs. Apical segments which are damaged or missing are directly reformed at the next moult.

If the spider succeeds in extracting all of its legs, it then hangs from its silk thread and periodically flexes the legs. If it is prevented from doing this, the entire limb may harden and become permanently inflexible. The cuticle is very pale at first and sometimes has a faintly bluish colour but, after a few hours, it reverts to its normal tint. Prior to a moult the legs often appear darker, because of the formation of the new hairs and spines which can be seen below the surface.

It is the old 'skin' or exuvium which is often mistaken for the corpse of a spider. Dead spiders are found very rarely and have a shrivelled appearance. Exuvia are transparent, with the carapace hinged to the crumpled abdomen or absent. If the carapace is present, then the family can often be determined by looking at the lenses of the eyes which are clearly visible on the front margin. Lycosids and thomisids with distinctive legs and spines can also be identified.

After ecdysis the relative proportions of the body are changed. The prosoma is now larger than before, while the abdomen is smaller. There is no metamorphosis in spiders (as found in most insects) except for minor variations in the larval stages. Some of the immature araneids have slightly different patterns from the later stages. It is noteworthy that the immature pattern of dark posterior triangle is

Tibellus oblongus exuvium

found in the adults of *Araneus marmoreus pyramidatus*.

In nearly all spiders (*Argiope* is an exception), the immature males have the same colour and pattern as the adult females, as is the case among many orders of animals. When the cuticle has regained its natural colour after the final moult, the male is either much darker than the female or has clearer markings (*Steatoda*, for example). In some species, the male has redder legs than the female. The males mature before the females and usually undergo fewer moults. In the araneomorph spiders, there is normally no further moult once the spiders are mature, although a post-adult moult has been reported for *Tegenaria*.

In some species the subadult male is as big or bigger than the female but, at his final moult, there is no growth and sometimes there is even a reduction of body size; the legs increase in length at the male's last moult. The females, on the other hand, do grow at their final moult, and the abdomen gets progressively larger with subsequent feeding and the production of eggs in the ovaries. Males, therefore, are generally smaller, darker, and more slender than their mates but their legs may be of equal or greater length than the females'. In the subadult male, the palp takes on a swollen appearance but it is not different in colour from the rest of the limb. On attaining maturity, the palp is dark with a more 'textured' outline and, in the more advanced families, it has a number of projections (apophyses) which, under the microscope, help to distinguish the species.

The epigastric region of the female, which previously had little or no markings present between the lungs, at maturity bears a dark reddish-brown patch of sclerotized tissue. This is the epigyne. It consists of variously shaped pockets and apophyses (for example, a scape) which enable the male palp to hold fast while copulation takes place. The haplogyne spiders of the families Oonopidae, Dysderidae, Segestriidae, and Scytodidae and the mygalomorph *Atypus* are the only spiders of the region where the females do not have epigynes when they are mature; maturity in these spiders must be assessed

Adult male
*Pardosa
monticola*
showing complex
structure of
mature palp

Linyphia (Neriene) peltata mating

Male *Pardosa nigriceps* courting

by size or by the possession of eggs. *Tetragnatha* females also only have the faintest signs of maturity in the epigastric region.

When the females attain maturity they probably emit a pheromone to which males of the same species are attracted, and which they can detect with the chemosensitive hairs on their legs. This has been recorded for some orb weavers, where considerable numbers of males have been attracted to the web of a freshly ecdysized female. Male hunting spiders are possibly capable of following chemically labelled silk drag lines left by a female in her wanderings.

Reproduction

Before the male can begin his courtship of the female, he must perform one of the strangest acts in the animal world. In both sexes the genital pore is located between the book lungs on the underside of the abdomen. The male, however, is provided with intromittent organs on both palps, but there is no internal connection between these and the testes. All males must, therefore, make a sperm web – a small triangle or rectangle of silk upon which is deposited a small drop of sperm. The palps are then dipped into this, the embolus taking up the liquid as a pen is filled with ink and storing it within the palp.

Then the male finds a female and, in many families, she is courted. In the nocturnal hunters there may be no courtship or just some leg tickling as a preliminary to mating but, in the sighted spiders of the Salticidae and Lycosidae, there is a good deal of dancing and prancing in front of the female, where the ornamented parts of the male are displayed and moved, often for some minutes. This has the effect of reducing predatory tendencies by the female and making her receptive to the male. In all the web makers courtship is undertaken by a purely tactile approach. The male locates the web of the female and, by various means, taps out a signal which brings the female out of her retreat and on to the silk lines. Males of some families have stridulating organs; theridiids have small spurs on the abdomen, near the pedicel, with a ridged area on the rear sloping surface of the carapace. When he is in the female's web, the male vibrates his abdomen and produces a high-pitched vibration. The stridulatory apparatus of linyphiids consists of a spur on the inside of the palp, with a series of ridges on the chelicerae. The lycosid, *Pardosa fulvipes*, has minute bristles on the coxae of a leg IV which are rubbed against the corrugated surface of his book lungs.

Once the female is receptive, the male approaches and, by crawling under or over the female (in the hunting species), the palps are applied one at a time or, in the more primitive spiders, both together, and the sperm is transferred to the female.

Copulation lasts from a few seconds to many hours; in some of the araneids courtship is greatly extended but the mating is very short. The courtships of some *Lepthyphantes* species (Linyphiidae) are relatively short but mating can proceed for up to seven hours. After this the spiders may part, the male leaving the web to recharge his palps and seek out another partner or, in other cases, the male may tear away part of the female's web, make a sperm web in the gap and subsequently go back to the same female. In most hunting spiders the male dashes away after copulation in case the female is feeling hungry. Apocryphal stories about the male being eaten by the female would quickly lead to the demise of the species, but *Argiope* females will sometimes eat their partners after copulation has been started and *Araneus diadematus* will do the same, although they probably only succeed in catching senile males, whose biologically useful days are at an end.

Some species, notably *Atypus*, *Eresus*, *Dictyna*, and *Tegenaria*, have a social life of sorts where the two sexes live fairly amicably together within the female's web. In the genus *Tegenaria*, they will also catch their own food on the web, but occasional squabbles will break out over which partner eats the prey. Both sexes of *Dictyna* seem to have permanently good relations and males have even been seen to make repairs to a shared web.

Egg laying

The males do not live long once they have matured irrespective of the longevity of the female. In *Tegenaria*, for example, the male dies and only then is eaten by the female. It is not known whether the same thing happens with all the other species mentioned, but it is recorded for *Atypus*.

The female lives on, catches more prey, and lays her eggs. This can take place long after the death of the male, and has given rise to ideas of parthenogenesis among spiders. This is unlikely, although the males of some species, especially tropical ones, are extremely rare. As far as is known, all the females produce fertilized eggs only after mating. A *Steatoda bipunctata* kept from maturity till death, however, continued to produce egg sacs for twenty-three months after mating, producing six in all.

Hunting spiders deposit their eggs into the retreat or on to a separate sheet to which a layer of silk is added as a cover. The eggs are fertilized shortly after they are laid. The lycosids bundle up their eggs and attach the sac to their spinners, while pisaurids carry the sac delicately in the fangs. Araneids and some other web makers lay their eggs in an inverted position, by depositing them from below on to a sheet of silk. Initially, the eggs are coated with a sticky substance which holds them together. This disappears after the retaining sheet is added. Papery silk is incorporated into the sacs of a number of spiders; it seems that the final layer of silk is dissolved to a slight extent by the spider's digestive juices and polished by the chelicerae. Incidentally, the action of the digestive juice on silk is the only way in which the weavers can sever the strands of silk they produce.

The fluffy, candy-floss-like silk which protects the eggs of many species is produced by a different behaviour. The spinners are applied to the sac and then the abdomen is raised high, to produce enough

Pisaura mirabilis on nursery web. Sac with cluster of young behind .

silk line to make a small loop when the spinners are pressed down to the sac again. This is repeated over and over again as the spider moves over the sac.

The female pisaurids differ from the other hunting spiders by weaving a nursery web around the sac after carrying it initially (*see* page 190 Pisauridae). The nursery tents of *Pisaura mirabilis* with the mother on the outer sheet, the dark spiderlings within, are a common sight in summer.

The life cycle of spiders

Spiders are found mature and active throughout the year. In spring, the majority of spiders from diverse families are adult. Many fewer are found in the summer although the females of the spring species are still active and guarding egg sacs, and immatures of the autumn-maturing species are growing fat on the abundance of insects. In late summer the larger weavers are highly conspicuous as is the exceptionally abundant *Linyphia triangularis*. The females of these species can be found up to the end of November in mild years. At about this time the numerous but often hidden midget spiders of the Linyphiidae are adult, and it is this family which can be found mature all through the winter.

Very little is known about the cycle of many individual species. In the cooler climates of Europe it is likely that the larger species require two overwintering periods before they are adult whereas, even in the rather limited region covered by this book, the same spiders in the south may be able to develop fully within nine to twelve months.

In principle, those spiders which mature in the spring, produce eggs in the summer which hatch within days or weeks into spiderlings; these develop and overwinter to become adult themselves the following spring. Summer-maturing spiders, however, make sacs in later summer; the spiderlings develop only to a limited degree before overwintering and possibly do not become adult until their second summer, after overwintering a second time. The smaller autumn species, such as *Meta segmentata*, are all found adult again the following autumn, but at least some of the autumnal arancids do not emerge from their egg sacs until late spring, becoming fairly large by their first autumn, but not fully adult until the end of the following summer. There is a strong possibility, at least in northern latitudes, that a brood of summer-hatching spiders will not all develop at the same rate. Some will be adult the following spring while others will remain immature during their second summer and become adult in the spring of the following year.

A large spider, such as *Dolomedes* may need three or even four years to become adult in the north of its range, although laboratory-reared animals, supplied with easily caught food may mature in one year. Hunting spiders are not very efficient predators, and do not catch as much prey in their own environment as they are clearly capable of eating in confinement. In a study of *Pardosa* spiders, many thousands of spiders were examined but very few were ever caught in the act of feeding, and this infrequency of finding wolf spiders feeding seems to be a characteristic of this genus. It was also found that *Pardosa lugubris* always took two years to mature in Scotland, and that in Holland spiders hatched in the summer took one year, but those from the autumn sac were not adult until the spring of the following year.

The longer winters in the north of the region prevent the spiders from feeding, and this lack of food is known to prolong the lives of spiders. Spiders like *Dolomedes*, which have restricted habitat preferences and long lives, may be very abundant at certain stages in their youth but the adults in the same sites are much less common. They are exposed to the many risks of a spider's existence for a longer time and thus a smaller proportion survive to adulthood. The spiderlings from a single egg sac, however, will vary considerably in the time they take to mature, some developing quickly and others feeding only intermittently and taking twice as long to become adult. While they spend a longer time 'at risk' they also may pass successfully through an unfavourable period of weather or shortage of prey, to produce a new generation in more favourable circumstances. Therefore, the life cycle may be under a year for the smallest species, twelve to eighteen months for many medium and larger species, especially the larger orb weavers, and up to a year longer for slow developers. The females of some species, such as *Steatoda bipunctata* and *Pholcus phalangiodes*, are capable of living for several years as adults, at least indoors.

Finding spiders

Spiders occur in all habitats where they can catch suitable prey or find shelter from the elements. *Atypus* occupies a silk-lined hole in the ground, *Meta* species are found in caves, and some of the linyphiids have been found deep in mines. They occur in abundance in moss and low vegetation such as grass and on flowers. Bushes support the webs of many spiders, as does the lower and sometimes higher foliage of trees. Several species are found on the trunks of trees, either camouflaged or on fine webs. The diurnal hunters can be found scampering on the bare ground, but often not far away from hiding places in nearby plants where they dash as we approach.

The bulk of the spiders described are found from spring till late autumn, but the small black linyphiids are found in sheltered habitats throughout the winter. Lycosids are most easily found on mild days in spring and early summer but the females, which live through the summer, are often found sheltering from direct sunshine under logs or in the shade of trees. The sun-loving jumping spiders are conspicuous only in warm conditions although they do venture out on cool but sunny days in the early spring.

Most species of spiders are nocturnal. Many web makers build silk-lined retreats in which they spend their days. These are constructed at the sides of their webs or connected to the snares in various ways so that finding the spider is a simple task. At night, most of these spiders come out on to the structure of the web. Nocturnal hunting spiders shelter under stones or similar debris on the ground. Whether hanging in their webs or in a protective cell, spiders in general show a preference for being inverted, and, if you are searching for the vagrants of the night, look first on the underside of a turned stone.

Several species show a curious preference for living in association with humans. We provide a suitable environment for some species, as long as it is not too warm and dry. Within the region, *Pholcus, Psilochorus, Scytodes,* and several *Steatoda* species are found only in houses. Other hangers-on include the notorious European house spiders, two of which have been given free rides to almost every part of the globe. Gardens also have their share and, even a small city garden may conceal twenty different species. As luck will have it, most of our sinister-looking species seem to be attracted to people; the evil-eyed *Dysdera* and *Drassodes lapidosus* frequent even small gardens. The large, hairy but not unattractive *Tegenarias* are persistent squatters and, in the autumn, the same specimen may have to be forcibly removed several times and yet will still manage to spend the winter indoors in some forgotten corner.

In the milder months their country cousins will be active. A walk in various habitats will, in general, reveal a variety of species. A real wood with a mixture of tree species and clearings with gorse or heather will hold a number of jumping spiders, wolf spiders, crab spiders, theridiids, and araneids. Sandy heathland is probably the most productive site of all. In southern England, a careful seach might produce several rarities in a few hours, or more likely in repeated visits over a period of years. Unfortunately, this habitat, which supports so many invertebrates, has been decimated in the last century in southern England. In the north, these heathy places are not so well populated but sometimes contain rarities of their own. It will be seen from the habitats of the species, that any wild and relatively undisturbed place can be a haven for spiders and, of course, their prey. Unfortunately these idyllic spots seem to attract those of our own species whose only wish is to destroy them, often for very little purpose.

In discovering spiders, make sure that you do not unwittingly join this group of vandals. Nearly all land to which there is public access belongs to someone, if not to the animals which depend on it for survival, and it cannot be stressed too strongly that the naturalists of earlier times may have been partly responsible for the extinction of species which had already suffered reduction or loss of habitat. Habitats should be left as they are found; stones and logs can be replaced after inspection and, in repeated visits, these same microhabitats will perhaps yield new species. Vegetation need not be damaged even if you seach it thoroughly. Spiders in webs can be removed for closer scrutiny and replaced on their webs with little difficulty.

Equipment and methods

There is a number of ways of observing spiders; for those to whom exercise is anathema, they can simply wait for the spiders to show themselves. For those with less patience for this rather time-consuming method, a slow pace gazing intently at the vegetation can be productive. For the more cryptically coloured species, an entomologist's sweep-net may be used. This should have a net made from strong white material which allows the captured spiders to be seen clearly. It is swept from side to side across the tops of grass or heather and sweeps all before it. The same device can be held under the foliage of trees and bushes while these are firmly shaken a couple of times over the bag. Thorny bushes, such as gorse, will need beating with a stick, but not so hard as to cause damage to the plant or the spiders may be damaged, too.

For clumped plants, a search can be made by grubbing; the vegetation is parted carefully and the unwary occupants may be caught as they try to get back into cover, or disperse in all directions. Moss and fallen leaves (litter) can be gathered up carefully and sorted on a large plastic sheet. This cannot be done in windy weather.

The spiders must be temporarily confined so that they can be placed under a lens and examined. Scientific and entomological suppliers will stock sweep-nets and glass or plastic tubes. Some arachnologists are so skilled that they can persuade most of the spiders to run into the tube which is swiftly corked. A more convenient device, but one which still needs a little practice to use, is the 'pooter' or aspirator. This consists of a glass compartment attached to an arm's length of flexible tubing, with an intervening filter to keep the quarry in the chamber where it can be inspected. These can be purchased from a few sources, or made from lengths of glass and rubber tubing. The power of the inhalation needs to be judged carefully or the specimen may be damaged, or possibly escape. Once confined, a finger over the end of the tube prevents escape and the spiders can be viewed. Some species will dash up and down in their desire to escape but most usually settle down within a few seconds. Spiders will eat one another and they should be examined one at a time.

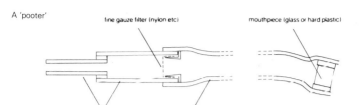

A 'pooter'

fine gauze filter (nylon etc)

mouthpiece (glass or hard plastic)

glass tubing

rubber or plastic tubing (flexible)

To examine spiders in the field you must have a good hand-lens It should be constructed from durable materials and have achromatic lenses. A times ten lens is most convenient to use. The viewing distance is such that the lens will produce a sharp image of a specimen in a 10 millimetre diameter tube. Higher powers will not do this and, with the larger species (over 8 millimetres), it is not possible to see the whole animal. These lenses can be obtained from opticians or from entomological suppliers but do not be tempted to buy inferior quality lenses. Cheaper lenses will tend not to give such a sharp image and will be tiring to use. The casing should have provisions for attaching a neck strap, and this should be used at all times to avoid losing your lens.

The fascinating behaviour of spiders can be observed in the field to a certain extent, if you sacrifice the urge to see a great number of species to concentrate on a few, and to get to know these in more detail. Where the sweep-net succeeds in producing the greatest number of species, it fails in destroying some useful means of identifying the catch; the weavers are knocked out of their webs, and the webs are destroyed. These webs are of great value in determining the family to which the specimen belongs until you become familiar with the appearance of the spiders themselves.

The biology of even some of the more common species is poorly understood. By keeping spiders in captivity you can learn more about spiders' habits and use this knowledge to supplement field observations. All of this should be recorded in a notebook, together with the site and date of capture. The specimens can be transported home in a small tube with a piece of vegetation or even paper for them to cling to. Only one animal should be confined per tube, which can be sealed; do not provide air holes or the spider may die from desiccation. Provided the tube is kept cool, and not exposed to the sun, most spiders will live for weeks in such conditions, but they should be put in larger containers so that they can feed and moult reasonably freely. More detailed information on keeping spiders can be found in Frances Murphy's *Keeping Spiders, Insects and other Land Invertebrates in Captivity*. Although spiders will not need feeding more than once or twice a week, it is difficult to find suitable food and you should not keep more spiders than you can feed.

Photographing spiders

Spiders make good subjects for the camera because of their interesting behaviour and attractive patterns and colours. Although they
are not able to fly away the moment they are in focus, some are
rather reluctant sitters and will dash off before the session is over.
As you become more familiar with the different habits of the various
families, their weaknesses can be exploited.

Slow, fine-grained films such as Kodachrome with a film speed of
25 or 64 ASA/ISO produce the best image quality but Ektachrome
64, which can be home processed, also gives good results. Most of
the subjects will be smaller than 15 millimetres across, including the
legs, so you will need a macro-lens and some form of extension.
With this optical arrangement and because of the need for a small
lens aperture to give good depth of field, a lot of light will be required
for the slow film. Sunlight is not bright enough to give good results,
but there are many small flashguns available which will provide
enough light to give good results even in dull weather or at night
(provided a supplementary light is used for focusing).

Most of the photographs in this book were originally taken at a
reproduction ratio of 1:1·5. This means that the spider appears on
the film 50 per cent larger than in life; measurements made on the
film itself must be reduced by one-third to find its true size. Macro-
lenses are available in two focal lengths from many manufacturers
– 50 millimetres and 100 millimetres or thereabouts. To achieve the
desired magnification the 100-millimetre lens is much more useful,
because the working distance from the front of the lens is about 150
millimetres and those species with good eyesight are not frightened
away so easily at this distance. My 'spider outfit' consists of a Pentax
MX body fitted with a plain ground-glass screen, type SE; this is
absolutely essential for macro work, because focusing is simplified.
A 100-millimetre Pentax macro-lens is mounted on a single 100-
millimetre extension tube; occasionally for larger subjects, a 50-milli-
metre tube is employed. In combination these components give a
range of magnification from times 0·5 or smaller, to times 1·5. For
field work I have used an old Sunpak GX 30 flashgun, but any similar
unit would be suitable. This enabled me to use an aperture of between f22 and f32 for the photographs. For specimens which cannot
be shot in the field for various reasons, and which can be photo-
graphed on a substrate, I use a Pentax LX camera with a plain
focusing screen, sometimes with a high-power finder, and Pentax
flashguns AF 280T and AF 400T. Together, this equipment permits
automatic, through-the-lens exposure accuracy with flash. For larger
magnifications using bellows and reversed lenses, there is no need
to do extensive calculations or prolonged tests. For spiders on webs,
however, manual exposure is desirable. To obtain the correct expo-

sure at short distances, you will need to carry out a preliminary test with your own equipment using different apertures from f11 down to the smallest opening of the lens. Larger apertures will not need testing, because they will not give sufficient depth of field, and the results will lack sharpness. Once you have worked out the correct aperture for your equipment, it is a good idea to stick a data label on the back of the flashgun as a reminder.

The best results are obtained with a flashgun mounted near the front of the lens, and a device to mount the flash on the filter ring of the lens is available. This maintains a more-or-less constant exposure as the lens is extended and different magnifications are produced. This setup also has the advantage of producing a decent modelling of the subject without the need for additional flashguns.

Good natural history shots are gained more by knowing your subject than by photographic expertise. Once the calculations have been done the photography should take care of itself; the main problem is to find new species and to take interesting shots of them. Only persistence and patience will achieve this.

All the species in this book can be accurately identified from a good photograph so this method may be used to establish identities of spiders (as with other groups) without collecting the specimen. In some instances this is illegal in Britain: all animals on National Trust property are protected, for example. *Dolomedes plantarius* and *Eresus niger* are protected by the endangered species list.

How to use the book

Many of the spiders and harvestmen described in this guide have a wide distribution, not only throughout Europe, but in the northern hemisphere. As you travel south and east in Europe, however, many more species are found: these may be identifiable at least to family, especially the easily recognized jumping spiders, which abound in warm climates. Apart from the numerous members of the Linyphiidae (money spiders) which occur in northern Europe, I have attempted to describe all the spiders and harvestmen which can be recognized and identified by their shape and markings. The bulk of the linyphiids are small and lack distinctive markings, and only those which can be distinguished by pattern or form have been included. In the remaining families I have only left out one or two species which are very rare and occur in isolated or inaccessible places.

The region covered comprises the lowland areas of north-west Europe, Scandinavia, and Finland. Only northern France is covered, although many of the animals described occur as far south as the Mediterranean.

In the 'Illustrated key', the most conspicuous features of each family are detailed and you should examine the specimen or its web and compare these features with the abbreviated descriptions. The most useful features of the spider are its eyes, because their arrangement is different in nearly every family. Some of the families have distinctive spinners or legs which allow them to be identified quickly. Then you should look through the photographic section of the book for that family to find a match with the specimen. In some families, the males are different in appearance from the females and, where this is the case, the male is described (sometimes illustrated) after the female. In those cases where the male is similar, he may be darker or more strongly marked and is not described separately; in all cases, the males are smaller and slimmer, with longer legs and noticeably swollen palps.

The habitats given are typical ones for each species but, very occasionally, you will find individuals in the 'wrong' place. Males of web-making species wander about searching for females at their appropriate season, and most ballooners are weavers (see page 237). The overall form of these spiders should place them in their correct family, especially if they have been previously seen on webs. More rarely, spiders are found in quite unsuitable places where they have ventured by accident: a specimen of *Zelotes rusticus* was found in a full bottle of whisky, *Zora spinimana* in a matchbox in a wood, and specimens from a variety of families are sometimes discovered in the pockets of my coat or in my car after a spider-watching excursion.

I have chosen to express the time of year in which both sexes are adult by season, rather than by month. This allows for inconsistencies in the weather which delay or accelerate the season. Before this period the immatures will be found and, in many cases, they will be identifiable at least to family, and, where the species has unique markings, to species. The females of many species will continue for a month or more after the males have died and, in rare cases, may be found much later. Where the females live for several years, they will, of course, be found at all times of year.

The nomenclature of the spiders is based on *British Spiders* Volume III by G. H. Locket, A. F. Millidge, and P. Merrett except for the Segestriidae (split off from the family Dysderidae), the Liocranidae whose members were previously included in the Clubionidae; the Hahniidae were grouped with the Agelenidae, and in the Araneidae, the spiders known as *Araneus* are now split into a number of new genera, as quoted here.

The harvestmen are too few in number to cause serious problems of identification. The nomenclature is based on *British Harvestmen* by J. H. P. Sankey and T. H. Savory with revisions.

The actual lengths of the spiders, excluding appendages, is shown by scale bars next to the photographs (red–female; blue–male) in units of 5 millimetres, with broken lines to indicate size range.

Illustrated key to spider families

Atypidae
purse-web spiders living inside tubular web, half buried in ground
page 45

Eresidae
one rare cribellate species living in tubular web buried in ground, small upper 'roof' extends from tube
page 50

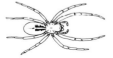

Amaurobiidae
larger cribellates making tubular retreat with rough collar on walls, trees, and in litter
page 52

Dictynidae
small cribellate spiders making aerial webs or snares in litter
page 54

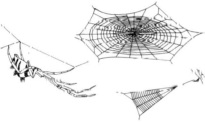

Uloboridae
cribellate orb weavers. *Uloborus* makes complete orb with stabilmentum; *Hyptiotes* makes segment of orb web on bushes and trees
page 58

Oonopidae   Dysderidae

Oonopidae, Dysderidae
six-eyed hunting spiders. Nocturnal. *Oonops* very small; *Dysdera*, *Harpactea* larger. All with reddish coloration
pages 62 and 63

Segestriidae
elongated spiders making tubular retreat with radiating trigger threads
page 64

Scytodidae
spitting spiders; nocturnal hunters around buildings
page 66

41

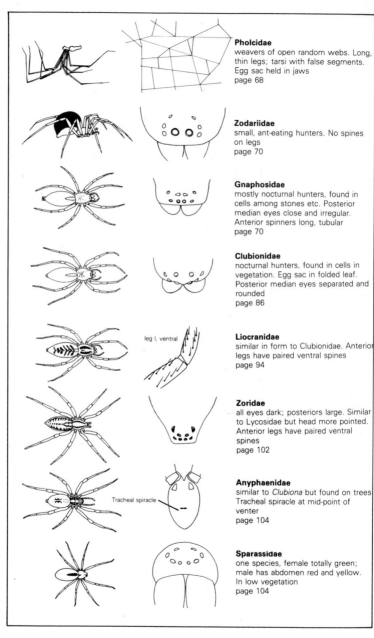

Pholcidae
weavers of open random webs. Long, thin legs; tarsi with false segments. Egg sac held in jaws
page 68

Zodariidae
small, ant-eating hunters. No spines on legs
page 70

Gnaphosidae
mostly nocturnal hunters, found in cells among stones etc. Posterior median eyes close and irregular. Anterior spinners long, tubular
page 70

Clubionidae
nocturnal hunters, found in cells in vegetation. Egg sac in folded leaf. Posterior median eyes separated and rounded
page 86

Liocranidae
leg I, ventral
similar in form to Clubionidae. Anterior legs have paired ventral spines
page 94

Zoridae
all eyes dark; posteriors large. Similar to Lycosidae but head more pointed. Anterior legs have paired ventral spines
page 102

Anyphaenidae
similar to *Clubiona* but found on trees Tracheal spiracle at mid-point of venter
page 104

Tracheal spiracle

Sparassidae
one species, female totally green; male has abdomen red and yellow. In low vegetation
page 104

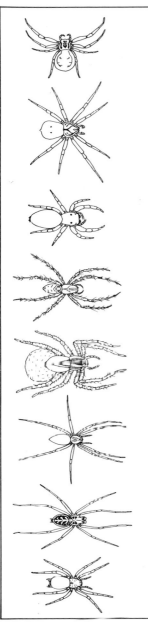

Thomisidae
crab spiders. Legs I, II longer and
stouter than III, IV. Abdomen broader
posteriorly. On flowers and ground
page 106

Philodromidae
legs subequal. Flattened bodies. On
ground, low plants, and trees
page 124

Salticidae
jumping spiders. Four very large
anterior eyes. Legs usually short and
stout, but leg I sometimes enlarged.
Diurnal
page 134

Oxyopidae
all legs with long spines. Head high
anteriorly. On low plants
page 162

Lycosidae
wolf spiders. Four large eyes on top
and front of head, anterior row of
small eyes. Female carries egg sac
attached to spinners. On ground
page 164

Pisauridae
nursery web spiders. Eyes smaller
than Lycosidae. Legs I, II held
together when at rest. Female carries
sac below sternum
page 190

Agelenidae
sheet web and tubular retreat.
Spinners long and two segmented.
Includes the European house spider
page 192

spinners from below

Hahniidae
small spiders with spinners in
transverse row. Small sheet web
page 192

spinners from below

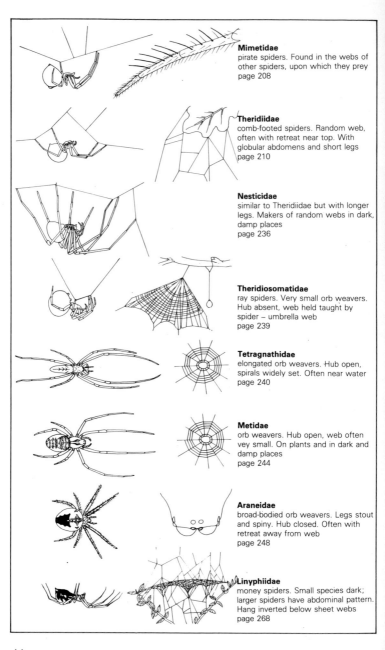

Mimetidae
pirate spiders. Found in the webs of other spiders, upon which they prey
page 208

Theridiidae
comb-footed spiders. Random web, often with retreat near top. With globular abdomens and short legs
page 210

Nesticidae
similar to Theridiidae but with longer legs. Makers of random webs in dark, damp places
page 236

Theridiosomatidae
ray spiders. Very small orb weavers. Hub absent, web held taught by spider – umbrella web
page 239

Tetragnathidae
elongated orb weavers. Hub open, spirals widely set. Often near water
page 240

Metidae
orb weavers. Hub open, web often vey small. On plants and in dark and damp places
page 244

Araneidae
broad-bodied orb weavers. Legs stout and spiny. Hub closed. Often with retreat away from web
page 248

Linyphiidae
money spiders. Small species dark; larger spiders have abdominal pattern. Hang inverted below sheet webs
page 268

ORDER ARANEAE THE SPIDERS

Suborder Mygalomorphae (Orthognatha)

Family Atypidae

The atypids are medium-sized, robust spiders. They occupy a closed, tubular web which is mostly below ground-level.

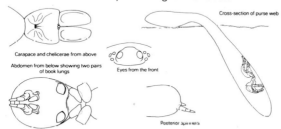

Cross-section of purse web

Carapace and chelicerae from above

Abdomen from below showing two pairs of book lungs

Eyes from the front

Posterior spinners

The three European *Atypus* species are the only representatives of the suborder Mygalomorphae found in northern Europe. Almost every aspect of their appearance is distinct from that of any other spider found in the region; the spiderlings can be assigned to the genus with ease.

The major differences lie in the articulation of the chelicerae and the possession of two pairs of book lungs (there is only a single pair in most araneomorph spiders) The chelicerae are more massive than in any other European species although, in males of some salticid, and both sexes of some tetragnathid and dysderid genera, they are almost as long. The mygalomorph chelicerae hinge in the vertical plane whereas those of the other genera move horizontally and usually have smaller fangs.

The spider excavates a deep hole in soft earth or detritus which is then lined with a thick silken tube. This subterranean section varies in length from 15 to 50 centimetres below the surface. The aerial portion of the tube is from 5 to 12 centimetres long and covered in soil particles, so that it is very difficult to detect. As the potential prey walks over the exposed tube, the spider rushes to the top and transfixes it with the long fangs. Gradually, the tube is severed and the prey pulled inside

Male *A. affinis* spiders become adult in the autumn, leave their tubes, and go in search of the tubes of females. When they find one, the front legs and palps are drummed against the tube (*see* photograph). If he is not repulsed, the male will tear the tube and enter. The male and female will cohabit for some months throughout the winter but, as the male becomes more senile and dies, he will be eaten by his mate. The eggs are laid in a sac, which is attached to the upper part of the chamber, and hatch in the late summer. The spiderlings remain in the tube with the female until the early spring of the following year, when they can be seen leaving the tube, trailing thick bands of silk as they climb short vegetation and disperse. According to Bristowe, W.S in *The World of Spiders*, eighteen months elapse between mating and the exodus of the spiderlings from their mother's web. Those that survive will take four years to reach adulthood; the males will live a few more months, but the females may produce additional sacs and continue to live for another two to five years, so that their total lifespan may be nine years. Some North American mygalomorphs have a suspected longevity in excess of twenty-five years.

Atypus affinis Eichwald

Size female 10–15 mm; male 7–9 mm

Female Carapace Brown to greenish brown, glossy. **Abdomen** Dark reddish brown with small greyish spots. **Legs** Coloured as carapace, glossy with fewest hairs on basal segments. Articulations between coxae-trochanters-femora white. **Spinners** With three subequal segments.

Habitat Tube usually under cover of low vegetation, in sandy or chalky substrates. On chalk hillsides, tube can often be found on sunny side of mounds of ant, *Lasius flavus* (Fabricius). **Season** Autumn, but older females all year. **Distribution** Recorded throughout British Isles, but very local in northern England and with one record for Scotland. Most common in southern counties where colonies are often found. Northern limit in Europe is Denmark.

Atypus piceus (Sulzer)

Size female 10 mm; male 9 mm

Distinguished from *A. affinis* by darker spinners: apical segment longer than both basal segments. Tube not normally as long as that of *A. affinis*.

Habitat and **Season** Similar to *A. affinis*. **Distribution** Absent from Britain. Recorded from France, Germany, Holland.

Atypus muralis Bertkau

Size female 12 mm; male 9 mm

Probably does not occur within region but is distinctive from *A. piceus* and may be found. Tube intermediate in length between *A. affinis* and *A. piceus*. Spinners four-segmented, each segment subequal in length.

♀
Atypus affinis

♂
Atypus affinis

47

Suborder Araneomorphae (Labidognatha)

Infraorder Cribellatae

The cribellates comprise a diverse group of web-making spiders. They all possess a cribellum and calamistrum which are responsible for the characteristically bluish silk found in the webs.

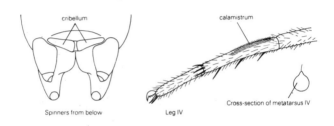

Spinners from below   Leg IV

Although the cribellum and calamistrum are difficult to see in the field, the bluish silk, peculiar to this group of spiders, and especially noticeable in the webs of the Amaurobiidae, soon identifies them. The silk itself is not coloured; it is more likely that the extreme fineness of the individual strands composing this spidery wool (about a hundredth of the diameter of the lines used in an araneid orb web, or 0·015 microns) influences the colour we see. This special silk is supported on two strands of normal silk. To manufacture it, the spider places the tip of one of the fourth legs on the distal end of the metatarsus of the opposite leg, bends both legs to bring the calamistrum near its cribellum, and then straightens the rear legs which pulls them away from the cribellum. This draws the fine strands out. The action is very rapid and is known as carding. In the course of carding its silk, the spider will occasionally alternate its legs and use both calamistra.

When it is fresh, the cribellate silk is very adhesive even though it is not coated with any glue. It is sticky because of its structure, in the same way that the hooked seeds of plants seem to be adhesive. Some insects, such as wasps, will not stick to the viscid silk of the araneids but they will become entwined in cribellate silk. Cribellates are not preyed upon by parasitic insects, cocooned as they are within

Amaurobius silk

Amaurobius simi-
lis carding silk

their webs. It is not known for certain how these spiders avoid becoming entwined in their own webs.

Even in northern Europe, it can be seen that the cribellate families are, in some cases, remarkably similar to some of the ecribellates, notably the Uloboridae/Araneidae and the Amaurobiidae and Agelenidae, especially *Coelotes*. The relationships are complicated by 400 million years of evolution, but it seems possible that the cribellates are more primitive, and that at least some of the ecribellates have evolved from cribellate ancestors. Convergent evolution has perhaps brought about the similarity of web structure and other behaviour in various groups. In spite of the complications, it is convenient to group the cribellates together, at least for field identification.

Family Eresidae

Eresus niger, the only species of the genus to be found in the region, is one of our most attractive and, unfortunately, rare species. In Britain it was originally discovered in 1816 in heathland on the border of Hampshire and Dorset. Up to 1906, only six males and a single female had been found. The original habitats have now been destroyed but, in 1979, two males were found in Dorset, and the second British female (*see* photograph) was found in 1980. The males resemble the females until their final moult, when they leave their burrows and go in search of females. The females never leave their hiding places and their webs are rather small and inconspicuous.

The spiders appear to feed mainly on other spiders and on beetles including the fiercely predatory tiger beetle. The males mature in autumn or spring and are short lived as adults. The females probably become mature at three years old, and produce one egg sac. This has a covering of cribellate silk to which bits of earth and prey remnants are attached. The mother moves this to the roof during the daytime, then takes it back into the tubular retreat at night, possibly to maintain an even temperature for the eggs. The young spiders spend a considerable time with their mother, overwintering in her tube until their sixth instar. It is reported that the female may die at this time and be eaten by her offspring (*see Coelotes* page 202). The complete life-cycle is thought to take a minimum of four years.

Eresus niger (Petagna)

Size female 9–16 mm; male 8–11 mm

Shares similarities with *Atypus* in that it lives in vertical tube in ground, has long life, and sometimes can be found in colonies. Web consists of tube lined with brownish silk which emerges from ground to form roof. Shelter is continued with strands of bluish, cribellate silk which are anchored to ground or nearby objects. Catching area of web can be very small and unobtrusive, making it difficult to find. **Female Carapace** Black with sprinkling of pale hairs. **Abdomen** Velvety black with few lighter hairs on front margin. Two rows of pits dorsally. **Legs** Black with light grey pubescence. Occasionally with small tufts of white hairs.

Male Carapace Black with orange-red hairs on sides of thorax or sometimes covering thorax completely. **Abdomen** Bright orange with three pairs of black spots; posterior pair much smaller than others. In some specimens these are ringed with white hairs. Sides, posterior margin, and venter black. **Legs** Black with rings of white hairs at joints. Sometimes with orange hairs on legs III and IV.

Habitat South-facing slopes among heather, under stones, etc well protected from wind. **Season** Autumn and possibly spring. **Distribution** Very rare as far north as Denmark. Protected species in Britain.

Facies

Carapace from above

Cross-section of web

♀
Eresus niger

♂
Eresus niger

Family Amaurobiidae

This family is represented in the region by five species of *Amaurobius* (including *A. erberi* (Keyserling) recorded from Belgium in the nineteenth century) and a single species of the smaller *Titanoeca*. Amaurobiids are large, robust spiders. The bluish cribellate web is most easily recognized in this family. They are all mature in the autumn, the males announcing their presence to prospective mates by drumming on the web with their palps. *Titanoeca* males use their legs to pull at the female's web when they conduct their springtime courtship. Amaurobiids are all nocturnal.

Amaurobius fenestralis (Stroem)
Size female 7–9 mm; male 5–7 mm
Carapace Brown, head usually darker. Sometimes with darker lines radiating from fovea. **Abdomen** Dark cardiac mark with very faint, lighter median line; surrounded by lighter area, mottled with white. Sides and rear greyish brown. Covered with short fine hairs. **Legs** Coloured as lighter parts of carapace with darker annulations.
Habitat Trunks of trees, under stones. **Season** Autumn. **Distribution** Common and widespread throughout.

Amaurobius similis (Blackwall)
Size female 9–12 mm; male 6–8 mm
Abdomen Cardiac mark has broader dividing band which is usually clear. Following chevrons usually thinner and clearer.
Habitat Principally crevices in walls but also under stones and bark. **Season** Autumn. **Distribution** As *A. fenestralis*

Amaurobius claustrarius (Hahn)
Size female c. 11 mm; male c. 8 mm
Similar to *A. fenestralis* and *A. similis* but with shorter cardiac mark, about one-third length of abdomen.
Habitat Under stones in damp places. Most frequent on mountains. **Season** Autumn. **Distribution** Absent from Britain. Widespread in Europe but generally less common than *A. fenestralis* and *A. similis*.

Amaurobius ferox (Walckenaer)
Size female 12–16 mm; male 9–12 mm
Largest and darkest of European species.
Female Abdomen Distinguished by dark abdomen. Dividing band of cardiac mark when visible, is very wide. Sides of this reduced to dark spots. **Legs** Too dark to distinguish any annulations. **Male** Almost identical to female. **Legs** Reddish brown and may have visible annulations. **Palp** Bulb conspicuously white.

Habitat Most frequently in houses, cellars, or gardens. **Season** Autumn to spring. **Distribution** Widespread in Britain, but rarer in the north. Widespread in Europe and North America.

Titanoeca obscura (Walckenaer)

Size female 5–7 mm; male c. 5 mm
Female Carapace Dark reddish brown; head darker. **Abdomen** Brown. **Legs** Dark reddish brown to black, covered with light pubescence. Spines few and confined to ventral side of legs. **Male** Coloration similar to female, but abdomen bears two pairs of light blotches – one pair near front margin, other at the mid-point.
Habitat Under stones, especially in chalky places, or in low vegetation or detritus. **Season** Spring. **Distribution** Absent from Britain. Widespread and common in Europe.

♀
Amaurobius fenestralis

♀
Titanoeca obscura
with egg sac

Family Dictynidae

None of the members of this family exceeds 5 millimetres in length and many are barely 2 or 3 millimetres. *Dictyna* species are by far the most common of the group, but even some of these are rare. Some of the *Dictyna* species are not easy to distinguish in the field because the patterns are composed of fragile hairs which are easily rubbed off. Only those with distinctive colours may be identified with certainty.

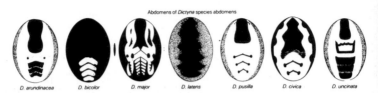

Abdomens of *Dictyna* species abdomens

D. arundinacea   D. bicolor   D. major   D. latens   D. pusilla   D. civica   D. uncinata

In the genus *Lathys* there are two species: *L. humilis* has two colour forms – as illustrated, it can be found in trees and bushes, but specimens found in damp detritus are often almost uniformly brown. This causes confusion with the much rarer *L. stigmatisata* which occupies a similar biotope at ground-level. *L. stigmatisata* has only been found in one or two places on the coast of southern England; it appears to be rare but widespread in Europe.

The genus *Argenna* comprises two species, *A. subnigra* and *A. patula*. Both are rare, are no bigger than 3 millimetres, and have no conspicuous field characteristics except that *A. subnigra* females have the epigyne consisting of two separated white discs which are sometimes distinct. The spider occurs under stones. *A. patula* is a brownish species with two lines of light streaks running the length of the abdomen; the spider has been found in detritus on the banks of tidal rivers or under stones on estuaries.

Altella lucida Simon is another rarity of about 1·5 millimetres which lives under detritus on dry heathland.

These species can best be determined by microscopic examination.

Dictyna arundinacea (Linnaeus)
Size female 3 mm; male 2·5 mm
Carapace Dark brown; head covered with rather coarse white hairs forming five longitudinal rows. **Abdomen** With short, coarse, white hairs. Two main areas devoid of hairs – cardiac area and similar region at rear of abdomen. Posterior region sometimes crossed by thin white lines. **Legs** Brownish yellow with pubescence.
Habitat On low, especially dry or dead vegetation. **Season** Spring and early summer. **Distribution** Common and widespread throughout.

Dictyna pusilla Thorell
Size female c. 2 mm; male c. 2 mm
Very similar to *D. arundinacea* but light border of median areas usually narrower, and sometimes with no posterior mark. **Legs** Dark ring apically on all segments.
Habitat and **Season** As *D. arundinacea*. **Distribution** Rare and local in England, Wales. Locally abundant in Scottish Highlands. Widespread but uncommon in Europe.

Dictyna major Menge
Size female 3–3·5 mm; male c. 3 mm
Larger than *D. arundinacea* and with abdominal markings.
Abdomen Cardiac mark with three spikes posteriorly followed by light space and faint bars or light bars with dark borders posteriorly. Thinner markings give abdomen lighter appearance than in other members of genus.
Habitat Sandy shores among detritus or low vegetation. **Season** Spring and summer. **Distribution** Scotland only. Very local in north.

Dictyna uncinata Thorell
Size female c. 2·5 mm; male c. 2 mm
Very similar to *D. arundinacea* and often found with it.
Abdomen Cardiac mark followed by pair of curved marks and posterior dark area with one or two light transverse lines.
Habitat, **Season**, and **Distribution** As *D. arundinacea*.

Dictyna civica (Lucas)
Size female c. 3 mm; male c. 2·5 mm
Resembles *D. uncinata* in abdominal pattern.
Legs Femora dark, remaining segments light brown with obscure annulations.
Habitat Walls. **Season** Spring. **Distribution** Absent from Britain and Scandinavia. Widespread elsewhere.

♀
*Dictyna
arundinacea*

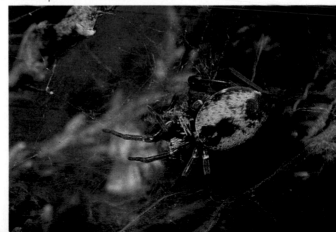

Dictyna latens (Fabricius)
Size female c. 3 mm; male c. 2 mm
Carapace Dark brown to black. With white hairs on head. **Abdomen** Dark brown to black, thickly covered by white hairs dorsally and on sides. Dorsal dark area is continuous, widest at its middle and with irregular edges. **Legs** Dark brown to black. With coarser hairs than *D. arundinacea*. **Habitat** Low vegetation and bushes, especially heather. **Season** Spring and early summer. **Distribution** Widespread but uncommon in Britain. Absent from Scandinavia. Widespread elsewhere.

Dictyna bicolor Simon
Size female 3 mm; male 3 mm
Carapace Dark reddish brown, with white hairs on head. **Abdomen** Black to dark brown with few white hairs. Posteriorly are four, light, contiguous marks reaching the spinners. **Legs** Femora very dark brown, other segments light brown with fine pubescence. **Habitat** Under stones or in detritus. **Season** Spring. **Distribution** Absent from Britain. Rare in Germany and Holland. More common in southern Europe.

Dictyna ammophila Menge
Size Male and female 2 mm
Very similar to *D. bicolor* but without lighter marks on abdomen which is uniformly dark.
Habitat Sand-dunes, under stones, moss etc. **Season** Spring. **Distribution** Poland and France. Very local.

Heterodictyna puella (Simon)
Size female c. 3 mm; male c. 2·5 mm
Female Carapace Greyish brown with broad light border. White hairs on head. **Abdomen** White with striking red cardiac mark, sometimes reduced to a spot. Sometimes followed by obscure reddish marks. **Legs** Pale yellow with fine pubescence on apical segments. **Male Carapace** Reddish brown with faintly lighter borders. **Abdomen** Variable, sometimes almost uniformly pink or with darker median stripe, widest posteriorly. **Legs** Pale brown with fine pubescence as in female.
Habitat Bushes. **Season** Spring to late summer. **Distribution** Very local in southern counties of England and Wales. Not recorded elsewhere in region but found around western Mediterranean.

Heterodictyna flavescens (Walckenaer)
Probably not distinguishable in the field from *H. puella* and has been recorded once only from County Durham in Britain. Absent from Denmark and further north. Uncommon to the south.

♀
Dictyna latens
with egg sac

♀
Dictyna bicolor

♀
*Heterodictyna
puella*

Heterodictyna walckenaeri Roewer

Size female 4–5 mm; male 3–4 mm

Female Carapace Yellow-brown; thorax greenish with light borders. White hairs sparse on head, but also present on clypeus. **Abdomen** Greenish with light hairs anteriorly and at sides. With paler green cardiac mark and posterior chevrons. **Legs** Yellow to greenish yellow. **Male Carapace** Reddish brown with lighter borders. **Abdomen** Similar to female. **Legs** Orange to brownish yellow.

Habitat Bushes. **Season** Late summer and early autumn. **Distribution** Local in England and confined to London and home counties. Widespread in Europe; absent from north, common in south.

Lathys humilis (Blackwall)

Size female c. 2 mm; male c. 2 mm

Carapace Black. **Abdomen** Reticulated with white spots dorsally, and with uniformly wide median band, constricted at middle. In some specimens this is absent anteriorly and posterior stripe is broken into chevrons. **Legs** Pale with very clear, thin annulations.

Habitat Trees and bushes. **Season** Spring and early summer. **Distribution** Widespread in Britain, locally common in south. Absent from Scandinavia. Widespread elsewhere.

Family Oecobiidae

The only species of the genus *Oecobius* to be found in northern Europe is an introduction, established in some hot houses but also found in the entymology department of the British Museum (Natural History). *O. annulipes* Lucas is a pale species, about 2·5 millimetres long, with an almost circular carapace; the ring of eyes is placed on a dark patch some way from the anterior margin. The abdomen is rather elongated with pairs of dark patches on both sides and in the middle. The legs are rather long, with annulations, which are fainter in the male. The web is a circular sheet, about 30 millimetres across, on flat surfaces and in corners. The spiders run very fast when disturbed. The species is found in all parts of the world, occurring outdoors in warm climates and seeking the shelter of buildings in cooler countries.

Family Uloboridae

Uloborus walckenaerius and *Hyptiotes paradoxus*, the sole members of this family in northern Europe, are unique among the spiders of the region in not possessing poison glands. To overcome this deficiency, the spiders wrap their prey very securely. I have watched *Uloborus* wrapping a small grasshopper for more than thirty minutes before feeding on it. (Both of them are very locally distributed –

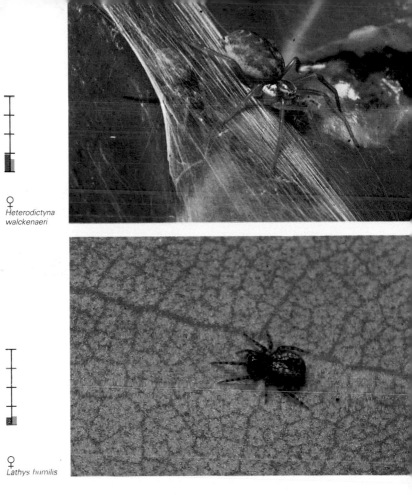

♀
*Heterodictyna
walckenaeri*

♀
Lathys humilis

Uloborus is confined to a few heathland sites in southern England although *Hyptiotes* is more widespread.)

The eyes of the uloborids are distinctive; those of *Uloborus* are in two rather separated, curved rows. The anteriors are very close to the front margin, the posteriors almost a third of the carapace length behind. *Hyptiotes* has the oddest eyes of any spider in the region. It is difficult to assign them to rows but the larger, rather protuberant posteriors are more-or-less in the mid-line of the carapace, and the anteriors are also well removed from the front of the head. In both cases all the eyes are dark.

Considering the size and shape of *Uloborus*, and the stabilmentum in the web, it may well be confused with *Cyclosa*, except that *Uloborus* makes an almost horizontal web whereas *Cyclosa*'s is almost vertical. *Hyptiotes* is known as the triangle spider because of its unique web, and the spider is so different in shape and features from any other native species that confusion is impossible.

Uloborus walckenaerius Latreille

Size female 4–6 mm; male 3–4 mm

Carapace Thickly covered by white hairs but with several dark bands running longitudinally. **Abdomen** Continuing pattern on carapace with white lines curving over sides. Each line has three or four tufts of white hairs which curve upwards. Ventrally with brown median band and pair of transverse bands which continue up sides. Bands absent on pale specimens. **Legs** Dark greyish brown with rather vague annulations of white hairs. I and II longer than III and IV.

Habitat Horizontal or slightly inclined web on low plants, especially heather. Has stabilmentum. Spider hangs below hub with forelegs close together making small angle with stabilmentum. Long, slender egg sac placed at side of web, hanging vertically surrounded by mass of fine strands. **Season** Early summer. **Distribution** Very local in central southern England. Local in France, Belgium, Holland, Germany.

Hyptiotes paradoxus (C. L. Koch)

Size female c. 6 mm; male c. 4 mm

Female Carapace Very broad and rather high. **Abdomen** Short and oval. High near mid-point and with several very small tubercles or tufts of hair running along edges of dorsal side. **Legs** Short and stout. Overall colour very variable, ranging from ginger to black. Markings are vague and consist of darker transverse lines which are found on dorsum and sides. **Male** Coloured as female or lighter. **Abdomen** short, rather cylindrical, and thickly covered with short hair. Legs are about same length as female and equally stout. Palpal organs conspicuously large and, together, equal volume of carapace.

Habitat Branches of evergreen trees and bushes usually 1·5 m or more above ground. In England associated with yew or box. Triangular web stretched by spider bridging loop at extremity of stretching thread. When prey strikes web, slack in loop is released, jerking web and further entrapping prey. This is done several times and spider lets out more silk from spinners and gathers in slack each time; spider continues to advance towards prey. Egg sac has tufted appearance and is attached to branches or tree trunk. **Season** Mid- to late summer. **Distribution** Very local and scattered in Britain, absent from Scotland and Wales. Widespread in Europe but rare in north.

♀
*Uloborus
walckenaerius*
wrapping prey

♀
*Hyptiotes
paradoxus*

♂
*Hyptiotes
paradoxus*

Families Oonopidae, Dysderidae, Segestriidae, Scytodidae

Unlike any other group of native spiders, members of these four diverse families have six eyes rather than eight and, for convenience, have been grouped together.

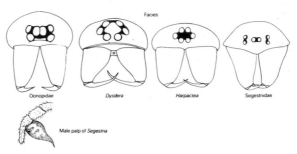

They are the haplogyne spiders of the region. The females do not show any external sign of maturity and the epigyne is absent; consequently, in females, size is the only indication of adulthood (which, given the normal variations among spiders, is not infallible) unless the spider is accompanied by a male or has an egg sac. Males are not often seen but their simple palpal organs are exposed and are not covered by the cymbium.

Nomadic species of these families do not indulge in courtship and the male uses his palps simultaneously – this is thought to be primitive. Bristowe reports, however, that *Oonops* males hold their palps close together, but only use one at a time.

Family Oonopidae

Two small, pink spiders are native to the region, although three other genera have been accidentally transported to Britain with plants and occur in hot-houses. All of these introductions have dorsal and ventral scuta and one, *Diblemma donisthorpei* O.P.-Cambridge, is distinguished by a single pair of eyes on the front of the carapace.

Oonops pulcher (meaning 'beautiful oval eyes') only occurs outdoors, and has been found in the webs of other spiders such as *Amaurobius*. *O. domesticus* walks with the front legs stretched out in front taking several steps at a leisurely pace followed by twice as many at a run. The egg sac is made within the mother's cell, the transparent silk of the sac revealing the two pink eggs. Probably several similar batches of eggs are laid. Both spiders are nocturnal and spend their days in a small silk cell which consists of few threads.

♀
*Oonops
domesticus*

Oonops domesticus de Dalmas
Size female 2 mm; male c. 1·5 mm.
Coloration pink or brownish red, with slightly lighter abdomen. Tibiae
I have five pairs of ventral spines.
Habitat Exclusively within houses in region, but in southern Europe
occurs under stones etc. **Season** Probably most times of year. **Distribution** Widespread in Britain but uncommon (unless it occurs in
your house!) Absent from Scandinavia. Widespread elsewhere.

Oonops pulcher Templeton
Differs from *O. domesticus* in having four pairs of ventral spines on
tibiae I
Habitat Under stones and in detritus. **Season** Spring. **Distribution**
Absent from very few counties in Britain. European records as for *O.
domesticus*.

Family Dysderidae

The three spiders of this family are generally large, elongated animals.
Dysdera spiders are free living and nocturnal, and are found in silk
cells during the day. The large divergent fangs and small eye grouping
give them a slightly mygalomorph appearance but the fangs are
articulated in the araneomorph, horizontal plane. This is an adaptation
which enables them to catch and eat woodlice, which most spiders
reject. The sexes mate without preliminaries, and the female wraps
her yellow eggs in silk within her retreat. The two species are very
similar. *Harpactea* is more elongated than *Dysdera*, particularly in the
male. The general habits are the same but *Harpactea*'s food preferences are not known, and the spider has no obvious morphological
adaptations for any particular group. The pink eggs of this species

are kept within the female's retreat without any wrapping, and are rather large compared with the spider which is the smallest member of the family.

Dysdera crocata C. L. Koch
Size female c. 12 mm; male c. 10 mm.
Carapace Brownish red, glabrous, and finely textured. **Abdomen** Light greyish to pinkish brown. Smooth and rather glossy. With two depressions at front. **Chelicerae** Fairly long and divergent. Fang is also long. **Legs** Lighter than carapace but same colour. With two short spines dorsally at basal end of femur IV.
Habitat Under stones and logs in warm situations. Sometimes in gardens. **Season** All year. **Distribution** Widespread and fairly common in Britain. Absent from Scandinavia. Widespread elsewhere.

Dysdera erythrina (Walckenaer)
Slightly smaller than *D. crocata*. Distinguished by absence of dorsal spines on femur IV.
Habitat As *D. crocata* but more tolerant of ants such as *Lasius flavus* (Fabricius). **Season** As *D. crocata*. **Distribution** Absent from Scotland and Scandinavia. Widespread elsewhere.

Harpactea hombergi (Scopoli)
Size female 7 mm; male 6 mm
Carapace Black, head glossier than thorax. **Abdomen** Greyish brown to black. Elongated, especially in male. **Legs** Pale brown with femora darkened except at base, and tibiae and metatarsi darkened mainly at base. **Palps** Dark brown.
Habitat Under stones, bark etc. **Season** Probably all year. **Distribution** Widespread and fairly common throughout.

Family Segestriidae

The three *Segestria* species make tubular webs which are characterized by the dozen or so radiating threads which proceed from the mouth of the tube.

Segestria senoculata (Linnaeus)
Size female and male 7–10 mm
Carapace Dark brown; head darker, almost black. Glabrous. **Abdomen** Elongated. Greyish to light brown with darker-lobed median band and some spots at sides. **Legs** Light brown with darker annulations. Front legs distinctly darker than III and IV.
Habitat Under stones, in holes in walls, under bark. **Season** Spring. **Distribution** Widespread and common throughout.

♀
Dysdera crocata

♂
Harpactea hombergi

♀
Segestria senoculata

Segestria bavarica C. L. Koch
Size female 10–14 mm; male 8–10 mm
Resembles *S. senoculata* but usually larger and slightly darker. **Abdomen** Median band narrower anteriorly and has in its centre line a row of light dashes, reinforced by white hairs. Some specimens generally hairier than *S. senoculata* and gaps between lobes also have white hairs giving an impression of chevrons. **Legs** Darker with less clear markings than *S. senoculata*.
Habitat Usually under stones, in walls, or cracks in cliffs, etc. **Season** Spring mainly, but both sexes can be found at most times of year. **Distribution** Very local in southern central and south-west England, usually on coast. Widespread in Europe, not confined to coast.

Segestria florentina (Rossi)
Size female up to 22 mm; male up to 15 mm
Almost uniformly black, apart from pubescence on abdomen which makes it appear grey, and the slightly lighter fourth legs. Chelicerae have distinctive metallic green sheen, hence specific name.
Habitat As *S. senoculata* and *S. bavarica*. **Season** Mid- to late summer. **Distribution** Very local in southern England and south Wales. Often near ports. Also Belgium, France, Holland, and countries to south.

Family Scytodidae

Scytodes thoracica is instantly recognizable because of the similarity in size of the prosoma and opisthosoma. The spider has been given the name of 'spitting spider' because of its method of attacking its prey. It is able to project a spray, over a distance of 10 millimetres, composed of gum and poison which cements the prey to the substrate, allowing the slow-moving spider to close in and deliver its fatal bite. It is possible that the spider locates the direction and distance of prey using the long trichobothria which are present on the distal ends of the metatarsi.

Scytodes thoracica Latreille
Size female 4–6 mm; male c. 4 mm
Carapace Oval and very high. Pale yellow-brown with black markings. **Abdomen** Not much larger than carapace. Similar in colour and with several pairs of spots in median line. Front pairs usually joined to form bars. Rows of smaller spots continue over sides. **Legs** Coloured as carapace with clear black annulations.
Habitat Houses. **Season** Early summer and possibly at other times. **Distribution** Southern England and Wales. Common in some places. Most of Europe except extreme north.

♀
Segestria bavarica

♀
*Segestria
florentina*

♀
*Scytodes
thoracica*

Family Pholcidae

These are long-legged spiders which make tangled webs inside buildings (in warmer climates they also occur out of doors).

The family is represented in the region by three species in two genera. The species may be separated by size, and the genera by the shape and colour of the abdomen which is long, tubular, and grey in *Pholcus*, but globular and bluish in *Psilochorus*. The carapace is subcircular with the eyes in a compact group near the front margin. The slender legs lack spines, but are clothed with many, regularly spaced long hairs. The tarsi are segmented and allow a limited amount of flexibility. The spiders hang inverted in their webs and, if disturbed, gyrate at great speed.

This is a primitive family, the males having rather large and exposed palpal organs although these are more complex than those of the preceding families. The female epigynes are visible but simple.

The male encounters a female's web in his wanderings and rather subtly vibrates his body to indicate his presence. The female approaches him and hangs head down while he inserts both of his palps together. The copulation lasts several hours and the two spiders part. The female's egg sac is more reduced than in any other family; the twenty or so eggs have very few strands of silk around them so that they are clearly visible as they are held in the female's chelicerae. Therefore, the young do not moult until they are free of the sac.

Pholcus phalangioides (Fuesslin)
Size female and male 8–10 mm
Carapace Almost circular; very pale with dark-grey patch over foveal region. **Abdomen** Tubular. Pale grey with darker dorsal marks. Clothed with fine, short hairs. **Sternum** Uniformly grey. **Legs** About five times body length, with long, fine hairs. Pale brown, with femora and tibiae lighter apically. Patellae dark. Tarsi flexible. **Epigyne** Like an inverted т.
Habitat Buildings. **Season** Early summer; females at most times of year. **Distribution** Absent from north of region. Widespread and fairly common elsewhere. Most common in southern Britain; also recorded from Scotland. All warmer parts of world.

Pholcus opilionoides (Schrank)
Size female and male c. 5 mm
Similar to *P. phalangioides*.
Sternum Greyish with lighter spots – one in middle and four laterals opposite coxae. **Epigyne** Broadly triangular.
Habitat and **Season** As *P. phalangioides*. **Distribution** Absent from Britain and north of region. More common to south.

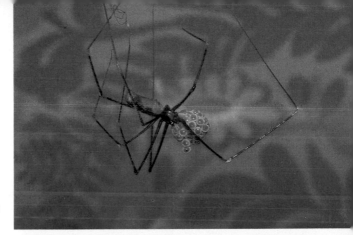

♀
*Pholcus
phalangioides*
with
egg sac

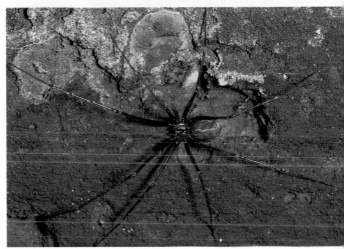

♀
*Psilochorus
simoni*

Psilochorus simoni (Berland)

Size female and male c. 2·5 mm
Carapace Pale with dark median band covering head and tapered posteriorly. **Abdomen** Short and very high; spinners ventrally placed. Bluish green or blue, covered with fine hairs. With paler dentate cardiac mark. **Legs** Brown with lighter apical patches on femora and tibiae. With long fine hairs.
Habitat Dry cellars. **Season** Probably most times of year. **Distribution** Widespread but infrequent in England and Wales. Also recorded from France, Belgium. Thought to be of American origin.

Family Zodariidae

This small family is represented within the region by the genus *Zodarion*. Most of the *Zodarion* species occur in the lands around the Mediterranean. The spiders are small and fast moving, and are believed to feed exclusively on ants, among which they may be found running. Two species occur in the region, *Z. gallicum* and *Z. germanicum*, but neither is common. The female constructs an oval egg sac suspended by a stalk, within an outer silk shell to which small pieces of vegetable debris have been fastened.

Eyes from above

Zodarion gallicum (Simon)
Size female c. 3·5 mm; male 2·5 mm
Carapace Dark to reddish brown, sometimes lighter anteriorly. **Abdomen** Dorsally black with fine pubescence. Ventrally very pale. **Spinners** Anteriors moderately long and joined at bases. **Legs** Rather slender, without spines, but with covering of fine hairs. Yellow-brown with femora somewhat darkened, especially in males.
Habitat Dry, sandy places. **Season** Summer? **Distribution** Absent from Britain and Scandinavia. Rare in France.

Zodarion germanicum (C. L. Koch)
Size female c. 5 mm; male 3·5 mm
Very similar to *Z. gallicum*.
Habitat In moss, under stones in fairly dry places in pine woods. **Season** Summer? **Distribution** France and Germany, especially on high ground.

Family Gnaphosidae

Gnaphosids are brownish to black spiders with irregular posterior median eyes and rather long tubular spinners.

Facies

Carapace from above

Spinners from below

Zodarion sp

Carapace In most genera it is broad anteriorly although it may be rather pointed in others. **Eyes** The eyes are set in two rows with the anterior medians dark while the others are pearly. The posterior medians may be oval, triangular, or (in *Callilepis*) reduced to slits. **Abdomen** The abdomen is narrowly oval and rather pointed posteriorly. It may be either uniformly coloured with a shiny appearance or have a pattern of white spots. **Legs** Gnaphosid legs are of medium length, rather stout in some genera, and have few spines. They often have a pubescence and scopulae on the apical segments. **Spinners** The anteriors are prominent, tubular, and widely spaced.

The spiders of this family are mostly nocturnal and may be found within a silk cell under stones or in detritus in dry situations. They are nearly all adult in the earlier part of the year. Males make their cells next to those of subadult females and mate with them immediately after they have moulted. Subsequent meetings of the two sexes may result in copulation with little visible sign of courtship, save some brief leg 'tickling'. Once the mating is completed, the males will dash away at some speed. Females make their egg sacs in the summer; the eggs are contained in a thick-walled sac which is enclosed in the retreat. The mother stays with it until the young hatch. The females of *Herpyllus* can live for more than a year as adults, and it is possible that some of the other genera may, too.

Genus *Drassodes*

Five species of this genus are found within the region. *D. lapidosus* is the most common species and also the largest. All are brown in colour, have no definite markings, and consequently they are difficult to identify.

Drassodes lapidosus (Walckenaer)

Size female 10–18 mm; male 10–13 mm
Carapace Greyish to reddish brown with black border line. Covered thickly with short hairs. **Eyes** Posterior medians closely spaced. **Abdomen** Coloured as carapace; also with pubescence. Sometimes with greyish cardiac mark. **Legs** Similar in colour to carapace.
Habitat Under stones. **Season** Spring principally, but also at other times of year. **Distribution** Generally common and widespread throughout.

Drassodes cupreus (Blackwall)

Identical to *D. lapidosus*.
Habitat In Britain restricted to heathland, at least in south. Occurs in Europe.

Drassodes pubescens (Thorell)

Size female 6–8 mm; male 5–7 mm
Smaller than *D. lapidosus* and usually paler, especially carapace and legs.
Habitat Under stones, in woods and more exposed places. **Season** Spring to early summer. **Distribution** Rather uncommon but widespread throughout.

Genus *Haplodrassus*

Previously included with *Drassodes*, haplodrassids may be distinguished by the coppery coloured hairs on the abdomen and lighter chevrons.

Haplodrassus signifer (C. L. Koch)

Size female c. 8 mm; male 6–8 mm
Carapace Brown to almost black. **Abdomen** Dark brown to black with coppery sheen. In some specimens several pairs of small, light spots surround darker median stripe, followed by obscure chevrons. **Legs** Brown.
Habitat Often in sandy places – heathland and dunes. Under low vegetation and stones. **Season** Spring and early summer. **Distribution** Common and widespread throughout.

Haplodrassus umbratilis (L. Koch)

Greatly resembles *H. signifer* but is slightly smaller.
Distribution New Forest in England. Widespread in northern Europe.

♀
*Drassodes
lapidosus* with
egg sac

♀
*Drassodes
pubescens*

♀
*Haplodrassus
signifer*

Haplodrassus dalmatensis (L. Koch)

Size female 5 mm; male 4·5 mm
Smaller than *H. signifer* but with clearer markings.
Habitat Under stones and detritus on heathland. **Season** Spring.
Distribution Widespread but very local in southern Britain. Widespread in northern Europe.

Haplodrassus silvestris (Blackwall)

Size female 8–10 mm; male c. 8 mm
Resembles *H. signifer* but carapace and legs more reddish.
Habitat Under stones, bark, or fallen leaves in woods. **Season** Spring.
Distribution Widespread but rare in Britain. Widespread throughout.

Haplodrassus minor (O.P.-Cambridge)

Size female 4 mm; male c. 3·5 mm
Smallest member of genus, resembling *H. signifer*.
Habitat Shingle beaches on east and south coasts. **Season** Early summer. **Distribution** Rare and local in Europe.

Genus *Herpyllus*

The three native species (one in Britain) are characterized by the somewhat greasy appearance of the hair on the abdomen. The males are distinguished by the presence of a dorsal scutum.

Herpyllus blackwalli (Thorell)

Size female 10 mm; male 8 mm
Carapace Dark brown. Narrowed in front and with fine pubescence. **Eyes** Posteriors equally spaced. **Abdomen** Brownish grey with thick, but short, greasy looking pubescence. Male has dorsal scutum, clearly visible in thin specimens. **Legs** Brown with thick pubescence. Rather short and stout.
Habitat In Britain around houses but under bark etc in Europe. **Season** Autumn, but females are long lived and found throughout year.
Distribution Widespread throughout.

Herpyllus scutulatus (L. Koch)
and Herpyllus quadripunctatus (Linnaeus)

Size female 10–16 mm; male c. 8 mm
Similar to *H. blackwalli* but larger. Males may be distinguished by length of abdominal scutum: in *H. scutulatus* it is about one-third length of abdomen; in *H. quadripunctatus* it is about half length of abdomen.
Distribution Absent from Britain. Most of northern Europe.

♀
*Haplodrassus
dalmatensis*

♂
*Herpyllus
blackwalli*

Genus *Callilepis*

This is a small genus with only a single species in the region. Like *Herpyllus*, the legs are strong, especially the anteriors which are also furnished with noticeable spines. The abdomen has a distinctive pattern composed of areas of glistening hairs. The spider is known to feed on ants using a specialized technique of biting at the base of the antenna, then waiting briefly for the poison to take effect. The prey is then removed to a retreat and consumed without external damage. The spider has an ant-like movement but is rather stout in appearance.

Callilepis nocturna (Linnaeus)
Size female 3·5 mm; male c. 3 mm
Carapace Broad, but narrowed anteriorly. Dark brown but thickly covered with light, coarse hairs which are easily rubbed off. **Eyes** Posterior medians reduced to slits. **Abdomen** Black with broad patch of light hairs on anterior margin. Two small spots at mid-point and further pair of larger patches near spinners. **Legs** Reddish brown, the front pair stronger and darker than III, IV. All with number of spines. **Habitat** British record refers to sandy bank near sea. Among stones in pinewoods in Europe. **Season** Spring. **Distribution** Only site in Britain is in Devon. Not uncommon in Europe and widespread.

Genus *Phaeocedus*

This genus contains just one species, with a subspecies described from southern France. The spider is widespread but apparently rare throughout. It is rather ant-like in movement and resembles a *Micaria* but without the iridescence. The males are usually better marked than females. The food preferences of this species are not known.

Phaeocedus braccatus (L. Koch)
Size female c. 6 mm; male 4·5 mm
Carapace Brown to black, with patches of white pubescence. **Abdomen** Black with fine pubescence. In male there is usually distinct pattern; very faint in females. Pair of light spots on anterior border, with two pairs of transverse spots in front of mid-line. **Legs** Brownish. Femora I and II dark, and apical segments also darkened.
Habitat Detritus and under stones. Ant-like when running. **Season** Early to mid-summer. **Distribution** Rare and local in southern England. Widespread but rare in Europe.

Genus *Zelotes*

This is a large genus (fifty-four species in France) and the only black spiders of 5 millimetres and over which occur in the region. There is some variation in the amount of black pigmentation on the legs which helps to distinguish some of the species. The carapace is noticeably narrowed anteriorly and, consequently, the eye rows are rather short. The carapace is usually glossy, the abdomen less so.

There are about fifteen species found within the region, most of which are superficially very similar. Apart from the first two described here, *Z. rusticus* and *Z. electus*, the remaining species can be distinguished in some cases by the markings of the legs.

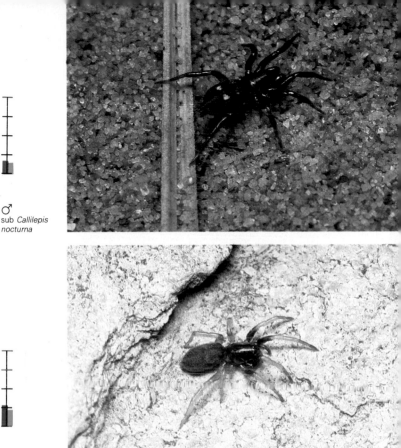

♂ sub *Callilepis nocturna*

Phaeocedus braccatus immature

Zelotes rusticus (L. Koch)
Size female 8·5 mm; male 6·5 mm
Carapace and Legs Orange-brown. **Abdomen** Greyish brown with faintly orange-brown cardiac mark.
Habitat Under stones, sometimes around buildings. **Season** Spring and summer? **Distribution** Scattered and very rare in England and Wales. France, Germany, Holland, Sweden.

Zelotes electus (C. L. Koch)
Size female 4–5 mm; male 3·5–4·5 mm
Carapace Dark to mid-brown. **Abdomen** Brownish black, with fine pubescence. **Legs** Femora light brown, darkened apically. Patellae, tibiae, and metatarsi dark brown, tarsi lighter. Legs rather stouter than in other British species.
Habitat Under stones or among low vegetation or lichens in sandy areas. Most British records from coastal dunes. **Season** Spring and early summer. **Distribution** Widespread around coasts of Britain, sometimes locally common. Widespread in Europe.

Zelotes pedestris (C. L. Koch)
Size female 7 mm; male c. 5 mm
Body black. Widespread in southern England and Europe.

Leg showing amount of black pigmentation

Zelotes lutetianus (L. Koch)
Size female c. 7 mm; male c. 5 mm
Body dark brown. Damp places. Widespread but rare in Britain. Widespread in Europe.

Leg showing amount of black pigmentation

Zelotes pusillus (C. L. Koch)
Size female c. 4 mm; male c. 3·5 mm
Body very dark brown. Widespread in dry places in Britain and Europe.

Zelotes villicus (Thorell)
Absent from Britain. Widespread in Europe.

Zelotes praeficus (L. Koch)
Size female c. 5 mm; male c. 4·5 mm
Body very dark brown to black. Uncommon in southern England. Widespread in Europe.

Leg showing amount of black pigmentation

Zelotes petrensis (C. L. Koch)
Size male and female c. 6·5 mm
Body black. Rare and very local in south-east England. Widespread in Europe.

♀
Zelotes electus
with egg sac

♀
Zelotes pedestris

♀
Zelotes pusillus

Zelotes latreillei (Simon)
Size female c. 8 mm; male 5–8 mm
Body glossy black. Widespread in Britain and not uncommon. Widespread in Europe.

Leg showing amount of black pigmentation

Zelotes apricorum (L. Koch)
Size female 7–9 mm; male c. 6 mm
Body glossy black. Widespread and fairly frequent in Britain. Uncommon in Europe.

Zelotes serotinus (L. Koch)
Size female c. 8 mm; male c. 6 mm
Body glossy black. Very local in Britain on heathland. Fairly widespread in Europe.

Genus *Poecilochroa*

These are attractively marked spiders with similar patterns in both sexes. The slight differences in the patches of shining white hairs on the abdomen make identification straightforward. These spiders appear to be less nocturnal than some of the preceding species.

Poecilochroa variana (C. L. Koch)
Size female c. 8 mm; male c. 6 mm
Carapace Dark reddish brown with median band of dense white hairs, and patches on margins. **Abdomen** Almost matt-black with patches of dense white hairs; these consist of anterior band, two transverse bars in middle, and short band above spinners. **Legs** Femora black, remaining segments reddish brown. With white pubescence, especially on III and IV.
Habitat Dry, sandy places, in detritus or under stones. **Season** Spring and summer. **Distribution** Absent from Britain. Widespread in Europe.

Poecilochroa conspicua (L. Koch)
Resembles *P. variana* closely.
Carapace Black. **Abdomen** Lacks posterior bar above spinners. **Legs** Femora black, tibiae brown, metatarsi and tarsi lighter.
Habitat Trees and bushes. **Season** As *P. variana*. Distribution Absent from Britain and Scandinavia. Widespread elsewhere.

♀
Zelotes apricorum
with egg sac

♀
Poecilochroa
variana

Genus *Aphantaulax*

One species, *A. seminiger* Simon, has a close resemblance to *Poecilochroa*, but with uniformly dark legs. The carapace is black and somewhat glossy; the abdomen has an anterior white band, two transverse white patches near the middle, and two small spots above the spinners. The spider is found on the Atlantic coast of France. A subspecies, *A. s. trimaculatus* Simon, occurs in the same area and as far north as Brittany. This spider lacks the posterior markings and has a metallic glint to the abdomen. Like *Poecilochroa*, it is diurnal.

Genus *Gnaphosa*

Fifteen species of this genus are found within the region but only one is common in Britain. They are rather similar in their grey-brown coloration, with stout brownish legs and the abdomen thickly covered with grey hair. Their stronghold appears to be in montane habitats; Norway has several endemic species. The similarity of colouring makes them impossible to distinguish in the field.

Gnaphosa leporina (L. Koch)
Size female 9 mm; male c. 6 mm
Carapace Dark brown to black. **Abdomen** Greyish brown, thickly covered with short grey hairs and sparsely covered by long black hairs. **Legs** Colour as carapace. With coarse hairs and ventral spines. **Habitat** Damp, bare areas of heathland. **Season** Summer. **Distribution** Uncommon and scattered in Britain. Widespread in Europe.

Genus *Micaria*

These are small spiders with an ant-like appearance and very speedy gait. They appear to be active only in bright sunshine. The body is adorned with patches of squamose (flattened) hairs with a strong and clear metallic lustre in some species. This distinguishes them from the otherwise rather similar *Phrurolithus* species in the next family, Clubionidae.

Micaria fulgens (Walckenaer)
Size female c. 6 mm; male c. 5 mm
Carapace Dark brown with grey hairs on thorax, iridescent red and yellow hairs on head and chelicerae. **Abdomen** Black with vague transverse bands of light grey hairs on dorsum and sides.**Legs** I and II mid-brown; III and IV darker. Femora with dark dorsal stripe on I and II; light stripe of hairs on IV. Metatarsi and tarsi I, II darker. **Habitat** Among stones in dry places. **Season** Spring. **Distribution** Absent from Britain. Very widespread in Europe.

Micaria pulicaria (Sundevall)
Size female 3–4 mm; male c. 3·5 mm
Carapace Black with radiating lines of white hairs; moderately iridescent. **Abdomen** Black; very iridescent. Short, white, transverse line anteriorly with parallel one ventrally. At mid-point is second transverse line which runs on to sides. Followed by median row of three white dots. **Legs** Brown in female; reddish brown in male. Femora I and II black, III and IV dark brown. **Habitat** Sunny gardens, wasteland etc. **Season** Spring to early autumn. **Distribution** Common and widespread throughout.

♀
*Gnaphosa
leporina*

♀
Micaria fulgens

♂
Micaria pulicaria

Micaria scintillans (O.P.-Cambridge)
Size female c. 5 mm; male c. 4 mm
Similar to *M. pulicaria*.
Abdomen Wider lines and no white spots. **Distribution** Local in counties bordering south coast. France.

Micaria silesiaca L. Koch
Size female c. 5 mm; male c. 4 mm
Similar to *M. pulicaria*.
Abdomen Even more obscure bars. **Legs** Rather uniformly brown with lighter patches on patellae and basal parts of tibiae I and II.
Habitat and Distribution Rare in sandy places in south and east of England. Absent from France. Most of Europe.

Micaria formicaria (Sundevall)
Size female 7·5 mm; male c. 5 mm
Largest *Micaria* in region.
Carapace Iridescent like *M. fulgens*. **Abdomen** Iridescent like *M. pulicaria*, with white transverse lines. **Legs** I darkened on femora, metatarsi, and tarsi; III and IV uniformly brown.
Habitat Dry, sandy places. **Season** Mid- to late summer. **Distribution** Absent from Britain and Belgium. Widespread elsewhere.

Micaria subopaca Westring
Size female c. 3 mm; male c. 2·5 mm
The smallest British *Micaria*.
Carapace Dark brown with very few white hairs. **Abdomen** Iridescent with single white transverse line. **Legs** All femora darkened.
Habitat Trunks of trees, especially pines if exposed to sun. **Season** Spring to late summer. **Distribution** In Britain locally common in Hampshire, Surrey, Sussex. Mainly northern in Europe.

Micariolepis dives (Lucas)
Size female 3–4 mm; male 2–3 mm
Carapace Brown, head darker, and lateral dark spots. Purplish iridescence on head. **Abdomen** Yellow-brown with darker areas anteriorly, laterally, and posteriorly. With blue or green iridescence. **Legs** Yellow. Femora basally dark or with dark streaks. Metatarsi dark. Long and thin with conspicuous spines on leg I only.
Habitat Under stones and in detritus, in dry and sunny places. **Season** Early summer. **Distribution** Absent from Britain, Scandinavia. Uncommon elsewhere.

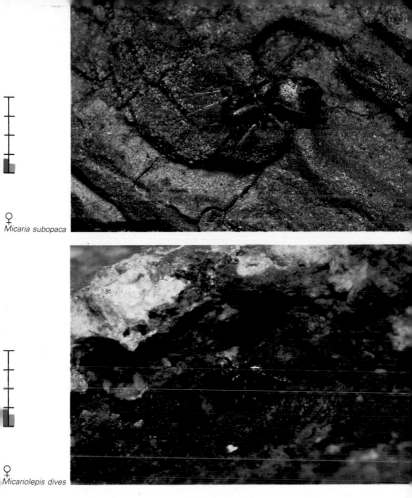

♀
Micaria subopaca

♀
Micariolepis dives

SUPERFAMILY CLUBIONOIDEA

Families Clubionidae, Liocranidae, Zoridae, Anyphaenidae

The members of this superfamily have been included in the family Clubionidae at various times, usually as subfamilies. The families contain genera of similar appearance and habits, but they are fairly easily distinguished in the field.

Family Clubionidae

The members of this family are medium- to small-sized spiders, mostly brown in colour with no pattern, and nocturnal habits.

Eyes viewed from the front

Carapace from above

Spinners from below

Carapace It is oval, with the head protruding somewhat. The carapace is fairly bulbous and has a silky pubescence in *Clubiona*, but is more bulbous and glabrous in *Cheiracanthium*. **Eyes** These are pearly, with the anterior medians slightly darker. They occur in two rows, the posterior medians widely spaced and not irregular. In *Clubiona*, the anterior row appears to comprise six eyes; in *Cheiracanthium*, the eyes are in three groups, similar to the araneids. **Abdomen** The abdomen is oval. It is slim and almost unmarked in *Clubiona*, but broader and with a median stripe in *Cheiracanthium*. **Chelicerae** In females, they are of moderate size or bulbous basally. Males have more attenuated chelicerae, especially in *Cheiracanthium*. **Legs** These are moderately long and rather slender. There are dorsal spines on the femora in *Clubiona*, but not in *Cheiracanthium*. The legs are uniformly coloured. Apical segments have scopulae. **Spinners** The spinners are fairly long, and occur in a compact group and of equal length. The posteriors are thinner than the anteriors. They are not as tubular as in Gnaphosidae.

Genus *Clubiona*

Twenty-four species of *Clubiona* are found within the region and, considering the lack of distinctive markings on all but two – *C. corticalis* and *C. compta* – they are not easy to distinguish in the field. The depth of colour does not vary to the extent that it does in other families, and the relative tone of the legs, abdomen, and chelicerae is a good guide to the species.

All the species are adult in spring and early summer, a few at other times as well. Many are typical of damp habitats and low vegetation but *C. brevipes* and *C. compta* frequent trees and bushes. Some of them make silk retreats habitually, others only for moulting. Their nocturnal habits and plain appearance has, perhaps, discouraged much investigation into their biology. It is known that there is little courtship by the male, but he uses his longer, more attenuated

Clubiona egg sac

chelicerae to hold the female prior to, and during the hour-long mating. The females of the more aerial species silk up a leaf in which to lay their pale-yellow eggs, without any further covering. Those species which inhabit the lower vegetation layers have a very characteristic way of folding over the end of a blade of grass to form a tetrahedral retreat, lined with white silk. The female remains on guard until the young have hatched. The spiders probably live for about one year.

Clubiona corticalis (Walckenaer)

Size female c. 0 mm; male 0–10 mm
Female Carapace Yellow-brown. **Abdomen** Brown, with lighter dorsal area enclosing dark cardiac mark. Followed by several light chevrons. **Legs** Coloured as carapace. **Male** Similar to female. **Palp** Extremely bulbous ventrally
Habitat Under bark, stones etc and around houses. **Season** Spring to summer. **Distribution** Common and widespread in England, Wales, Europe.

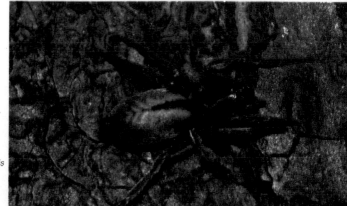

♀
Clubiona corticalis

Clubiona reclusa O.P.-Cambridge
Size female 6–8 mm; male c. 6 mm
Typical member of genus in its uniform brown coloration.
Carapace, Chelicerae, Legs Similar in colour. In male legs and chelicerae often lighter than carapace. Chelicerae noticeably small in male.
Habitat Low vegetation in wet places. **Season** Spring and early summer. **Distribution** Common and widespread throughout.

Clubiona stagnatilis Kulczynski
Size female 6–8 mm; male c. 6 mm
Similar to *C. reclusa*
Female Chelicerae Dark. **Male** Chelicerae Almost black.

Clubiona pallidula (Clerck)
Size female 8–11 mm; male 6–8 mm
Carapace Dark greyish brown. **Abdomen** Dark reddish to purplish brown. **Legs** Coloured as carapace but with femora lighter.
Habitat As *C. reclusa*. **Season** Summer. **Distribution** Absent from Scandinavia. Widespread elsewhere.

Clubiona phragmitis C. L. Koch
Size female 8–11 mm; male 5–10 mm
Carapace Yellow-brown; head darker. **Abdomen** Greyish brown, thickly covered with silky hairs. **Chelicerae** Dark and enlarged basally, less so in males. **Legs** Yellow-brown.
Habitat As *C. reclusa*. Female constructs egg sac retreat in high vegetation, such as *Phragmites* heads. **Season** Spring and summer. **Distribution** Locally abundant throughout.

♀
*Clubiona
phragmiti*

♀
Clubiona reclusa

♂
Clubiona stagnatilis

♀
Clubiona pallidula

Clubiona terrestris Westring
Size female 6 mm; male 5 mm.
Carapace Light yellow-brown; head darker. **Abdomen** Light reddish brown dorsally, yellow-brown at sides and below. **Chelicerae** Dark brown. **Legs** Very pale.
Habitat Among low vegetation, under stones, etc. **Season** Adults at most seasons. **Distribution** Common and widespread throughout.

Clubiona neglecta O. P.-Cambridge
Size female 6–8 mm; male 4·5 mm
Slightly darker than *C. terrestris* on body, but with pale legs.
Distribution Less common than *C. terrestris* but equally widespread throughout.

Clubiona lutescens Westring
Size female 6–8 mm; male c. 6 mm
Rather dark reddish or yellowish brown.
Distribution Common and widespread throughout.

Clubiona compta C. L. Koch
Size female 4–6 mm; male c. 4 mm
Smaller, lighter version of *C. corticalis*.
Abdomen Almost identical to *C. corticalis*.
Habitat Trees and bushes, occasionally under loose bark. **Season** Spring to mid-summer; some females throughout year. **Distribution** Common and widespread throughout.

Clubiona brevipes Blackwall
Size female c. 6 mm; male c. 5 mm
Carapace Very dark brown to black. **Abdomen** Reddish brown with darker cardiac mark. Darker in male. **Legs** Light yellow-brown or yellow with metatarsi III and IV darkened apically.
Habitat Foliage of oaks and other trees and bushes. Sometimes under loose bark. **Season** Spring and early summer. **Distribution** Common and widespread throughout.

♀
Clubiona terrestris

♀
Clubiona compta

♀
Clubiona brevipes

Clubiona trivialis C. L. Koch
Size female c. 4 mm; male c. 3·5 mm
Carapace Yellowish to reddish brown. **Abdomen** Reddish brown.
Legs Pale reddish brown.
Habitat Exposed places, on low vegetation, heather, gorse, etc. **Season** Adults all year. **Distribution** Fairly common and widespread throughout.

Clubiona subtilis L. Koch
Size female 3–4 mm; male c. 3 mm
Carapace Brown. Darker in male. **Abdomen** Yellowish with brown cardiac mark, sometimes browner posteriorly. **Legs** Pale yellow-brown.
Habitat Grasses and moss in wet places. **Season** All year. **Distribution** Widespread but scattered in Britain; locally common in south. Widespread in Europe.

Clubiona diversa O.P.-Cambridge
Size female c. 4 mm; male 3–4 mm
Male and female similar. Resembles *C. subtilis* but rather broader.
Abdomen Much paler markings than *C. subtilis*.
Distribution Generally less common than *C. subtilis*.

Genus *Cheiracanthium*

The spiders of this genus have more robust bodies but thinner legs than *Clubiona*. *C. erraticum*, the most frequently found species, also has a clear abdominal pattern. The spiders are usually found in a silk retreat during the day and when about to moult. In the spring the adult male seeks out the retreat of the female, and constructs his own retreat adjoining the female's. In the case of *C. pennyi*, once the female had moulted, the male drummed with his palps and first legs on the female's retreat. After a short delay this was repeated; then he tore open the silk, entered the retreat touching the female's legs, and added silk to her retreat as well as to her legs and chelicerae before mating. In the summer, the female makes a globular retreat, with the eggs in a separate compartment at the top of the sac, while the spider occupies the lower chamber. The eggs are pink. *C. virescens* makes her egg sac beneath stones.

♀
Clubiona trivialis
with egg sac

♀
Clubiona subtilis

Cheiracanthium erraticum (Walckenaer)
Size female c. 7 mm; male c. 5 mm
Carapace Light brown but some specimens greyish with two lighter patches on head and irregular light border. **Abdomen** Greyish at sides, with broad light-yellow median band enclosing dull reddish-brown median stripe. **Legs** Light yellow-brown; apical ends of tarsi darkened.
Habitat Among grass and low plants, often in cell. In summer, females construct spherical egg sac, in which they enclose themselves with pink eggs. **Season** Spring. **Distribution** Commonest *Cheiracanthium*. Widespread and fairly common throughout.

Cheiracanthium pennyi O.P.-Cambridge
Very similar to *C. erraticum*.
Habitat and Distribution More open places. In southern England on heather, but very rarely. Absent from Scandinavia. Widespread but uncommon elsewhere.

Cheiracanthium virescens (Sundevall)
Size female 5–8 mm; male c. 6 mm
Carapace Brown with slight greenish tinge. **Abdomen** Greenish to reddish brown with faintly darker cardiac mark. No further marks posterior to this. **Legs** Similar in colour to carapace.
Habitat Under stones or on heather etc in dry, sandy places. **Season** Spring. **Distribution** Widespread but uncommon throughout.

Cheiracanthium punctorium (Villers)
Size female 10–15 mm; male 8–12 mm
Similar greenish coloration to *C. virescens* but much larger.
Habitat Moist places. **Season** Mid-summer. **Distribution** Absent from Britain. Widespread in Europe.

Cheiracanthium oncognathum Thorell
Size female c. 12 mm; male c. 10 mm
Resembles *C. punctorium*. Females usually lack red-brown median stripe but males retain it.
Habitat Woodland edges, on bushes. **Season** Spring. **Distribution** Absent from Britain, Holland, Belgium. Widespread elsewhere.

Family Liocranidae

The spiders of this family were placed with the clubionids, and strongly resemble them. The liocranids differ in having several pairs of ventral spines on the tibiae and metatarsi of legs I and II. Except for *Apostenus fuscus* and *Liocranum rutilans*, they tend to have clear markings, especially on the carapace.

♀
*Cheiracanthium
erraticum*

♀
*Cheiracanthium
virescens*

Genus *Agroeca*

The five species of northern Europe are rather similar and are found in low vegetation. The carapace has dark, streaked lateral bands and the abdomen has some faint chevrons. The ventral spines are reduced in this genus. The male's courtship consists of waving the first two pairs of legs in front of the female and then vibrating them at high speed. These two actions are then repeated a number of times. The egg sacs of *A. brunnea* and *A. proxima* are very distinctive, and are seen more often than the spiders. The eggs are laid on to a stalked platform, covered with silk, and a lower empty chamber is provided for the spiderlings to occupy once they have hatched. The outside is then covered with soil which the spider carries up from the ground in the chelicerae and places on the sac. Fine strands of silk hold it in place. Occasionally sacs are found without the outer layer of earth.

Agroeca brunnea (Blackwall)
Size female c. 8 mm; male c. 7 mm
Carapace Reddish brown, head covered with golden hairs. Faintly dark submarginal bands. **Abdomen** Thickly covered with short golden hairs. Very faint dark cardiac mark and chevrons posteriorly. **Legs** Reddish brown, sprinkled with short golden hairs. Apical segments rather darker.
Habitat Wet places, often in woods. **Season** Autumn in Britain. All year in Germany. **Distribution** Widespread but infrequent in Britain. Widespread in Europe.

Agroeca proxima (O.P.-Cambridge)
Size female c. 6 mm; male c. 5 mm
More greyish brown than *A. brunnea*. **Carapace** Dark markings clearer. **Abdomen** Pattern clearer. **Legs** Similar in colour to carapace, with golden hairs.
Habitat Dry places. Often on heathland and bordering woods. **Season** Late summer and autumn. **Distribution** Widespread and fairly common throughout.

Agroeca inopina O.P.-Cambridge
Size female 5–7 mm; male c. 4 mm
Carapace Much darker marginal bands than *A. proxima*. **Abdomen** Darker than *A. proxima*. **Legs** Greyish brown, lighter at ends of segments. Some specimens have very faint broad annulations, especially on rear legs.
Habitat Coastal dunes. Woods. **Season** Late summer and autumn. **Distribution** Local in southern England and Wales. France, Belgium.

♀
Agroeca brunnea

♀
Agroeca proxima

♂
Agroeca inopina

Agroeca lusatica (L. Koch)

Size female 6 mm; male 4·5 mm
Resembles *A. inopina.*
Legs Brown with lighter femora and patellae.
Habitat and Distribution In England from sandhills at Sandwich, Kent. Widespread in Europe. **Season** Autumn.

Agroeca cuprea Menge

Size female c. 6 mm; male c. 4.5 mm
Carapace and Abdomen With copper-coloured hairs.
Legs Reddish brown with darker marks on basal segments.
Habitat and Distribution Extremely local in southern England, on coast and in Breckland. Widespread in Europe.

Genus *Agraecina*

A single, rare species occurs in the region.

Agraecina striata (Kulczynski)

Size female c. 5 mm; male c. 3·5 mm
Carapace Similar markings to *Agroeca.* **Abdomen** Also similar to *Agroeca* but with pair of lighter stripes on each side. **Legs** Faintly annulated; metatarsi I have two pairs of ventral spines not three as in *Agroeca.*
Habitat Under stones etc in marshy places. **Season** Adults in early summer. **Distribution** Rare throughout.

Genus *Scotina*

This genus contains three species, all of which are found in Europe, and nowhere else. They are small spiders with well-developed ventral spines on the first two pairs of legs. All three occur in the ground layer in detritus or moss.

Scotina celans (Blackwall)

Size female c. 4 mm; male c. 3 mm
Carapace Black and shiny, with thin, light median and lateral bands.
Abdomen With dark grey pubescence. Female has obscure light spots posteriorly; male has lighter chevrons between spots. **Legs** In female femora brown; other segments darker; less distinctive on rear legs. In male paler and less distinctly marked; patellae, metatarsi, and tarsi sometimes darker.
Habitat Moss and detritus in woods. **Season** Late summer and autumn. Females overwinter and may be found in spring. **Distribution** Widespread but uncommon in Britain. Widely distributed in Europe.

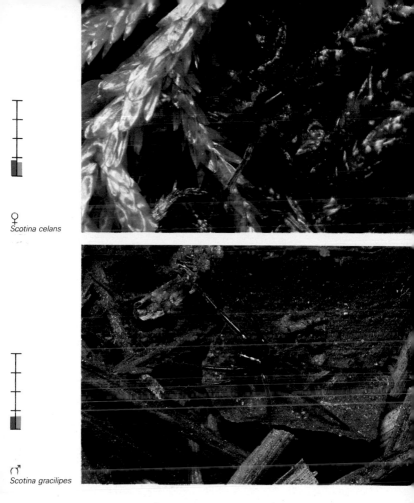

♀
Scotina celans

♂
Scotina gracilipes

Scotina gracilipes (Blackwall)

Size female c. 3 mm; male c. 3 mm
Carapace Uniformly dark brown to black, shiny. **Abdomen** Dark grey with faint, reddish-brown chevrons posteriorly in both sexes. **Legs** Femora reddish brown; patellae, tibiae, and metatarsi black and shiny; tarsi dark reddish brown. Darker segments of rear legs have annulated appearance. Similar in both sexes.
Habitat Drier and more exposed places, eg, under or on heather. **Season** As *S. celans*. **Distribution** Rather scattered but widespread in Britain. Not common. Widespread in Europe.

Scotina palliardi (L. Koch)
Very similar to *S. gracilipes* in size and colour.
Carapace Some specimens have obscure pattern like *S. celans*.
Distribution Rare and very local in central and east-southern England. Absent from Belgium. Widespread elsewhere.

Apostenus fuscus Westring
Size female 3 mm; male 3–4 mm
Similar in general form to *Scotina* spp.
Carapace Brownish with thin, dark border and sparse pubescence.
Abdomen Dark brown with long pale hairs. Cardiac mark lighter, and followed by pale chevrons. **Legs** Pale brown.
Habitat Moss and detritus in woods. Recently in Britain on coastal shingle. **Season** Spring to autumn. **Distribution** Absent from Holland. Widespread elsewhere.

Genus *Liocranum*

The two species in the region are distinguished from *Agroeca* by the broader eye region and head, and the chelicerae which are closer to *Clubiona*. The spider apparently does not make a retreat and the eggs are guarded by the female within a very flimsy cover or none at all. They are found in drier places than the preceding liocranids.

Liocranum rupicola (Walckenaer)
Size female c. 7 mm; male c. 6 mm
Carapace Brown to reddish brown with irregular dark lateral bands and dark border line. **Abdomen** With very clear pattern consisting of dark-grey cardiac mark followed by many oblique marks forming chevrons posteriorly. Lighter parts greyish brown. **Legs** Greyish brown with paler apices of most segments, almost like annulations on rear legs.
Habitat Under or among stones, under bark. Sometimes in houses.
Season Spring mainly, but also in autumn. **Distribution** Very local in southern Britain. Widespread in Europe.

Liocranum rutilans (Thorell)
Size female 8–10 mm; male 8 mm
Carapace and Abdomen Uniformly brown, without a pattern but with coppery coloured hairs. **Legs** Brown.
Habitat Dry, sandy places, under bark and stones. Also occasionally in houses. **Season** Spring. **Distribution** Absent from Britain, Belgium. Widespread elsewhere.

♀
Liocranium
rupicola

Genus *Phrurolithus*

Two small, highly active species which look ant-like as they run on the ground in sunshine. They lack the iridescence of the similar *Micaria*. The males of both species have a scutum which completely covers the dorsum.

Phrurolithus festivus (C. L. Koch)
Size female c. 3 mm; male c. 3 mm
Carapace Dark brown. Head black. Lightly covered with silky hairs.
Abdomen Dark brown to black with patches of white hairs; two anteriorly on shoulders, followed by chevron in front half, joined to large patches on sides, which continue back to spinners on venter. Small median spot above spinners. Male less well marked. **Legs** Yellow-brown, with femora I and II darkened. Other segments have faint white pubescence.
Habitat Under stones with ants and running on ground **Season** Early summer. **Distribution** Widespread and frequent throughout.

♀
Phrurolithus
festivus

Phrurolithus minimus C. L. Koch
Size female c. 3 mm; male c. 2·5 mm
Carapace Reddish brown. **Abdomen** Reddish brown to brown, often with two small patches of white hairs anteriorly as in *P. festivus*. Some specimens have thin lighter median stripe in cardiac area with dark patches near centre. **Legs** Uniformly reddish brown. Femora sometimes darker.
Habitat As *P. festivus*. **Season** Spring to summer. **Distribution** Very local in southern England. Widespread but uncommon elsewhere.

Family Zoridae

A single genus, *Zora* is found in the region. The spiders are characterized by the anteriorly pointed carapace with large, dark eyes set in two curved rows. The posterior row is so rounded that the eyes appear to be in three rows like *Pardosa*. Legs I and II have ventral spines in two rows like the Liocranidae.

Eyes from above

The courtship is a simplified version of *Agroeca*'s followed by a brief mating for a few minutes. The egg sac is found in summer near ground-level. As in *Liocranum* there is no outer covering, the exposed female guarding her sac under a stone or in a dried leaf.

Zora spinimana (Sundevall)
Size female c. 6 mm; male c. 4·5 mm
Carapace Light brown with pair of thin, dark-brown median bands enclosing lighter area covered by white hairs which are quite long in ocular region. **Abdomen** Pale brown with sprinkling of dark spots and patches of white hairs. These more-or-less disposed in rows. **Legs** Femora pale brown with dorsal streaks on I and II. Remaining segments dark greyish brown. Spiderlings and immatures have very distinct annulations.
Habitat Detritus, moss, and grass, especially in damp places. **Season** Autumn, early spring. Females into summer. **Distribution** Widespread and common throughout.

Zora nemoralis (Blackwall)
Size female 3·5–5 mm; male 3·5 mm
Carapace Dark bands wider than enclosing light bands. Dark marginal band wider. **Abdomen** Darker than *Z. spinimana*.
Habitat Woods and heather. **Season** Probably as *Z. spinimana*. **Distribution** Rare and local in England and Wales; more common in Scotland. Widespread in Europe.

♂
*Phrurolithus
minimus*

♀
Zora spinimana
with egg sac

Zora armillata Simon

Abdomen Lighter with smaller dark spots. **Legs** Yellow-brown with only apical portions of metatarsi dark.
Habitat Similar to *Z. spinimana*. **Season** Autumn? **Distribution** In England from three sites in fen country and Dorset. Also France and Sweden.

Zora silvestris Kulczynski

Size female and male c. 4 mm
Legs Clear dark spots on femora.
Habitat Heather. **Season** Spring and summer. **Distribution** Very local in south-east England. Holland, Sweden, Finland.

Family Anyphaenidae

This family has its headquarters in the Americas, and there are only six species of the genus *Anyphaena* throughout Europe. The single species of the region is easily recognized by the markings on the abdomen. The spider is superficially very like *Clubiona* species except that the tracheal spiracle, which is usually close to the spinners, occurs near the middle of the abdomen. The eyes are oval and pearly, except the anterior medians, which are circular and dark.

Anyphaena accentuata (Walckenaer)
Size female 5–7 mm; male 4–6·5 mm
Also a melanic form.
Carapace Pale yellow with black lateral bands; these have dentate outer edges and small white streaks radiating from fovea. Lighter median area has two black spots behind posterior eyes. **Abdomen** Pale yellow to pinkish brown. At mid-point are two pairs of black marks, rather variable in shape, remaining dorsal area sprinkled with few small dark spots. **Legs** Pale yellow with many small black marks, sometimes amounting almost to annulations.
Habitat Trees and bushes. **Season** Early summer. **Distribution** Widespread and common throughout.

Family Sparassidae

This family is represented by a single species in the region. The spiderlings are pale yellow or brown but gradually become green as they grow. The immatures resemble the female in colour and the splendid male takes on his gaudy adult coloration on completion of his final moult.

There is no courtship in *Micrommata*, and the mating can start with the male gripping the female's leg or abdomen in his chelicerae. The female remains quiescent throughout the long mating which lasts up to seven hours. The male changes palps several times during the copulation although each palp may only be used once. The male has a brief but colourful life and, consequently, is encountered less frequently than the female.

In mid-summer the females may be found in their egg sac retreats. These are made by silking together several leaves to form a relatively large space, in which the bright-green eggs are enclosed in a thin white sac, through which their colour and shape can be seen. This retreat is made on broadleaved vegetation, particularly oak saplings, although the spider does not venture very far above ground – less than 0·5 metre is typical. Females can be found until September in their retreats, and may be guarding their second sacs.

The spiders may be found among low vegetation during the day

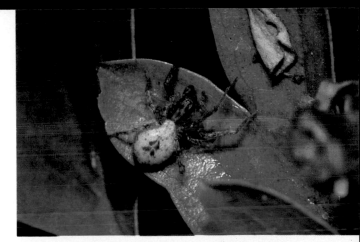

♀
Anyphaena
accentuata

Micrommata
virescens
immature

105

but, in captivity, they will also catch and consume prey at night. In spite of this, their development appears to be slow and half-grown spiders have been encountered in late July; an eighteen-month cycle may be expected in northern Europe.

Micrommata virescens (Clerck)
Size female 12–15 mm; male 8–10 mm
Female Carapace Deep green. Eyes conspicuously ringed with white hairs. **Abdomen** Bright yellow-green, with darker-green cardiac mark. Covered in fine white hairs. Newly moulted spiders and those guarding egg sacs are paler, with broad yellowish areas around green cardiac mark. **Legs** Coloured as carapace. With dense scopulae on metatarsi and tarsi. **Male Carapace and Legs** Dull green, thickly covered with silky hairs. **Abdomen** Tubular with red median band, darker on cardiac area, and edged with broad yellow bands. Sides red. Thickly covered with short silky hairs. **Spiderlings** Distinctively marked, and quite different from adults. **Carapace** Pale yellow-brown with two median bands, thin sublateral bands, and thin band of radiating streaks between. Markings all reddish. **Eyes** With rings of white hairs, fainter than adults. **Abdomen** Coloured as carapace on sides, with two white median bands. Covered with many red spots. **Legs** Coloured as carapace, with many small red spots.
Habitat Low vegetation in sheltered, damp places. Retreat on low bushes or trees. **Season** Spring and early summer. Males have short season. **Distribution** Uncommon but widespread throughout.

Micrommata virescens (or *roseum*) var. *ornata*
With red spots as in spiderlings of *M. virescens*. **Distribution** Absent from Britain. Throughout northern Europe.

Family Thomisidae

Thomisids are broad-bodied, crab-like spiders with legs I and II longer and more robust than III and IV. They are able to walk sideways, but are slow and awkward in their predatory behaviour. They are often brightly coloured.

Carapace The carapace often has two dark bands enclosing a lighter area behind the ocular region. These bands sometimes extend to the margins. **Eyes** The medians are smaller than the laterals, which are on tubercles of varying sizes within the genera. The posterior laterals face backwards. The anterior medians change colour as they are moved. **Abdomen** This is broadest at or near the posterior, and dorsally it has five depressions. It is often sparsely covered with spines. **Chelicerae** These are small. **Legs** I and II are twisted forwards, so that they articulate in the plane of the body (laterigrade).

♀
*Micrommata
virescens*

♂
*Micrommata
virescens*

107

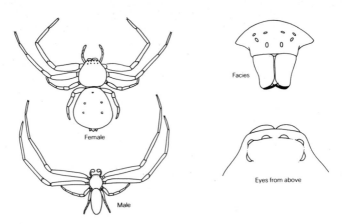

Female

Male

Facies

Eyes from above

The most conspicuous spines are situated on the prolateral surfaces of the tibiae and metatarsi. Legs III and IV are short and thin, and usually paler in colour. **Spinners** The spinners are small and inconspicuous.

The Thomisidae are all distinctly crab-like in appearance and movement. They may be split into two groups: the first group contains genera which show the most marked development of the family characteristics; and the second group contains two genera which are more uniform in appearance.

Genera *Thomisus, Pistius, Tmarus, Misumena, Misumenops, Synaema, Runcinia, Diaea, Heriaeus, Coriarachne*

These spiders show a great diversity of form and colour. *Thomisus, Misumena*, and *Synaema* occur in a variety of colours, the first two being capable of changing colour over a period of several days. The shape of the abdomen is the best means of identifying the spiders, although the coloration of the remaining genera varies only to a small degree and this, coupled with the overall form, serves to separate the females. The males of some of the genera are very small and, while they all have the abdominal humps characteristic of their genus, these are much less obvious on the male's smaller abdomen. Legs I and II in males are very long and may be as much as twice the body length. These long laterigrade legs make it impossible for the spiders to fold their legs over the carapace when they are alarmed, as the spiders of many other families do; in such circumstances, they fold the legs in front of the head.

Heriaeus, which is distinctive because two species are found in the region (all the other genera have only one), is also atypical in that it is covered with long fine hairs. The remaining genera are superficially smooth and sometimes shiny in appearance although their bodies are usually covered in very short spines.

Typically, their protective coloration allows the thomisids to frequent exposed positions on flowers where they ambush pollinating insects. The small size of their chelicerae belies the fact that their poison is very potent to arthropods. They are capable of preying on the most formidable of insects, such as bumblebees. This prowess is equalled only by the web builders which are able to bind their prey while their poison slowly takes effect.

When an insect approaches, a crab spider will extend its long anterior legs and align itself with the prey. It then waits for the insect to walk within its grasp. So apparently lethargic are the thomisids, that a nearby insect will be unmolested if it does not walk into the welcoming but predatory legs, and some fortunate insects manage actually to walk over the spider without being caught. Once the prey is grabbed, however, escape is impossible.

Thomisids have been seen to grasp such large flying insects (including fleshflies and bees) that they have been carried aloft, hanging on for grim death. Indeed, death follows within seconds of the embrace and brings the flight to an abrupt halt. After a few seconds, the legs relax their grip, and the prey is held by the chelicerae alone while it is consumed. The prey is not mutilated in any way and finishes up as a dry but perfect husk.

In spite of this horrifying ease with which they will take prey larger than themselves (including other spiders), they are perfectly harmless to humans, even though they will adopt their predatory pose as we approach – only to scuttle away crab-fashion when they realize their error.

Their sight is good enough to enable males and females to recognize one another at close distances, although their courtship (in summer) appears to be more of a tactile nature. The tiny male walks about on the abdomen and carapace of the female before copulating; in some species, the mating is interspersed with perambulations. The two palps are used alternately by the male, which must almost disappear below the female to inseminate her. After a period ranging from five to forty-five minutes (depending on the species) the spiders separate. The male wanders off while the female rids herself of any frail strands of silk laid down by her mate during his movements.

The egg sac is similar in each genus, and consists of a thick sheet of white silk enclosing the buff-coloured eggs; it has a lenticular shape. The mother sits on guard until her death. The spiderlings, which closely resemble the adults, probably mature in their second year, although some may become adult in the following spring. All the species of the region are described.

Thomisus onustus Walckenaer

Size female 7 mm; male 3 mm

Females variable (and changeable) in colour. Pink, yellow, or white, or in combination. Males more constant in colour. Tubercles on carapace and abdomen identify species.

Female Carapace With broad bands, lighter median and darker lateral. **Eyes** Subequal in size; laterals on tubercles. **Abdomen** With large posterior tubercles and smaller triangular region at rear. **Legs** I, II sometimes uniform, sometimes with large white areas. III, IV lighter with faint annulations. **Male Carapace** Dark brown with narrow lighter median band. Warty texture. **Eyes** Laterals on large pointed tubercles. **Abdomen** Brownish orange with small tubercles. **Legs** I, II very long; femora lighter, other segments dark. III, IV lighter.

Habitat Flowers, especially cross-leaved heath (*Erica tetralix*). **Season** Early to mid-summer. **Distribution** Southern England. All Europe, more common in south.

Pistius truncatus (Pallas)

Size female 9 mm; male 5 mm

Mottled brown in both sexes. Male smaller and darker than female. **Carapace** Uniform brown with lighter spots. **Eyes** Laterals larger than medians. Tubercles small and rounded. **Abdomen** Similar to *Thomisus*, but tubercles less pronounced. Uniform brown with lighter spots, sometimes forming faint chevrons at rear. Truncated posteriorly. **Legs** I, II dark brown with faint dark and light annulations. III, IV pale with patellae IV darkened.

Habitat Bushes and lower branches of trees (eg oak). **Season** Early to mid-summer. **Distribution** Not found in Britain for more than a century. Uncommon but widespread in Europe.

Tmarus piger (Walckenaer)

Size female 6 mm; male 4 mm

Sexes similar in colour. Single posterior prominence on abdomen much reduced in the male. **Carapace** Brownish with broad grey lateral bands. Covered in small spines arising from tubercles. **Eyes** All on tubercles; laterals largest. **Abdomen** Mottled grey with single large blunt tubercle. **Legs** Coloured as carapace with spines arising from black spots. No clear annulations.

Habitat Twigs and branches of bushes and conifers where its shape and colour camouflage it. **Season** Early to mid-summer. **Distribution** Absent from Britain and Scandinavia. France, Germany, Belgium, Holland.

Thomisus
onustus mating

♂
Pistius truncatus

♀
Tmarus piger

Misumena vatia (Clerck)
Size female 10 mm, male 4 mm
Females variable and changeable in colour, white, pale green, or yellow. Smooth form of body with oval abdomen are characteristic. Male much darker than female.
Female Carapace With irregular white median band. Coloured as abdomen. **Eyes** Laterals on small rounded tubercles. Fairly small, sometimes with yellow pigment in ocular area. **Abdomen** Oval, broader posteriorly. Sometimes with red lateral lines. **Legs** Unmarked, coloured as carapace; III, IV paler. In white specimens tarsi are yellow. **Male** Carapace Dark brown with thin yellow median band. **Eyes** On lighter region and with small tubercles laterally. **Abdomen** Pale with darker edges and two median lines. **Legs** I, II with darker femora; remaining segments annulated. III, IV pale, almost unmarked.
Habitat Typically on white or yellow flowers. **Season** Early and mid-summer. **Distribution** Commonly found in all Europe especially south.

Misumenops tricuspidata (Fabricius)
Size female 6 mm; male 3 mm
Both sexes resemble female *Misumena vatia*.
Female Carapace and Legs Greenish. **Abdomen** Subtriangular with brown flask-shaped mark dorsally. **Male** Carapace Brown with lighter median band. **Abdomen** With darker sides; dorsal pattern less clear than female. More angulate posteriorly than male *Misumena vatia*.
Habitat and Season As *M. vatia* but less common. **Distribution** Absent from Britain and Scandinavia. France, Germany, Belgium, Holland.

Runcinia lateralis (C. L. Koch)
Size female 6 mm; male 3 mm
Both sexes have attenuated appearance and are rather pale in colour.
Female Carapace Grey with white central line and dark lateral bands. **Eyes** Ocular region rather broad with frontal keel prominent. **Abdomen** White with reddish sides and two median lines converging anteriorly. **Legs** Grey with darker streaks. **Male** Carapace Pale brown, marked as female. **Eyes** Similar to female. **Abdomen** Shape as female; coloured brown and very faintly marked. **Legs** I, II with pale femora, other segments lighter basally with broad dark annulations apically. III, IV pale and unmarked. **Palps** Very small.
Habitat Bushes, flowers, grasses. **Season** Early and mid-summer. **Distribution** Only in France. Uncommon.

Misumena vatia
mating

Runcinia lateralis
mating

Synaema globosum (Fabricius)

Size female 8 mm; male 4 mm

Both sexes with similar markings. Small size and overall darkness of male make his pattern less easy to discern.

Carapace Black and shiny. Sparsely covered with bristles. **Eyes** Anterior laterals largest and on larger tubercles than posterior laterals. With light rings. Ocular area pale brown. **Abdomen** Subcircular in plan with broad dentate folium. Sides white, yellow, or orange. Mottled ventrally. **Legs** I, II darker than III, IV but all legs annulated in both sexes.

Habitat Usually on umbellifers or bushes. **Season** Early to mid-summer. **Distribution** Absent from Britain and Scandinavia. France, Germany, Belgium, Holland.

Diaea dorsata (Fabricius)

Size female 6 mm; male 4 mm

Combination of green prosoma and legs, with brown abdomen characterize immatures and females.

Female Carapace and Legs Bright green without other markings. With few long bristles. **Eyes** All on light rings. Lateral tubercles very small. **Abdomen** Dorsally dark brown, sometimes marked with paler spots. Sides and venter pale brown. **Male Carapace** Light brown with long bristles. Faint lateral bands. **Eyes** As female. **Abdomen** As female but more often with folium spotted with pale brown. **Legs** Brown to greenish brown with femora and tibiae sometimes spotted with dark brown. III, IV lighter and unmarked.

Habitat Trees; yew, oak, pine, etc. **Season** Early summer. **Distribution** All Europe but uncommon in north.

Heriaeus hirtus (Latreille)

Size female 9 mm; male 5 mm

Green spiders with whole body covered thickly in white hairs.

Female Carapace Bright green with thin white median line. **Eyes** On white rings. Lateral tubercles small. **Abdomen** Subtriangular, emphasized with white lines on bright green. Sometimes with red cardiac mark as in male. Several white lines posteriorly. **Legs** Coloured as carapace. **Male Carapace** As female, narrowed in front. **Eyes** As female. **Abdomen** Pale yellow, sometimes with red cardiac mark. **Legs** As female.

Habitat Typically hairy vegetation such as grasses, flowers. **Season** Early summer. **Distribution** France, Germany, Belgium.

H. oblongus

Very similar to *H. hirtus*, but female has narrower abdomen. Difficult to distinguish from *H. hirtus* in field.

Distribution France, Germany.

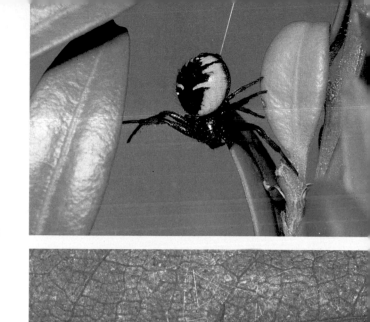

♀
Synaema globosum

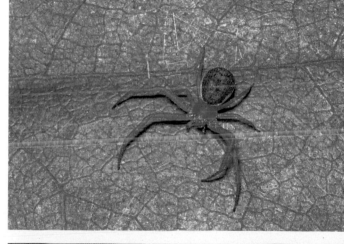

♀
Diaea dorsata

♂
Heriaeus hirtus

Coriarachne depressa Thorell

Size female and male c. 5 mm
Extreme flatness of this rare species makes it unlike any other thomisid. Male darker than female.
Carapace Dark brown. Very flattened. **Eyes** Laterals on low tubercles. Ocular region pale. **Abdomen** Scarcely wider than carapace. With several pairs of depressions, those in middle deeper than front and rear pairs. Sides have white wrinkles converging towards centre. Whole abdomen greatly flattened, with desiccated appearance. **Legs** I, II robust and rather short. Tibiae rather bulbous with long spines. Tarsi also with long spines.
Habitat Under bark, stones, or in litter. **Season** Spring and early summer. **Distribution** Absent from Britain. Widespread but rare in Europe.

Genera *Xysticus, Oxyptila*

The species of these two genera differ from those of the first group in the uniformity of their general appearance.

Genus *Xysticus*

Carapace This usually has dark, broad, lateral bands. The lighter median band has a dark triangle running back from the posterior eyes. It is sparsely covered with long acuminate spines. **Eyes** The laterals are larger than the medians and are on low tubercles. **Abdomen** This possesses a brown folium containing overlapping lighter triangles which are sometimes reduced to pairs of lateral transverse lines. The sides are wrinkled, except in fat or gravid females. It is sparsely armed with long spines. **Legs** The legs are not so disparate in size as in the first group of genera. Legs I, II are about 30 per cent longer than III, IV in females and 50 per cent longer in males. I, II are armed ventrally with many rather long spines.

Genus *Oxyptila*

Carapace In these spiders the dark triangle is reduced or absent. The spines are shorter than in *Xysticus* and frequently they are blunt or even club shaped (clavate). **Eyes** The ocular region is more rounded and pushed forwards, so that the carapace is not as circular as in *Xysticus*. **Abdomen** Usually this bears a sharp ridge anteriorly where it overhangs the carapace. The pattern is very faint, at best consisting of widely spaced pairs of spots. The spines are very short and blunt or clavate. It is wrinkled at the sides and rear. **Legs** The legs are shorter and more robust than *Xysticus*. I, II are about 20 per cent longer than III, IV in females, 30 per cent in males. **Sternum** Some species have a pattern of spots and bars. Males are not more elongated than the females in this genus (as is normally the case in spiders) but are even more dumpy with scarcely longer legs; they are, however, usually darker.

The individual species of *Xysticus* and *Oxyptila* are not easy to distinguish in the field because of their overall similarity and the great variability of many of the species. For this reason, a selection of the more common or more easily identified species is given, although additional species may be found in Britain and Europe.

Their predatory techniques are identical to those of the first group in this family, and the laterigrade legs enable them to run crab fashion to escape capture. With the exception of *X. lanio*, a reddish species found in trees, *Xysticus* spiders are denizens of the ground-layer and low vegetation. *Oxyptila* spiders are always found in the ground-layer, in detritus and so on, but there is evidence that the genus is nocturnal, because they have been swept from higher vegetation at night. Neither genus has representatives which frequent flowers, so they seldom meet the fierce prey taken by spiders of the previous group, but *Xysticus* species will feed on ants which are avoided by most spiders.

When the sexes meet, the female assumes a submissive posture with the forelegs folded in front of her head. The male climbs over the female and turns many times, while he spins a thin silk covering, known as the 'bridal veil', which apparently ties the female to the substrate. The male then crawls under the female, lifting her slightly, to insert his palps. After the two part the female easily rids herself of this token binding.

Xysticus attaches her egg sac to low plants, and she can be found clutching the smooth white sac during the summer months. Normally, only one sac is made and the female probably dies before the spiderlings emerge. *Oxyptila* females do the same except that the sac is attached to the lower side of a stone or other object at ground-level. The spiderlings may take two years to mature.

Acuminate spine
of *Xysticus*

Blunt spine (*left*) and
clavate spine (*right*) of *Oxyptila*

Xysticus cristatus (Clerck)

Size female 7 mm; male 5 mm
Most common British thomisid. Females occur in wide range of browns, so that members of genus are hard to identify with certainty. **Female Carapace** Median triangle about two-thirds length of carapace, ending in sharp, dark point. **Abdomen** Typically with clear pattern of overlapping triangular patches on darker folium. Sometimes very pale. **Legs** Same general hue as abdomen, sometimes with faint streaks and spots, or with stronger markings in dark specimens. **Male** As female but darker.
Habitat Ground or low vegetation. **Season** Spring and early summer. **Distribution** Common throughout.

Xysticus kochi Thorell

Occurs in same situations as *X. cristatus* but less commonly. Darker, more greyish brown.

Xysticus audax (Schrank)

Size female 8 mm; male 4 mm
Sometimes considered to be form of *X. cristatus*, as genitalia of both species very similar, but habitat and markings appear to be consistently different.
Female Carapace Median triangle about half length of carapace and rounded behind or fading out. Lateral bands black. **Abdomen** Always with strongly marked pattern. **Legs** With extensive areas of black especially on femora and tibiae. **Epigyne** More strongly sclerotized than *X. cristatus*. **Male** Darker.
Habitat Frequent on gorse and heather on heathland. Usually in higher vegetation than *X. cristatus*. **Season and Distribution** as *X. cristatus*.

Xysticus erraticus (Blackwall)

Size female 7 mm; male 5 mm
Much less well-marked than *X. cristatus*, and rather variable in colour. **Female Carapace** With thin lateral bands. Median triangle faint or absent. **Abdomen** Pattern faint, sometimes reduced to spots. Usually with faint cardiac mark. **Legs** Unmarked or with faint stripes. **Male Abdomen** With clear folium and distinct cardiac mark. **Legs** I, II femora and patellae dark brown, remaining segments and all III, IV light brown.
Habitat Usually in ground-layer. **Season** Spring to late summer. **Distribution** Less common than *X. cristatus*. Widespread in Europe.

♂ and ♀
Xysticus cristatus

♀
Xysticus erraticus

♂
Xysticus erraticus

Xysticus lanio C. L. Koch

Size female 7 mm; male 5 mm
Found in higher vegetation than other species of this genus. Female characterized by reddish sides of abdomen.
Female Carapace Rather like *X. audax* but paler. **Abdomen** Folium brown, almost unmarked. Sides reddish. Very broad and rounded posteriorly. **Legs** Light-brown, blotched and spotted with dark brown. **Male Carapace** Black, with ocular region light brown. Median Y-shaped mark in light brown. **Abdomen** Folium black broken by transverse white lines and with white sides. **Legs** I, II femora and patellae black, remaining segments light brown. III, IV light brown with darker spots.
Habitat Bushes and lower branches of trees, especially oak. **Season** Spring and early summer. **Distribution** Fairly common throughout Europe.

Xysticus ulmi (Hahn)

Size female 6 mm; male 4 mm
Characteristic shape and pattern of abdomen, and damp habitat make spider easily recognizable.
Female Carapace With median triangle elongated. Lateral bands thinner and marbled. **Abdomen** Rather elongated, overhanging carapace to greater extent than other species. Folium has median band on anterior half, followed by two or three clear transverse lines. **Legs** Finely spotted. **Male** Similar to female, but darker. **Legs** I, II with black femora and patellae. III, IV pale brown with fine spots.
Habitat Low plants only in damp places, such as fens. **Season** Spring and early summer. **Distribution** Local but widespread in Europe.

Xysticus bifasciatus C. L. Koch

Size female 10 mm; male 7 mm
Large size and robust form make it easily identified. Male is as large as females of other species.
Female Carapace Rather like *X. ulmi* but with more bristles. **Abdomen** Pink with brown folium. Laterally elongated spots at rear sometimes quite clear. **Legs** Robust with dark lines and spots especially on femora and tibiae. **Male Carapace** As female but much darker. Rather bulbous. **Abdomen** Dark-brown folium with two lighter spots midway, followed by transverse thin line. **Legs** I, II with femora and patellae darkened.
Habitat Low vegetation on warm grassy heaths. **Season** Spring and early summer. **Distribution** Rare in Britain. Widespread in Europe.

♀
Xysticus lanio

♀
Xysticus ulmi

♀
*Xysticus
bifasciatus*

Xysticus sabulosus (Hahn)

Size female 8 mm; male 6 mm

Only one of group where both sexes are adult in early autumn. Older females almost totally black.

Female **Carapace** Lateral bands broad. Median area with obscure pale markings. **Abdomen** Reddish brown with darker border posteriorly. Three or four short lateral stripes at rear. Sides light grey. **Legs** Light grey with large black spots. I, II darkest on apical segments. On III, IV spots almost amount to annulations. **Male** Very dark brown or black with few small white spots on body and legs. **Legs** I, II almost uniformly black, not lighter on apical segments like males of other *Xysticus* species.

Habitat Ground or low plants on heathland. **Season** Late summer and early autumn. **Distribution** Uncommon in Britain. Widespread in Europe.

Genus *Oxyptila*

Carapace The ocular region is produced forwards and rounded anteriorly. **Abdomen** This is without a folium, but has spots and bars. It does not overhang the carapace so much as in *Xysticus*. It is truncated and has a strong edge anteriorly. **Legs** III, IV are only slightly shorter than I, II. Some of the species have the spines clavate, otherwise they are short. On the body they are stubbly, appearing broken and not acuminate.

Habitat They are found in low vegetation and detritus. **Season** Males may be found in spring and early summer, females all year. **Distribution** These spiders are widespread in Europe.

Oxyptila scabricula and *O. nigrita*

Size female and male 2–3 mm

Both small and dark. Covered with soil particles.

Oxyptila trux, O. simplex, O. atomaria

Size females up to 6 mm; males c. 4 mm

Largest British species. Rather pale in colour, even males.

Oxyptila praticola (C. L. Koch)

Distinctive pattern on sternum.

Oxyptila brevipes

Similar pattern on sternum to *O. praticola* but less well defined; lighter in female, darker in male than *O. praticola*.

♀
*Xysticus
sabulosus*

♀
Oxyptila atomaria

♀
Oxyptila praticola
with egg sac

Family Philodromidae

These are flattened, rather slim-bodied spiders with legs of subequal length. They are capable of rapid and erratic movements.

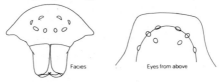

Facies   Eyes from above

Carapace This is almost circular, with the head raised in front slightly. It is covered in plumose hairs and usually has lateral bands. **Eyes** These are small and equal in size and occur in two rows. The posterior medians form a hexagonal group with the anterior row. (This is more marked in *Thanatus* and *Tibellus*.) All eyes are dark. **Abdomen** It is rather elongated (particularly in *Tibellus*), widest just behind the middle, and rather pointed posteriorly. It is clothed in plumose hairs. **Legs** These are subequal in length, leg II being longest. The apical segments have scopulae. **Chelicerae** The chelicerae are small.

Genus *Philodromus*

The spiders of this genus have leg II slightly longer than the others. They are rather sedentary spiders, well camouflaged and lie in wait for their prey on the foliage of bushes and trees. Once disturbed, they are capable of fairly sustained dashes at very great speed, living up to their name. Their leg scopulae help them to execute lightning changes of position without needing to fall on a safety line, although this option is not denied them. Like the thomisids, they can move sideways, but only, it seems, to escape capture. Unlike the thomisids, they will actively grab nearby prey and do not just rely on it coming to them.

There is little apparent courtship in this genus, and mating entails the insertion of one palp only for about thirty seconds, after which the spiders part. The egg sacs are rather variable within the genus; *P. histrio* and *P. fallax* cover their sacs with local materials, but the remaining species tend to lodge them in the crook of some foliage without any further covering other than a thick sheet of white silk. The female guards this until her death. *P. aureolus*, one of the commonest species, and often found in abundance, constructs a thin sheet of silk like a roof to protect her on the vigil.

P. histrio differs from the other species in becoming mature within a year, and recognizable spiderlings can be found in the summer, becoming almost full grown, but still immature by the autumn. They suffer great losses in the winter, and the adults are few and far between. Of the remaining species, some individuals probably take two winters to mature in the north of the region, and quite small spiderlings can be found alongside adults and even females on sacs.

Philodromus dispar Walckenaer

Size female 5 mm; male 4 mm
Specific name indicates disparity in appearance of male and female.
Female Carapace With dark lateral bands and white margins. **Abdomen** Light brown with faint pattern; sides very light. **Legs** Pale grey. Tibiae I with four or five pairs of ventral spines. **Male Carapace and Abdomen** Black with iridescent blue sheen. Sides white. **Legs** As female.
Habitat Trees, oak, pine, etc. **Season** Spring and early summer. **Distribution** Common in England; absent from Scotland. All Europe.

♀
*Philodromus
dispar*

♂
*Philodromus
dispar*

♀
Philodromus cespitum with egg sac

Philodromus aureolus (Clerck)

Size female 6 mm; male 4 mm

Female Carapace Light median band, darker margins. **Abdomen** Sometimes approaching *P. cespitum* in markings, but females on sacs usually with pale-yellow dorsum and darker sides. Two small dark flecks above spinners. **Legs** Pale brown with darker spots. Tibiae I with two pairs of long spines ventrally followed by small pair apically. **Male** Greyish brown overall with purple and green iridescence.
Habitat Bushes and trees. **Season** Spring and summer. **Distribution** Often abundant. All Europe.

Philodromus cespitum (Walckenaer)

Size female 6 mm; male 4 mm

Previously considered to be subspecies of *P. aureolus*.
Female Carapace Like *P. aureolus*. **Abdomen** With distinct cardiac mark followed by chevrons. **Legs** Similar to *P. aureolus*. **Male** Not easily distinguishable from *P. aureolus* but often with less iridescence.
Habitat, Season, Distribution As *P. aureolus*.

Philodromus collinus C. L. Koch

Size female 6 mm; male 5 mm

Female Carapace Similar to *P. aureolus*, with patches of white plumose hairs. **Abdomen** Reddish brown with broken median band of white hairs, tapering to spinners. Some faint black chevrons at rear. Also pair of white spots at sides, on dark bands. **Legs** Greyish brown. **Male** Indistinguishable from *P. aureolus* or *P. cespitum*.
Habitat Trees, eg pines. Sac made at end of branch. **Season** Early summer. **Distribution** Uncommon in south-east England. All Europe.

♂
Philodromus aureolus

♀
Philodromus cespitum with egg sac

♀
Philodromus collinus

Philodromus fallax Sundevall
Size female 6 mm; male 5 mm
Superbly camouflaged to match sandy habitat.
Carapace Pale brown, with darker lateral bands punctuated by white spots. **Abdomen** With prominent cardiac mark and many white spots. **Legs** Pale brown with large black spots.
Habitat Coastal species typical of foredunes. Usually on sand or in marram. **Season** Early spring. **Distribution** Uncommon and local in England, Wales. Only in northern Europe.

Philodromus histrio (Latreille)
Size female 7 mm; male 6 mm
Most handsomely marked *Philodromus*, with unvarying pattern, very similar in both sexes. Males can be confused with *Oxyopes heterophthalmus*.
Carapace Similar in pattern to other *Philodromus* spp, with addition of dark median line. **Abdomen** With distinct cardiac mark flanked towards rear by two pairs of white spots. **Legs** Greyish brown with brown blotches.
Habitat Usually heather. **Season** Early spring. **Distribution** Local from south coast to Scotland. Throughout Europe.

Philodromus emarginatus (Schrank)
Size female 6 mm; male 5 mm
Lack of any distinctive markings and pinkish-brown colour characteristic.
Female Carapace Greyish brown with pink area on head. **Abdomen** Very faint pattern like *P. cespitum* dorsally; sides with adjacent dark and light spots. **Legs** Greyish brown with darker spots and bars. Femora have long pale hairs ventrally. **Male** Similar in colour to female, but spots less distinct, and ventral hairs reduced or absent on femora.
Habitat Conifers and heather. **Season** Early summer. **Distribution** Infrequent and local, with same range as *P. histrio*. Throughout Europe.

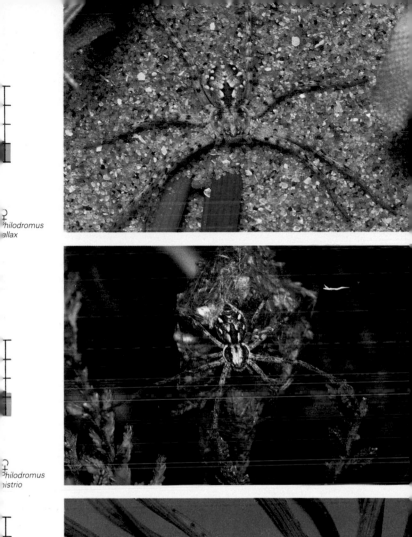

Philodromus rufus Walckenaer
Size female 5 mm; male 4 mm
Both sexes similar to *P. dispar* females but paler.
Carapace Like *P. dispar*, but with pattern fainter. **Abdomen** Pattern made up of small brown dots. Sides light. **Legs** Pale greenish yellow. **Habitat** Bushes and lower branches of trees. **Season** Early summer. **Distribution** Rather rare and local in south-east England. Widely distributed in Europe.

Philodromus margaritatus (Clerck)
Size female 6 mm; male 5 mm
Broad-bodied, rather flattened species occurring in two pattern forms but same colour.
Female Coloration whitish green and black or grey. **Carapace** With faint white spots on darker lateral bands, or with large black spots over lateral eyes and at posterior sides. **Abdomen** Greyish median band with indistinct chevrons, or with darker shoulders and transverse row of black spots. **Legs** With large black or grey spots. Femora dorsally with short spines, ventrally with long hairs. **Male** Similar to female but lacking ventral hairs on legs. Two forms found in both sexes.
Habitat Bark and foliage of lichen-covered trees. **Season** Early summer. **Distribution** Rare in Britain. More common in Europe.

Philodromus poecilus
Similar to *P. margaritatus*.
Abdomen Grey with black and white spots, and with black band anteriorly. **Legs** I, II have femora and patellae streaked with black ventrally.
Habitat As *P. margaritatus*. **Distribution** Absent from Britain. Widespread in Europe

Genus *Thanatus*

These are similar in appearance to *Philodromus*, but with leg IV longer than the others, and an eye grouping with the posterior laterals more removed from the others. The two British species are rare, and the commoner *T. striatus* is distinguished by the long fine spines covering the dorsal surface of the body. All the species have a distinctive cardiac mark.

They occur at ground-level, often in sandy habitats and in exposed places, although within the cover of thick vegetation.

♀
Philodromus rufus

♀
Philodromus margaritatus

♂
Philodromus margaritatus

Thanatus striatus C. L. Koch

Size female 5 mm; male 4 mm

Smallest species of *Thanatus* occurring in Europe.

Female Carapace With dark lateral bands and light median band bisected by further dark band. Covered with many long erect hairs. **Abdomen** Pale brown with long cardiac mark, flanked at rear by two sinuous lines which converge to spinners. With many erect hairs. **Legs** With many dark spines and pale plumose hairs. **Male** With less distinct pattern than female.

Habitat Low vegetation in damp places. **Season** Early summer. **Distribution** Rare in England and Wales. Widespread in Europe.

Thanatus sabulosus (Menge)

Female Same size and markings as *T. striatus*. **Male** Black with lighter border on front of abdomen.

Habitat Heather in sandy woodland. **Season** Adult in April. **Distribution** France, Germany.

Thanatus formicinus (Clerck)

Size female 8–12 mm; male 7 mm

Large species very rare in southern England, recorded from only two sites. Less hairy than *T. striatus*.

Female Carapace Similar to *T. striatus*. **Abdomen** Conspicuous cardiac mark edged in white. Posterior lines much reduced. **Legs** Greyish-brown. **Male** Similar to female.

Habitat Low vegetation. **Season** Early summer. **Distribution** Widespread in Europe.

Thanatus arenarius Thorell

Size female 6 mm; male 5 mm

Similar to *T. formicinus* but smaller.

Distribution Absent from Britain, Holland. Widespread elsewhere.

Genus *Tibellus*

A distinctive genus with two species in the region. Unfortunately, they are rather variable, and some specimens are not easy to assign to a particular species. The elongated abdomen, long legs, and round carapace are found in both sexes, and these spiders could be confused with *Tetragnatha* species which have similar habits of stretching themselves along thin pieces of vegetation. *Tibellus* has a different eye pattern and very small chelicerae, however. *Tibellus* spiders are never metallic.

They are characteristic spiders of long grass, where they lie along leaf blades to ambush their prey.

♀
Thanatus striatus

♀
Thanatus formicinus

Courtship is minimal but mating is more extended than in *Philodromus*, taking up to half-an-hour, with the male using both palps several times each. The egg sac is built at the top of suitable plants and guarded by the mother. Immatures of all sizes can be very common in the typical habitat but adults are less frequently seen. Like *Philodromus*, they probably take two years to mature. The spiderlings achieve their lankiness as they grow and, when small, can be confused with *Thanatus* immatures. (Also compare with *Micrommata* immatures.)

Tibellus maritimus (Menge)
Size female 10 mm; male 8 mm
Female Carapace Pale brown, covered with white hairs. Broad median band. With large dark spots opposite legs, sometimes absent.
Abdomen With dark median stripe running entire length. When present, dark spots are large, with about six on each flank. **Legs** Unspotted except dorsally at base of femora. Absent in some specimens. **Male** Similar to female. **Abdomen** Extremely thin.
Habitat Coastal dunes in marram but also inland in coarse grasses.
Season Early summer. **Distribution** Less common than *T. oblongus* but widespread in Europe.

Tibellus oblongus (Walckenaer)
Size female 10 mm; male 8 mm
Less obviously spotted than *T. maritimus*.
Female Carapace Usually without spots, but some specimens resemble *T. maritimus*. **Abdomen** With dark median stripe and typically pair of spots flanking central line at posterior end. Sometimes with two pairs of spots and less frequently with many (up to thirty) very small spots over whole length of abdomen on each side. **Legs** Sometimes with femoral spots, otherwise plain; light brown. **Male** Similar to *T. maritimus*.
Habitat Grasses in damp places. **Season** Early summer. **Distribution** Very common throughout Europe.

Family Salticidae

These are medium to small spiders with square-fronted carapaces bearing four large eyes. They are most active in warm, sunny weather and are popularly known as jumping spiders.

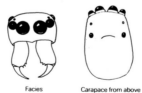

Facies   Carapace from above

Carapace The carapace is longer than it is wide (very much so in some genera) and it is rounded posteriorly. Usually it is fairly high and has steep sides. The head often has a metallic sheen or is textured. The carapace is clothed with normal or flattened (squamose) hairs. In some genera squamose hairs may appear iridescent. **Eyes** These are

134

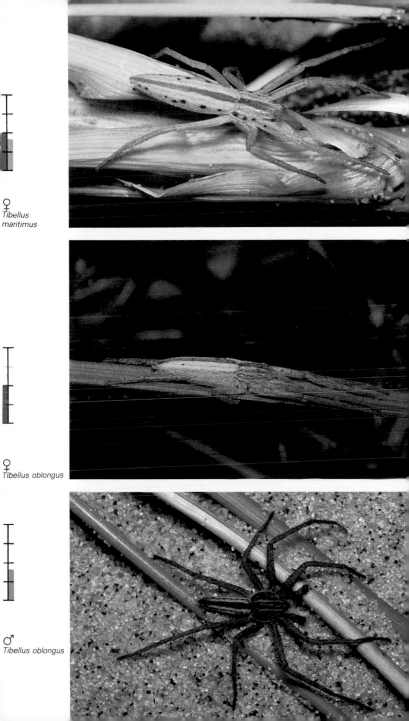

♀
*Tibellus
maritimus*

♀
Tibellus oblongus

♂
Tibellus oblongus

arranged in three rows. The anterior medians are always very large and have a green patina in those species which are found in vegetation. The anterior laterals are smaller, set higher on the head, and have a dull magenta coating in those spiders with green median eyes. The eyes of the second row (posterior medians) are tiny and probably vestigial. The posterior laterals are nearly as large as the anterior laterals and are set on the edges of the head. The eyes are all dark (but *see below*). **Abdomen** The abdomen is widest at the mid-point and tapers to the spinners but it may be squatter or more elongated in some genera. Usually it bears distinctive markings composed of normal or squamose hairs. **Legs** For jumping animals, these are remarkably short and stout. In some genera the first pair of legs are thickened although these are never used for jumping but for the capture of prey. **Chelicerae** The chelicerae are small in all females, but very large in the males of some genera.

The Salticidae, or jumpers as they are affectionately known among arachnologists, comprise the largest family of spiders and about 4000 species have been described. The behaviour of nearly all of them is strongly influenced by their exceptionally acute vision. Their curiosity is almost greater than their fear, even when attempts are made to catch them for closer examination. When they are pursued, many of them will stop and turn on their pursuer for a long, hard stare.

The eyes of spiders are termed 'simple', in contrast to the 'compound' or multifaceted eyes of insects, but this does not necessarily mean that they are unsophisticated. The anterior median eyes of the salticids are capable of more degrees of movement than our own, and the change in colour which can be observed under a lens, from black to pale brown, is caused by the movement of the eye capsule within the head. These eyes are able to move forwards and backwards, for focusing; to either side or up and down, as in our own eyes; and a curious rotational movement used for prey or mate determination. They are probably sensitive to colour and polarized light, and have the greatest visual acuity to be found in any arthropod, as well as the greatest range of movement.

The remaining eyes are less spectacular. They cannot move and do not have very good resolving power but, together, they give the spider a 360-degree field of view, where at least movement can be detected. The anterior laterals give binocular vision to the front with monocular vision to the sides. The posterior laterals give the broadest angle of view, which covers the sides and rear, and give a small binocular overlap in the median line at the rear. Consequently, the jumping spiders have an all-round view of their environment without having to move their heads. When movement is detected, they orient so that the anterior median eyes can scan the disturbance in great detail. If these eyes get dirty the spider will clean them carefully with a palp.

Salticids stalk their prey by creeping ever closer, then jumping the final few centimetres and grabbing the prey with the forelegs. Large prey does not always intimidate them but they rarely, if ever, succeed in catching anything much larger than themselves. Unlike the *Pardosa* species which are capable of jumping short distances as they run, salticids make their jumps from a standing start, using the rear legs or II, III, and IV in tandem to propel them forwards. They will do this to evade capture and are nimble enough to dodge sideways or backwards with almost equal dexterity. *Marpissa nivoyi* can move as swiftly backwards as forwards, and the elongated body makes it look like an animated shuttle. Binocular vision enables salticids to leap from twig to twig with great accuracy but, when they do misjudge the distance, they dangle at the end of a safety line, which is always made before a jump. In dull or cold weather and at night, they spin a small silk cell around themselves and remain there until conditions become more favourable.

As in all spiders the male matures before the female and sets about searching for a prospective mate. If the male comes across a female in a silk cell, about to moult, he will join her and mate once she has moulted. Males also encounter females in the open and actively court them. This varies in detail in each species (which presumably effectively prevents any hybridization) but broadly consists of the male throwing up his front legs, sometimes also raising his abdomen, and dancing to and-fro in front of the female. In species like *Euophrys*, where the males have decorated palps, these will add something to the display. The enlarged chelicerae of *Salticus* males and the distinctive head markings of *Aelurillus* enter into the rituals performed by the males. Their excitement is greater than their vision, for males will court one another – which results in some antagonistic but harmless sparring – and they can be deceived by mirrors, courting their own reflections with almost as much vigour as they would a female.

The female constructs an over-sized silk cell in which to lay her eggs and remains in the cell with them until they hatch. The young are blind at first but the eyes become fully developed at the second moult. At this stage, they are ready to leave the protection of their mother's cell and to fend for themselves. Although the female guards them, there is no other interaction such as feeding.

Genus *Salticus*

There are four species, of which two are very rare in Britain. They are black with patches of white hairs, giving the spiders a striped appearance. *S. scenicus* is the most common member of the whole family and may be used as a basis for comparison with the other members of the family. Males have greatly enlarged chelicerae.

Salticus scenicus (Clerck)

Size female c. 6 mm; male c. 5 mm

Female Carapace Black with patch of white squamose hairs behind anterior eyes and pair of spots behind posteriors. **Abdomen** Black with white anterior band and two pairs of oblique white stripes at sides, sometimes with additional pair of small spots above spinners. **Legs** Femora whitish in basal half, otherwise black. Speckled with white hairs, sometimes giving impression of annulations. **Male** Similar to female but with very long chelicerae.

Habitat Principally houses and gardens, but also on rocks and stones. Occasionally on trees. **Season** Early to late summer. **Distribution** Often abundant and widespread throughout the Northern Hemisphere.

Salticus cingulatus (Panzer)

Size female 6 mm; male 5 mm

Female Carapace Black, with larger areas of white squamose hairs. **Abdomen** Light grey with several black triangles in median line. Within these are number of light chevrons. **Legs** More clearly annulated than *S. scenicus*. **Male Abdomen** Pattern reduced, usually without chevrons. **Chelicerae** Almost as long as carapace.

Habitat Trees in woods and on heathland. **Season** Summer. **Distribution** Much less common than *S. scenicus* but widespread throughout.

Salticus zebraneus (C. L. Koch)

Size female 4 mm; male 3 mm

Male and **Female** Similar to *S. scenicus* but with white stripes less defined.

Distribution Very local in south-east England. Widespread in Europe.

Genus *Heliophanus*

Nine species are found within the region, with four in Britain, of which only two are common – *H. cupreus* and *H. flavipes*. They are all dark spiders, sometimes with a faintly metallic sheen to the abdomen, a thin white band anteriorly, and various white spots dorsally. They are usually found in undergrowth.

♀
Salticus scenicus

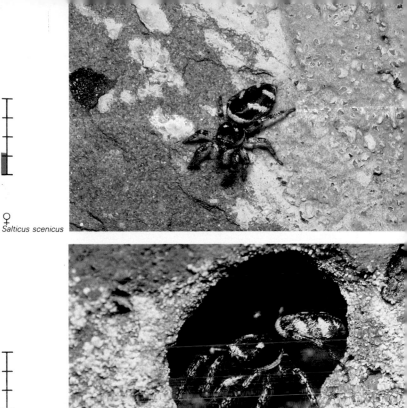

♂
Salticus scenicus

♀
*Salticus
cingulatus*

Heliophanus cupreus (Walckenaer)

Size female 6 mm; male 4 mm

Female Carapace Black with some whitish squamose hairs. **Abdomen** Black with thin white border at front and sides. With one or two pairs of white spots in posterior half. With coppery sheen. **Legs** Sometimes yellow-brown with much darker streaking, usually blackish (cf *H. flavipes*.) **Male** Carapace and **Abdomen** Usually without white hairs. **Legs** Usually darker than female and furnished with white squamose hairs.

Habitat Low vegetation in woods, wastelands, etc. **Season** Spring and summer. **Distribution** Common and widespread throughout.

Heliophanus flavipes C. L. Koch

Size female 6 mm; male 3·5 mm

Very similar to *H. cupreus*.

Legs Much paler than *H. cupreus* with black streaks usually confined to femora.

Heliophanus tribulosus Simon

Resembles *H. flavipes*.

Abdomen Has only two white dots posteriorly, sometimes forming single, short curved line above spinners. **Legs** Black basally with pale apical segments.

Habitat and Season Similar to *H. cupreus* and *H. flavipes*. **Distribution** Absent from Britain. France, Germany, Belgium.

Genus *Marpissa*

There are four elongated species, three of which are relatively large. None of the spiders is common in Britain. *M. nivoyi* was previously known as *Hyctia nivoyi*.

Marpissa muscosa (Clerck)

Size female 8 mm; male 8 mm

Carapace Dark brown with broad submarginal bands of light hairs. Pale brown band on clypeus. **Abdomen** Grey to brown with lighter median band outlined in darker dots or broken lines. **Legs** Dark brown, vaguely annulated with light hairs, and with many long silky hairs. Leg I much stouter. **Palps** With long white hairs.

Habitat Trees, especially pines, or fences etc. Cell under loose bark etc. **Season** Spring and summer. **Distribution** Uncommon but widespread in England. Widespread in Europe.

♀
Heliophanus
cupreus

♂
Heliophanus
tribulosus

♀
Marpissa
muscosa

Marpissa radiata (Grube)
Size female 8–10 mm; male 7 mm
Carapace Brown with head darker, and dark median band. Clothed with light hairs. **Abdomen** Light brown with darker stripes enclosing golden median band. Clothed with light hairs. **Legs** Uniform pale brown, with long light hairs. **Palps** Similar to legs.
Habitat Confined to reedbeds in England. Egg sac in heads of *Phragmites*, which female guards in summer. In wet places generally in Europe. **Season** Early summer. **Distribution** Fen country and Somerset in England. Widespread but uncommon in Europe.

Marpissa pomatia (Walckenaer)
Similar to *M. radiata* (and erroneously recorded from England in place of *M. radiata*).
Distribution Absent from Britain. Rarer than *M. radiata* but equally widespread.

Marpissa nivoyi (Lucas)
Size female c. 5 mm; male c. 4 mm
Carapace Noticeably long. Brown with two rows of white hairs. Median row of white hairs on head. **Abdomen** Elongated. Brown with three rows of black spots, sometimes joined. With two rows of white hairs and number of transverse lines at sides. **Legs** I enlarged and dark brown. Others paler with darker annulations.
Habitat Among marram on coastal sand-dunes or in marshes. **Season** Females all year, males in autumn? **Distribution** Very local on British coast; absent from Scotland. Uncommon in France, Belgium, Holland.

Dendryphantes rudis (Sundevall)
Size female c. 6 mm; male c. 5 mm
Carapace Black, thickly covered in brown squamose hairs, giving metallic lustre. **Abdomen** With brown metallic lustre, covered anteriorly and at sides with many patches of white squamose hairs; two pairs of small white dots posteriorly. With greyish-brown median band edged in black. Sides dark brown. **Legs** Dark reddish brown annulated in black. With many short, white squamose hairs. Leg I slightly enlarged.
Habitat Branches and trunks of conifers. Sac among needles at end of branch. **Season** Early summer. **Distribution** Absent from Britain. Widespread in Europe.

♀
Marpissa radiata
with egg sac

♀
Marpissa nivoyi

♀
Dendryphantes
rudis

Dendryphantes nidicolens (Walckenaer)

Same size as *D. rudis*.
Abdomen With oblique white lines.
Habitat As *D. rudis*. **Distribution** Absent from Britain. Widespread in Europe.

Pellenes tripunctatus (Walckenaer)

Size female 6 mm; male 4–5 mm
Carapace Black with white and brown hairs. **Abdomen** With long, fine white hairs. Brown with darker patches and white median band, broken into spots posteriorly. First of these broadens into curved transverse line. **Legs** Blackish with many long white hairs. Leg I stouter.
Habitat In Britain on shingle beaches. In Europe in variety of situations in ground-layer or low bushes. **Season** Summer. **Distribution** In Britain rare on eastern coast of Kent. Fairly common and widespread in Europe.

Pseudicius encarpatus (Walckenaer)

Size female 5·5 mm; male 4–5 mm.
Female Carapace Dark brown with white lateral bands and vague light median stripe. **Abdomen** Dorsally with pair of broad dark-brown stripes enclosing lighter median area, with vague chevrons. Sides thickly covered with white hairs. **Legs** Brown, with dark annulations, especially on III, IV. Few longish white hairs. **Male Carapace** Dark brown with median and lateral bands of white hairs. **Abdomen** Dark brown with widely spaced lateral bands of white hairs. Sides brown. **Legs** Similar to female, but darker and leg I more robust.
Habitat Woods; in moss and on bark of trees. **Season** Early summer. **Distribution** Absent from Britain and Holland. Uncommon in Europe, especially in north.

Genus *Ballus*

This is a small, stout species with pale legs and is found on foliage.

Ballus depressus (Walckenaer)

Size female 4 mm; male 3 mm
Carapace Black with pale-brown hairs. **Abdomen** Brown with dark median band in front half; with two transverse extensions, rear being most pronounced. Posteriorly with one or two dark bars. **Legs** Very pale; I with femora and patella darkened. Tibiae I darkened on inner side and apically. Others with black streaks and apical annulations on patellae and tibiae. Segments not very different in length. Leg I more robust in male.
Habitat Broadleaved trees and bushes. **Season** Summer. **Distribution** Uncommon in England and Wales. Widespread in Europe.

144

♀
*Pollones
tripunctatus*

♀
*Pseudicius
encarpatus*

♀
Ballus depressus

Genus *Bianor*

There is just one species and one subspecies in the region. The dark, metallic appearance, enlarged leg I, and rather stout form are characteristic.

Bianor aenescens (Simon)
Size female 4 mm; male 3·5 mm
Female Carapace Very dark with metallic appearance. Covered with white hairs. **Abdomen** Uniformly grey or brown, thickly covered with squamose hairs. **Legs** All femora darkened, other segments brown. Femora and tibiae I greatly enlarged. **Male Carapace** Black to dark brown; head pitted. **Abdomen** Very dark with patches of golden squamose hairs – on front margin and on two transverse lines near middle. **Legs** Femora and patellae I black with tibiae dark reddish brown. Last two segments have thickly set hairs, fine dorsally and very coarse ones below. Remaining legs have darker femora and other segments reddish brown.
Habitat Very low vegetation, among stones etc. **Season** Spring to autumn. **Distribution** Local and scattered in England. Rather rare but widespread in Europe.

Genus *Neon*

There are two small species found in detritus. Neither of them jumps. The posterior eyes are relatively large.

Neon reticulatus (Blackwall)
Size female c. 3 mm; male c. 2·5 mm
Carapace Brown, darker in ocular region and with short light hairs. Posterior eyes large and protuberant. **Abdomen** Dark grey to black, with light greyish-brown to yellow spots and bars. Some specimens appear greenish in field. Very faint chevrons in median area. **Legs** Rather pale brown with leg I darker. Leg I in male marked with large areas of black.
Habitat Moss and leaf litter. **Season** Females all year, males in early summer. **Distribution** Common and widespread throughout.

Neon valentulus Falconer
Very similar to *N. reticulatus*.
Legs Darker with heavy annulations in both sexes.
Distribution Much rarer. England, Sweden, Holland.

♂
Bianor aenescens

♀
Neon reticulatus

Genus *Euophrys*

Members of this genus are medium to small spiders, typically found under stones or in low vegetation. The males of some of the species have bright patches of hairs on the clypeus and palps. Of the eight European species, only *E. frontalis* is at all common. *E. erratica* is also known as *Pseudeuophrys callida* (Walckenaer).

Euophrys frontalis (Walckenaer)

Size female 3–5 mm; male c. 3 mm
Female Carapace Brown with darker borderline. Head dark brown or black. **Abdomen** Pale brown with black spots, those in midline triangular. **Legs** Pale brown, unmarked. **Male Carapace** Dark brown with black head. Thinly covered with short golden hairs. Anterior eyes surrounded with orange hairs. **Palps** Brownish with white hairs on upper and inner sides. **Legs** I, and to lesser extent II, black with metallic lustre. Tarsi white.
Habitat Low vegetation, under stones; in woods, on heaths, etc.
Season Spring and early summer. **Distribution** Common and widespread throughout.

Euophrys petrensis C. L. Koch

Size female 3 mm; male c. 3 mm
Female Carapace and Abdomen Dark brown to black, with white and orange hairs. Very vague pattern of chevrons on rear of abdomen. **Legs** Femora black, remaining segments orange-brown with black annulations. **Palps** Yellowish. **Male Carapace** Brownish with orange hairs around anterior eyes and thickly covering clypeus. **Abdomen** Similar to female. **Legs** I and II black, especially on more basal segments. III and IV brown with black annulations. **Palps** Black, tibiae with thick skirt of long white hairs.
Habitat Under stones or very low vegetation. **Season** Spring and early summer. **Distribution** In England, ·counties bordering south coast, Cumberland; Galway and Antrim in Ireland. Very local. Widespread in Europe.

♀
Euophrys petrensis

♀
*Euophrys
frontalis* with
eggs

♂
Euophrys frontalis

♂
*Euophrys
petrensis*

Euophrys erratica (Walckenaer)

Size female c. 4 mm; male c. 4 mm

Carapace Black with borderline of light hairs. Head covered with orange and brown hairs, with patch of white hairs centrally. **Abdomen** With light-brown and orange hairs. Pattern vague except for few chevrons at rear. **Legs** Light brown with darker annulations and rings of light hairs. Rear legs more clearly marked. **Palps** Uniformly light yellow in female; Male with light-yellow femora and patellae, the tarsi dark brown.

Habitat Walls and stony places. **Season** Early summer. **Distribution** Local and scattered in British Isles. Absent from central southern England. Absent from Holland. Widespread in Europe.

Euophrys aequipes (O.P.-Cambridge)

Size female 2–3 mm; male 2 mm

Carapace and Abdomen Black with many yellowish hairs. Appears dull yellow in field. **Legs** Pale yellow with clear, black annulations. Males have femora I black. **Palps** Yellowish in both sexes.

Habitat Sunny, stony places. Hunts on ground. **Season** Summer. **Distribution** Very local but widespread in England and Scotland. Widespread in Europe.

Euophrys lanigera (Simon)

Size female 4·5 mm; male c. 4 mm

Resembles *E. erratica* but has greyer appearance.

Abdomen More sharply defined pattern than *E. erratica*. In male brownish hairs which constitute pattern in female are all white. **Legs** In male less clearly annulated; leg I is black apart from brown tarsus. **Palps** Light yellow, with tarsus darker.

Habitat Buildings, sometimes gardens. **Season** Females all year; males principally summer. **Distribution** Widespread in England; recorded in south Wales. Locally common in south. Belgium, France.

Genus *Sitticus*

The four species described can most easily be distinguished by their habitats. They are rather plump spiders with white spots on the abdomen. They are less inclined to make silk cells than most of the other genera.

♀
Euophrys erratica

♂
*Euophrys
aequipes*

♀
Euophrys lanigera

Sitticus pubescens (Fabricius)
Size female 5 mm; male 4 mm
Female Carapace Dark brown to black with many light hairs. Light triangular spot occurs in median line, just in front of posterior eyes, with another pair behind. **Abdomen** With pattern of spots; two pairs of small ones in front, large pair behind midline and with two or three pairs posteriorly, sometimes forming oblique lines. Sides have patches of white hairs. **Legs** Vaguely annulated and with rings of light hairs. **Male** Darker. **Abdomen** Clearer spots.
Habitat Houses and gardens. Occasionally tree trunks (eg pines on heathland). **Season** Summer. Females throughout year indoors. **Distribution** Widespread but uncommon except locally in England and Wales. Very widespread in Europe and North America.

Sitticus floricola (C. L. Koch)
Size female 5 mm; male 4 mm
Abdomen Similar pattern to *S. pubescens* except that largest pair of spots are elongated laterally.
Habitat Low vegetation in swamps. Females construct egg sacs in heads of cottongrass, and probably other vegetation. **Season** Early summer. **Distribution** Scotland, Ireland, Delamere Forest in Cheshire, England. More common and widespread in Europe.

Sitticus rupicola (C. L. Koch)
Size female 5–7 mm; male 5 mm
Greatly resembles *S. floricola*.
Abdomen Sides thickly clothed with light-grey hairs, particularly clear on front margin and posteriorly. In median line are number of rather ill-defined chevrons.
Habitat Shingle beaches on coasts of southern and eastern England and Somerset. Among rocks in mountainous areas of Europe. **Season** Summer. **Distribution** Apparently absent or very rare within region.

Sitticus caricis (Westring)
Size female 3–4 mm; male 3 mm
Female Carapace and Abdomen Blackish, thickly covered with orange and white hairs, giving overall purple-brown colour. **Legs** Purple-brown sometimes with dark, but vague annulations. **Male** Similar to female but usually with clearer white spots on abdomen.
Habitat Low vegetation in marshes. **Season** Summer. **Distribution** Uncommon, with most records concentrated in south-east England. Uncommon but widespread in Europe.

Attulus saltator (Simon)

Size female 2·5–4 mm; male 2–3 mm

Tiny species with similar pattern to *Sitticus* spp.

Carapace Black, rather shiny. Broken line of white hairs centrally, broad line of white hairs on sides and continuing around front of head, encircling eyes. **Abdomen** White sides. A light, broken bar anteriorly, some brownish hairs in centre line, two large white spots and white patch over spinners. **Legs** Thickly covered in white hairs, with some darker spots and rings. Leg IV much longer than others. Male very similar, but leg I has tibia and metatarsus dark.

Habitat Sandy places. In Britain mostly coastal dunes. **Season** Spring and autumn. **Distribution** Widespread but very local on coasts of England and south Wales; also Surrey, Suffolk. Widespread but uncommon in Europe.

Philaeus chrysops (Poda)

Size female 7–12 mm; male 7–12 mm

Female Liberally covered with long white hairs. **Carapace** Black. **Abdomen** With broad black median stripe, tapering posteriorly. Sides light brown. **Legs** Black with vague lighter rings. **Male** Sometimes larger than female. **Carapace** Black. **Abdomen** Bright red with black median band. **Legs** Black with thick covering of hairs; predominantly orange on legs I and II, white on III and IV.

Habitat Among rocks and stones; sometimes low bushes. **Season** Summer. **Distribution** Absent from Britain. Rare in southern part of region and more common in southern Europe.

♀
Attulus saltator

♀
Philaeus chrysops

♂
Philaeus chrysops

Evarcha falcata (Clerck)

Size female 7 mm; male 5 mm

Female Carapace Black. Head has metallic lustre. Thorax clothed with brown hairs. **Abdomen** Brown with whitish sides. Sometimes with few black spots laterally. **Legs** Brown to black. With white and brown hairs. **Male Carapace** Black with brown hairs on head. Sides with broad white or light-brown band of hairs. **Abdomen** Reddish brown with black edges, sometimes dentate. Central area sometimes with lighter triangles or with pair of white spots in rear half. Sides with white band surrounding folium. **Legs** Anterior pairs stouter than III and IV. Femora I enlarged and totally black; others light basally. Remaining segments clothed with white and orange hairs.

Habitat Vegetation in woods; also on heather. **Season** Spring and summer. Males also adult in autumn. **Distribution** Common and widespread throughout.

Evarcha arcuata (Clerck)

Size female 7 mm; male 5–6 mm

Female Carapace Brown metallic on head, with whitish hairs on thorax. Clypeus has two rows of white hairs. **Abdomen** Brown with short median stripe anteriorly, followed by very oblique dark streaks in rear half. Thickly covered with white hairs. **Legs** Obscurely marked and with white hairs. **Male** Wholly dark brown to black with metallic lustre. Sturdy appearance. **Carapace** Clypeus has two rows of white hairs, which also surround eyes, and occur as stripes on chelicerae. **Legs** I has femur, patella, and tibiae enlarged.

Habitat Grass and heather in damp places, usually heathland. **Season** Summer. **Distribution** Local, but sometimes very common in southern England. Widespread in Europe.

♀
Evarcha arcuata

♀
Evarcha falcata

♂
Evarcha falcata

♂
Evarcha arcuata

Evarcha laetabunda (C. L. Koch)
Resembles *E. arcuata*.
Habitat Dry places. **Distribution** Absent from Britain. Widespread in Europe.

Aelurillus v-insignitus (Clerck)
Size female 7 mm; male 4–5 mm
Female Carapace Black, covered with greyish hairs. Anterior lateral eyes have patches of light hairs below them. **Abdomen** Similar to carapace; sometimes with two rows of lighter spots in median line. **Legs** Blackish with rings of light hairs. **Male Carapace** With two v-shaped rows of light hairs. Margins have light edges, and there are brownish hairs on thorax which are easily rubbed off, leaving larger part of carapace black and shiny. **Abdomen** Dorsally black with brownish median stripe. Sides also with brownish-black hairs. **Legs** Similar to female, but leg I and palps with light brown or golden hairs. **Habitat** Heathland and other sunny places. **Season** Spring and summer, occasionally to autumn. **Distribution** Local in England but sometimes common in counties bordering south coast; East Anglia and Fife in Scotland. Very widespread in Europe.

Phlegra fasciata (Hahn)
Size female 7 mm; male 6 mm
Female Carapace Black with light-brown margins and two light-brown stripes running from posterior eyes. **Abdomen** With two dark-brown bands along length. Sides and median band light brown. **Legs** Light brown with darker annulations. **Male** With very faint markings disposed as in female. Blackish dorsally with reddish-brown legs. **Habitat** Among low vegetation on sandhills. **Season** Summer. **Distribution** Rare and local on coasts of central southern and southeastern England. Uncommon throughout Europe and North America.

Genera *Synageles, Leptorchestes*, and *Myrmarachne* – ant mimics

While the behaviour of most salticids appears to be rather intelligent and considered, these three spiders which have a rather ant-like form, actually behave like ants, running about in the same manic way that ants do. In the field they are difficult to distinguish from their models, having the pedicel clearly visible from above. There is a constriction near the middle of the abdomen, giving a tripartite appearance to the body, and rather thin legs. *Synageles* and *Leptorchestes* differ in size but otherwise are similar. *Myrmarachne* males have greatly enlarged fangs.

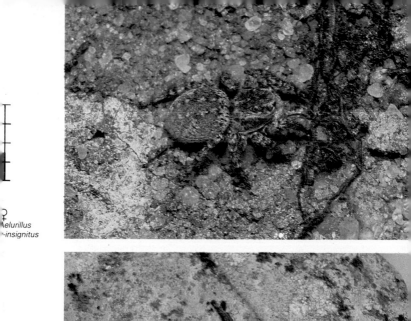

♀
*Aelurillus
v-insignitus*

♂
*Aelurillus
v-insignitus*

♀
Phlegra fasciata

Synageles venator (Lucas)

Size female c. 4 mm; male 3 mm
Carapace Black with iridescent sheen. Band of white hairs immediately behind posterior eyes. **Abdomen** Pedicel clearly visible. Black with transverse, light-brown stripe containing thin line of white hairs. Constricted in male. **Legs** Pale brown with longitudinal black lines. Leg I darker and stouter.
Habitat Among low vegetation on sandhills, fens, and cultivated sites. **Season** Females at most seasons; males in summer and autumn. **Distribution** Very local in southern England, not uncommon locally in south Wales. More frequent and widespread in Europe.

Leptorchestes berolinensis (C. L. Koch)

Size female 7 mm; male 6 mm
Closely resembles *S. venator* but larger and slimmer.
Carapace Thorax smoothly raised posteriorly, dorsally flat. **Chelicerae** Similar in both sexes. **Palps** Normal in female.
Habitat Sunny walls, under bark, etc. **Season** Summer. **Distribution** Absent from Britain. France, Germany, Belgium. [The species figured is *L. mutilloides* (Lucas) found to the south of the region.]

Myrmarachne formicaria (Degeer)

Size female 6 mm; male 6 mm (overall)
Female Carapace Head black with metallic lustre, abruptly raised from thorax which is orange-brown to black. **Abdomen** Anteriorly orange-brown to dark brown. Constriction marked by white hairs midway. Posteriorly darker. **Legs** Yellow- to orange-brown streaked with black. Leg II with least markings. **Palps** Black and spatulate.
Male Very similar to female, except that iridescent black chelicerae are hugely enlarged and flattened on dorsal surface. They project in plane of body and increase length of male by about 30 per cent.
Habitat Grassy banks exposed to sun. **Season** Early summer.
Distribution Very local in southern and eastern England. Widespread in Europe.

♀
Myrmarachne formicaria

♂
*Synageles
venator*

♂
*Leptorchestes
mutilloides*

♂
*Myrmarachne
formicaria*

Family Oxyopidae

This family, with many tropical members, consists of three rather similar species in the genus *Oxyopes*, represented in the region.

The oxyopids have affinities with the salticids and lycosids; they are found in low vegetation, such as heather, where they hunt during the day. They are capable of running and leaping through the undergrowth with great ease on their quite long, slender legs with the long, erect spines but they can catch nearby prey simply by leaping from a stationary site like a salticid. In July the females can be found tenaciously guarding their flattened egg sacs which are placed in a crook of twigs, exposed at the top of the plant. Large immatures can be found in the early autumn in England, suggesting a life-cycle in which they overwinter twice before becoming adult.

Facies

Oxyopes heterophthalmus (Latreille)
Size female 5–7 mm; male 5–7 mm
Superficially, male and female resemble *Philodromus histrio*.
Carapace Brownish. Two divergent median bands occur posteriorly stopping at head. Thin white band partly encircles head, which has thin median stripe that continues down clypeus. White borderline continues around head to form large patches below lateral eyes.
Abdomen Prominent cardiac mark (black in male) is edged in white which continues as line to spinners. Brown median band surrounds line. Sides are dark with forward-pointing streaks of white hairs. **Legs** Blackish, but thickly covered with brown and white hairs.
Habitat Heather. **Season** Early summer. **Distribution** In England in the New Forest and three heaths in Surrey where they are infrequent. France, Belgium.

Oxyopes lineatus Latreille
Size female c. 6 mm; male 4–5 mm
Carapace Much paler than *O. heterophthalmus*. White median bands continue thickly to lateral eyes. Borders are yellowish and almost devoid of hair. In male bands are surrounded by black, and black area in ocular region is clearly visible. **Abdomen** Less strongly marked than *O. heterophthalmus*, with oblique side bands faint in some specimens. Median band broader. **Legs** Very pale, with few hairs and no blotches.
Habitat Trees, bushes, and low vegetation. **Season** Summer. **Distribution** Absent from Britain. France, Holland, Belgium(?)

Oxyopes ramosus (Panzer)

Size female 6–10 mm; male 6 mm

Carapace Reddish brown; two white median bands almost parallel but broken into dots immediately behind head. With white hairs on margin continuing as thin stripes on clypeus. **Abdomen** Reddish brown, with broad median band paler. Three oblique side stripes. **Legs** Dark brown. Femora and patellae very dark, tibiae and metatarsi with annulations, tarsi with dark apical ring.

Habitat Similar to *O. heterophthalmus*. **Season** Early summer. **Distribution** Absent from Britain. Most of region, including Sweden, Finland.

♀
Oxyopes hetero phthalmus on egg sac

Oxyopes lineatus and egg sac

Family Lycosidae

Lycosids are medium to large spiders which are found running on the ground. The females carry their egg sacs attached to the spinners.

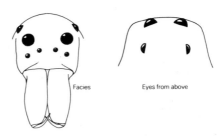

Facies

Eyes from above

Carapace The carapaces of wolf spiders vary in height within the genera. In plan view the thorax appears rounded and the head protrudes anteriorly. Lateral and median bands are nearly always present and they are composed of subcutaneous colouring, reinforced by hairs in most genera. **Eyes** Lycosid spiders' eyes are arranged in three rows; the anterior eyes are very small and set out in a straight or slightly curved row. The larger medians vary in their spacing but are always situated on the vertical front of the head. The posterior eyes are more widely spaced than those of the previous row and are set on the sides of the head which may be steep sided or sloping. All the eyes are dark. **Abdomen** The abdomen is oval, with a pattern composed of hairs which can become worn in old specimens. Frequently, there are small clumps of white hairs which form rows of spots on the dorsum. **Legs** In lycosids the fourth pair of legs is the longest, and this is emphasized by the posture of the spider because these legs are frequently held stretched out. In some genera the spines on the third and fourth pairs are longer and more erect than those on the anterior two pairs of legs. **Sternum** Frequently, the sternum has a light median band but this is very variable. Some *Pirata* species and *Hygrolycosa* have dark spots opposite the coxae.

Of the ten genera of lycosid spiders, *Pardosa* species are the most widespread and abundant. Unlike the others, they are often found in some numbers, although their gregarious nature is not extended into true sociability. While they will avoid other, similarly sized spiders, they will attack and devour small immatures of their own species. The immature stages tend to be found within the litter layer, while the older spiders are most active on the surface. This minimizes the destruction of the immatures which may require two winters to become adult.

If they are disturbed, the spiders run away at some speed, making small jumps when the ground demands it. They are known as wolf spiders because it was thought that they hunted in packs and ran down their prey. This idea was reinforced because it was known that their eyesight is better than average for their order. In the field, they are rarely seen with prey, which includes smaller animals, such as springtails and small flies, which the spiders catch when they approach closely. The more powerful species of *Trochosa* have been seen grappling with beetle larvae which are also fierce carnivores. *Alopecosa fabrilis*, the largest member of its genus in England, eats adult beetles and, when tackling large flies, the spider seizes them in its fangs and rolls over on its back, presumably to prevent the flies from crawling off.

In the early spring *Pardosa* subadults can sometimes be seen basking in the sun. They climb on to leaves up to 10 centimetres above the ground and adopt a curious posture: the first three pairs of legs are bent forwards so that the head appears to be resting on them. The fourth pair is stretched out behind, their claws gripping the edge of the leaf. Sometimes, these 'sleeping' spiders can actually be touched before they take fright and dive into the undergrowth.

Once they become adult, the males spend a great deal of time and energy searching out females and courting them. The courtship can be initiated in captivity by objects (stones, leaves, etc) with which a female has been in contact but, in the field, it appears to be sight which has a strong influence on his behaviour. The male stretches his legs and struts about until he confronts the female face to face. In detail, the procedure varies from species to species but, essentially, the male's semaphore display consists of vibrating his front legs (which often carry conspicuous markings) and jerkily raising his dark palps alternately or together. Periodically, his abdomen will vibrate as he gradually approaches the female. Although she appears to be fascinated by his behaviour, she may well make a mock attack on him. After several rejections, his persistence may be rewarded and, tickling the female's legs briefly, he climbs on to her from the front. He rests his abdomen on her carapace and leans over the side of her abdomen to insert his palps. These are used alternately, and the mating proceeds fitfully, for a considerable period of time in some species, before the two part.

After a few weeks, the female makes her first egg sac; a small sheet of silk is woven upon which the eggs are deposited. A second sheet is spun over them and joined to the lower sheet. Once the eggs are securely wrapped, the female holds the bundle between her third legs and fangs and rotates as she adds more silk. *Pardosa* and *Hygrolycosa* differ from the remaining genera in making coloured sacs, and it is this final coat which imparts the colour. In about three-quarters of an hour the sac is completed and attached to the spinners where it remains until the young emerge.

The burrowing genera have been seen to expose their sacs to the sun's rays from the mouth of the burrow, and *Pardosa* females (of species which are considered to be strictly ground living) will climb up low vegetation, particularly after wet weather, to dry and warm their egg sacs. The spiders orient themselves so that the sac is facing the sun; unlike the basking spiders, these females are easily disturbed and difficult to observe.

After the young have emerged from the sac and have moulted, they climb on to their mother's abdomen, and are carried about by her for several days. Once this happens, the sac (containing the white chorion from the eggs and the pink skins shed by the spiderlings) is released by the female, but the instinct to drag this about is so strong in some females that they may be seen with young clustered on their abdomens and a sac in tow as well.

Genus *Pardosa*

These spiders are the most common and abundant lycosids. They are found in most habitats provided they are not too dry. One species, *P. nigriceps*, is often found in bushes but, typically, members of this genus are found running on the ground in sunshine or basking. All *Pardosa* spiders are adult in the early spring. In most species the males disappear by June but the females are seen long into the summer and make two or three egg sacs which have a blue, green, or brown hue. The long fourth legs and, to a lesser extent, the third pair have more conspicuous spines than the anterior pairs. There is great sexual dimorphism in many species, with the male being very dark with contrasting legs. In the field the females are identified chiefly by the markings on the carapace and legs. Many species are found in Europe and a selection of the more common or distinctive species are described here. Previously, the genus was included in *Lycosa*, a name now restricted to large, burrowing species found in southern Europe and other warm climes.

Pardosa agricola (Thorell)
Size female 7 mm; male 6 mm
Female Carapace Light median band very irregular in width. Lateral bands clearly broken. **Abdomen** Often with lighter median band extending whole length. Venter with light-grey pubescence. Epigyne clearly visible (cf *P. amentata* which has similar but more obscure dorsal markings). **Legs** Clearly annulated. **Male** Darker than female, with less clear markings on carapace and abdomen. **Legs** Annulations obscure; tarsi I darkened almost to base.
Habitat On sandy banks of rivers and lakes; among vegetation or on sand itself. **Season** Spring. **Distribution** Chiefly in northern Britain, but also in north Wales, English midlands. All northern Europe.

Pardosa agricola forma _arenicola_ (O.P.-Cambridge)
Size female 7 mm; male 5 mm
Female Carapace Median band thin, pointed anteriorly. Lateral bands broken. **Abdomen** Like _P. agricola_ but less clear dorsally. **Legs** Annulations obscure. **Male** All markings much less clear than female. **Legs** Tarsi I darkened almost to base.
Habitat On shingle beaches in southern Britain; also recorded from dunes in Europe. **Season** Late spring. **Distribution** Uncommon in England, France, Sweden.

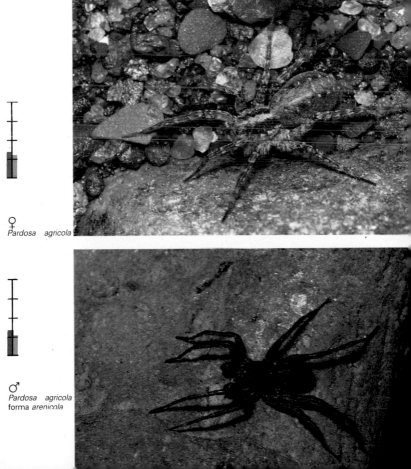

♀
Pardosa agricola

♂
Pardosa agricola
forma _arenicola_

Pardosa purbeckensis (F.O.P.-Cambridge)

Size female 8 mm; male 6 mm

Female Carapace With clear median and lateral bands; median thin and pointed anteriorly. Laterals entire. **Abdomen** Dark brown, sometimes with pairs of small white spots in posterior half. **Legs** Obscurely marked. **Male** Distinguished by leg markings. Femora with streaks basally and dorsally only; remaining segments pale and unmarked. Metatarsi and tarsi of legs I have many long, fine hairs.

Habitat Only on shores of estuaries or tidal mudflats where there is some vegetation. **Season** Spring, early summer. **Distribution** Widespread around British Isles. Holland, Belgium, Denmark.

Pardosa monticola (Clerck)

Size female 6 mm; male 5 mm
(*see also P. palustris*)

Female Carapace Dark brown with very light and clear bands. Median and lateral bands thin and almost parallel sided. Edges of carapace with thin, dark line. **Abdomen** Very variable. Usually with clear cardiac mark. Rest of abdomen almost uniformly brown, or with tapering brown area flanked by small black spots. Sides light grey. Epigyne subrectangular and less than third the width of abdomen (cf *P. palustris*). **Legs** Pale brown with variable and vague markings. **Male** Carapace and Abdomen Black with lighter median bands. Lateral markings often absent. **Legs** Femora with dark marks dorsally; remaining segments unmarked, pale brown.

Habitat Rather open places, eg dunes, grassy hillsides, where herbage is short. **Season** Spring. **Distribution** Common throughout.

Pardosa palustris var *herbigrada* (Linnaeus)

Size female 6 mm; male 5 mm

Some specimens indistinguishable from *P. monticola*, especially males. Females may be separated by epigyne which is subtriangular and wider than a third of abdomen. *P. palustris* has less distinct markings, and some specimens of *P. palustris* have same carapace markings.

Female Carapace With broad and often irregular pale bands. Median dilated anteriorly. Laterals very broad and extending to edges of carapace. **Abdomen** Cardiac mark and following brown patch edged with black, spur from which extends across sides of abdomen which are pale grey. **Legs** Pale grey to pale brown with vague annulations. **Male** Slightly darker than female but with pattern distinct, and with annulations present on legs.

Habitat Variety occurs only in heathery places. **Season** Spring to early summer. **Distribution** Confined to one habitat, but (like parent form) widespread throughout.

168

♀
*Pardosa
purbeckensis*

♀
*Pardosa
monticola*

♀
Pardosa palustris
var *herbigrada*

Pardosa bifasciata (C. L. Koch)
Size female 6 mm; male 5 mm
Female Carapace Three bands almost parallel. Median parallel sided and reaches broad pale region bounded by eyes. Lateral bands broad, with faint traces of darker submarginal band. **Abdomen** Cardiac mark white, surrounded by brown. Dorsal marks edged broadly with dark grey, mottled at sides. Ventrally with white hairs which largely cover epigyne. **Legs** I, II almost unmarked, brown with white pubescence; III, IV darker with a few spots. **Male** Generally darker than female.
Habitat Sunny open places, with sand or stones. **Season** Late spring to early summer. **Distribution** Absent from Britain. France, Germany, Belgium, Scandinavia.

Pardosa pullata (Clerck)
Size female 6 mm; male 4·5 mm
Often without any clear markings, female appearing totally black or dark brown. Male often has fairly clear median carapace band, and cardiac mark.
Legs Very pale brown without annulations. Slight darkening of femora.
Habitat Gardens, wasteland, marshes, etc. **Season** Spring, summer. **Distribution** Widespread throughout.

Pardosa prativaga (L. Koch)
Size female 6 mm; male 5 mm
Both sexes have annulated legs, very clear in some specimens.
Habitat and Season As *P. pullata*. **Distribution** Widely distributed.

Pardosa fulvipes (Collett)
Size female 6 mm; male 5 mm
Sometimes considered as variety of *P. prativaga* but leg annulations obscure, and usually with clearer markings on carapace and abdomen. **Habitat** Grassy places. **Season** Early to mid-summer. **Distribution** Scandinavia.

♂
Pardosa prativaga

♀
Pardosa bifasciata

♂
Pardosa pullata

♀
Pardosa fulvipes

Pardosa sphagnicola (Dahl)
Size female 6 mm; male 5 mm
Female Resembles *P. pullata* except for white hairs in spots on dorsal surface of abdomen and at sides. **Male** White hairs thickly cover sides of carapace and abdomen, and coxae of legs. **Legs** I, II, and palps also lightly covered in white hairs. Uniformly brown.
Habitat Damp, mossy places. **Season** Spring, early summer. **Distribution** Holland, Germany, Scandinavia.

Pardosa amentata (Clerck)
Size female up to 8 mm; male 6 mm
Female Carapace Variable, but typically with median band of irregular width, dilated anteriorly. Lateral bands often with dentate inner edges, and submarginal darker line. **Abdomen** Grey or brown sometimes with obscure markings, usually with two widely spaced rows of black dots. Ventrally epigyne obscured by hairs (cf *P. agricola*). **Legs** All segments marked. **Male** Much darker than female. **Palps** Black.
Habitat Open, moist places. **Season** Spring. **Distribution** Common and widespread throughout.

Pardosa nigriceps (Thorell)
Size female 6 mm; male 5 mm
Female Carapace Dark brown with broad, yellowish bands. Median dilated anteriorly, stopping at posterior eyes. **Abdomen** Markings variable but usually brown with yellow spots, forming typical *Pardosa* pattern. **Legs** Yellow-brown, marks on femora, remaining segments unmarked. **Male Carapace** Darker than female with conspicuous white hairs on face. Lateral bands covered in white hairs. **Abdomen** Dark brown with white hairs on sides. **Legs** Clear yellow-brown. **Palps** Covered thickly with black hairs.
Habitat Heaths, grassy and with heather. Unlike other *Pardosa* species, often found in tall bushes above 1 m. **Season** Spring. **Distribution** Common and widespread throughout.

♀
Pardosa nigriceps

♂
*Pardosa
sphagnicola*

♀
Pardosa amentata
with egg sac

♂ *Pardosa nigriceps*
courting

Pardosa lugubris (Walckenaer)

Size female 6 mm; male 5 mm

Female Carapace Dark brown with pale-brown median band, which reaches anterior eyes and tapers slightly at rear of carapace. Lateral bands thin and faint. **Abdomen** Dark brown, speckled with patches of golden hairs. **Legs** Annulated dark brown and gold, especially clear on femora, patellae, and tibiae. **Male Carapace** Black with almost parallel-sided median band of thick, white hairs. **Abdomen** Black with pattern of white hairs similar to, but less distinct than female. **Legs** Femora black, remaining segments pale brown.

Habitat Woodland edges or sunny places in woods. **Season** Spring. **Distribution** Common and widespread throughout.

Pardosa hortensis (Thorell)

Size female 6 mm; male 4 mm

Female Similar to *P. amentata*, but with less distinct markings. **Carapace** Greyish brown, median band very irregular in outline, but clearly defined. Lateral bands obscure and broken. **Abdomen** Speckled appearance, grey-brown. Pattern very obscure. **Legs** Grey-brown marked with irregular dark annulations. **Male** Darker than female on carapace and abdomen. **Legs** Rather light with clear marks only on femora. **Palps** Femora and patellae pale; tibiae and tarsi dark.

Habitat Open situations such as sandpits, clearings in woods, etc. **Season** Early spring. Males adult for 2 or 3 weeks only. **Distribution** Fairly widespread but local in Britain. France, Germany, Holland, Belgium.

Pardosa proxima (C. L. Koch)

Size female 6 mm; male 5 mm

Female Carapace Dark brown with yellow bands. Median rather short and tapered at both ends. Laterals usually broken. **Abdomen** Dark brown with only yellow cardiac mark clearly defined. **Legs** Yellowish with darker annulations, becoming more obscure apically. **Male** Similar to female but darker on body.

Habitat Grassy places, sometimes in damp spots. **Season** Spring. **Distribution** In Britain local in southern half of England. France, Holland, Belgium.

Genus *Hygrolycosa*

There is only a single species in the region. It is rather similar to *Pardosa*, but the legs, especially III and IV which do not have erect spines, are less spiny. The legs and carapace have a shiny appearance, unlike *Pardosa* spiders. The spots on the femora of the female's legs are characteristic only of this species. The egg sac is pale brown.

♀
ardosa lugubris

♀
Pardosa hortensis

♀
Pardosa proxima
with egg sac

Hygrolycosa rubrofasciata (Ohlert)

Size female 6 mm; male 5·5 mm

Female Similar to *P. nigriceps* in colouring. **Carapace** Pale yellow, with sinuous dark-brown submarginal bands. Irregular yellow median band flanked by wide, dark-brown bands. Shiny. **Abdomen** Reddish brown dorsally with faint pattern and pairs of white spots. **Legs** Coxae, femora, patellae pale yellow with large, dark-brown blotches. Remaining segments uniformly brown, getting lighter apically. **Male Carapace** Very dark brown, shiny, with very faint bands. **Abdomen** Rather similar to female but darker. **Legs** Coxae, femora, patellae, basal part of tibiae very dark brown. Remaining segments light brown. **Habitat** Damp places in woods. **Season** Early summer. **Distribution** In Britain very local in England. Widespread, fairly common in France, Germany. Holland, Belgium, Sweden.

Genus *Xerolycosa*

There are two species in northern Europe. They are similar in general features to *Pardosa*, but both have distinctive markings and live in dry habitats. The males of both species are lighter and more clearly marked than the females. The egg sac is white.

Xerolycosa nemoralis (Westring)

Size female 7 mm; male 6 mm

Both sexes have overall pink colour.

Female Carapace Rather circular, black with very clear pink-brown median stripe. Broadest behind posterior eyes, and narrows to front of head. Lateral bands composed of white hairs, which can become rubbed away. **Abdomen** Dark grey and pink-brown covered in small patches of white hairs. Two dark marks anteriorly at sides. **Legs** Dark pinkish brown, annulated clearly on femora. **Male** Similar in pattern (but not colour) to male *P. lugubris*. **Carapace** Black with pale-pink-brown median band which is almost parallel sided. Short lateral bands of same colour. **Abdomen** Pink-brown with two dark marks on lower front margin. Pattern very faint. **Legs** Pale pinkish grey with tibiae I covered in white pubescence.

Habitat Sandy heaths, woods, and on chalk. **Season** Summer. Females with egg sacs found up to September. **Distribution** In Britain rather local in south-east England. Widespread in Europe.

♀
Hygrolycosa
rubrofasciata

♂
Hygrolycosa
rubrofasciata

♀
Xerolycosa
nemoralis

Xerolycosa miniata (C. L. Koch)
Size female 6 mm; male 5 mm
Sexes similar.
Female Carapace Brown. Median band pale brown, covered in white hairs and distinctly narrowed at mid-point. Lateral bands confined to posterior half. **Abdomen** Lighter than carapace, with two widely spaced rows of white dots, composed of hairs, each pair joined by faint white bar. **Legs** Femora and sometimes tibiae annulated and covered with white hairs. Remaining segments brown. **Male** Lighter than female and with clearer markings. **Carapace** Median band white. Lateral bands clearer than in female. **Abdomen** Like female. **Legs** Femora I, II darker ventrally. Tibiae I, II with white hairs.
Habitat Sandy places. **Season** Early summer. **Distribution** Local in coastal dunes in Britain. Widespread throughout Europe.

Genus *Alopecosa (Tarentula)*

The abdomen is characterized by a clear cardiac mark and its shape and background colour vary among the species. The female makes a burrow in which she stays with her white egg sac.

Alopecosa pulverulenta (Clerck)
Size female 10 mm; male 8 mm
Female Carapace Dark brown with lighter median band. Lateral bands very faint or absent. **Abdomen** Variable. Cardiac mark brown with thin, dark border on brown median band, about half length of abdomen. Occasionally outlined in white hairs and followed by thin, white, transverse lines connecting white spots. **Legs** Femora faintly annulated. Remaining segments brown. **Male** Carapace Median band covered in white hairs. **Abdomen** Pattern less distinct than female. **Legs** Similar to female but leg I dark to tibiae; remaining segments lighter.
Habitat Open ground. **Season** Spring. **Distribution** Common and widespread throughout.

Alopecosa cuneata (Clerck)
Size female 8 mm; male 7 mm
Female Carapace Dark brown with lighter median band and clear lateral bands. **Abdomen** Cardiac mark longer than in *A. pulverulenta*, and very clearly defined, on much lighter median band. **Legs** Annulations faint or absent. **Male** Very like female. **Abdomen** Pattern even more clearly defined. **Legs** Tibiae I swollen. (Only found in this species.)
Habitat Open places. **Season** Early spring. **Distribution** In Britain local and uncommon in England. Widespread in Europe.

♀
*Xerolycosa
miniata*

♀
*Alopecosa
pulverulenta*

♂
*Alopecosa
cuneata*

Alopecosa accentuata (Latreille)

Size female up to 12 mm; male 9 mm

Female Carapace Dark brown with irregular median band, narrowed about half way. Lateral bands faint or broken, except anteriorly where they are well developed at sides of ocular region. **Abdomen** Cardiac mark short, but very distinct and with two pairs of thin lateral extensions. Paler median band contains thin dark chevrons. **Legs** Annulations clear on femora, less distinct on other segments. **Male Carapace** Similar to female but more clearly defined. Median band has white hairs which sometimes cover whole of head. **Abdomen** Usually less clearly defined than female. Median region sometimes thickly covered in white hairs. **Legs** No annulations. Sometimes covered in white hairs, but always with tibiae and metatarsi of leg I black with dense black hairs ventrally.

Habitat Open places on sand and chalk. **Season** Spring. Females adult in autumn and overwinter as adults. **Distribution** Common in suitable habitats. Widespread in Europe.

Alopecosa fabrilis (Clerck)

Size female 15 mm; male 12 mm

Female Carapace Median and lateral bands well defined, with darker regions streaked. **Abdomen** Similar to *A. accentuata* but with white spots conspicuous. Black ventrally. **Legs** Femora vaguely annulated, often with large dark spots apically. Remaining segments unmarked. **Male** Similar to female, but with lighter parts covered thickly with white hairs. **Legs** Covered with white pubescence from coxae to tibiae.

Habitat Sandy places where female constructs deep burrow lined with silk. **Season** In England both sexes are mature in autumn but adults are also found in early to midsummer in Europe. Female overwinters in burrow and lays eggs in spring. **Distribution** In England known only from two isolated heaths in Dorset and Surrey. Widespread and more common throughout Europe.

Genus *Acantholycosa*

Four species occur and they are found only in mountainous areas. These spiders are similar in shape to *Pardosa* but usually they are very dark or have markings more like those of *Alopecosa*. The legs are annulated, clearly in some specimens, and rather elongated. They are shy, elusive spiders which live among stones on screes or among the fallen limbs of trees in warm, dry places. In mid-Europe they are really outside the region, but *A. lignaria* (occurring on the edges of mountain forest) and *A. norvegica* (with more strongly annulated legs) are found in Scandinavia.

♀
*Alopecosa
accentuata*

♀
Alopecosa fabrilis
with prey

Genus *Trochosa*

Members of this genus are large, robust spiders. The median carapace band is widened anteriorly with two dark spots within it. The
four European species are difficult to identify, but *T. terricola* is the
most commonly encountered. The spiders are probably active at night
but males are found wandering in daylight in the spring and early
summer. The females excavate small burrows in which to make their
white egg sacs and in which they remain until the young emerge.

Trochosa ruricola (Degeer)
Size female 12 mm; male 8 mm
Female Carapace Dark brown with lighter median band broadened anteriorly and containing two darker streaks. Lateral bands thin. Abdomen Grey-brown with distinct light cardiac mark. Other markings usually very faint. Legs Grey-brown. **Male Carapace** Very dark brown with thinner bands than female. **Abdomen** Very dark brown, sometimes with more distinct pattern than female, but with cardiac mark very light. Legs As female but with tibiae, metatarsi, and tarsi of first pair dark brown.
Habitat Damp places. Usually found in retreat under stones etc. **Season** Adults at most times of year. **Distribution** Common throughout.

Trochosa robusta (Simon)
Size female 20 mm; male 18 mm
Similar markings, habitat, and season, but much rarer than T. ruricola. Largest Trochosa. **Distribution** Widespread. Absent from Scandinavia.

Trochosa terricola Thorell
Size female 8–14 mm; male 9 mm
Female Carapace Dark brown with reddish-brown bands. Median with two streaks behind posterior eyes. Laterals broader than T. ruricola. Abdomen Reddish brown with faint markings. Cardiac mark not lighter than surrounding area. Legs Reddish brown with faint annulations on femora. **Male** Similar to female T. ruricola except that cardiac mark not so light and tarsi of legs I lighter than tibiae and metatarsi.
Habitat Drier places than T. ruricola. **Season** Throughout year. **Distribution** Common throughout.

Trochosa spinipalpis (F.O.P.– Cambridge)
Size female 11 mm; male 9 mm
Very difficult to distinguish from T. terricola. **Abdomen** Deeper, more umber brown (dorsally and ventrally).
Habitat and Season As T. terricola. **Distribution** Widespread in Europe, but probably rare.

Genus Tricca

There are two rare species that have similar eye patterns to those of the Pisauridae. T. alpigena is a montane species with a very clear white cardiac mark; the tarsi I are thickly clothed in short hairs. Formerly this species was ascribed to Arctosa. T. lutetiana is a smaller species (male and female 6–8 mm) found in sandy habitats and detritus.

182

♂
Trochosa ruricola

♀
Trochosa terricola

Genus *Arctosa*

The five species of the region are characterized by a flattened carapace upon which the posterior eyes have an upward glance. There
is little sexual dimorphism. *A. perita* and *A. cinerea* have the habit of
making short dashes, then freezing with the legs spread-eagled.
Spiders of this genus make burrows in sand or detritus, or under
stones, but they are often found running on the ground. The egg sac
is white.

Arctosa perita (Latreille)
Size female 8 mm; male 8·5 mm
Overall coloration matches habitat.
Carapace Light brown to black. Lighter patches below posterior eyes at sides, sometimes with large patch behind posterior eyes dorsally. **Abdomen** Greyish cardiac mark, flanked by two large pink areas, followed by two small white spots. Median area of alternating dark and light transverse stripes flanked by two large light spots, followed by smaller ones. **Legs** Very clearly annulated except tarsi.
Habitat Sandy places inland and coastal where spider makes burrow, although both sexes frequently found running about. **Season** Autumn, spring, and early summer. **Distribution** Common and widespread throughout.

Arctosa leopardus (Sundevall)
Size female 9 mm; male 7 mm
Carapace Dark brown, covered to varying extent with gold hairs. Often with shiny appearance. Sometimes with lateral bands of white hairs. **Abdomen** Dark brown, usually with clear cardiac mark. Remaining dorsal area speckled with small patches of white and gold hairs. **Legs** Dark brown. Except for tarsi, segments have black annulations.
Habitat Marshy places, among moss and detritus. **Season** Late spring and summer. **Distribution** Infrequent and scattered in Britain. Widespread in Europe.

Arctosa cinerea (Fabricius)
Size female up to 17 mm; male 14 mm
Whole spider covered in white pubescence.
Carapace Grey-brown. Lighter patches below posterior eyes. **Abdomen** Brown, spotted with black or grey. Two rows of white spots in posterior half. **Legs** Brown with darker annulations.
Habitat Burrows beneath stones on sandy banks of rivers and lakes. **Season** Autumn, spring, early summer. **Distribution** Absent from southern half of England, and from Holland. Widespread elsewhere.

Genus *Pirata*

Pirata species are characterized by the Y-shaped median mark on the carapace. All are found in damp places where they make a tubular web in moss, etc. The lighter species have patches of bluish-white hairs on the carapace and abdomen. *P. piccolo*, at 3 mm, is the smallest lycosid in the region.

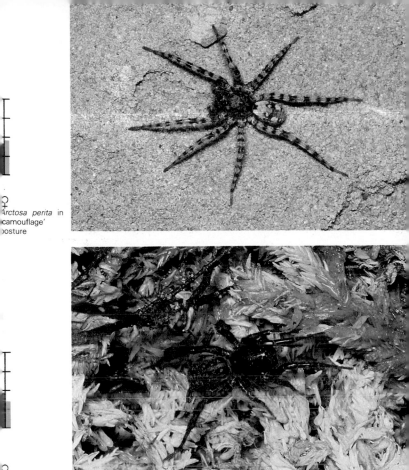

♀
Arctosa perita in 'camouflage' posture

Arctosa leopardus

♀
Arctosa cinerea

Pirata piraticus (Clerck)

Size female 4·5–9 mm; male 6 mm

Female Carapace Dark yellow-brown, sometimes with faintly greenish appearance. Median band with normally distinct, Y-shaped centre. Laterally with white hairs. **Abdomen** Reddish brown with yellow cardiac mark outlined in white hairs which converge at rear of abdomen. In posterior part, lines are flanked by white spots. Sides of abdomen are thickly covered in white hairs. **Legs** Yellow-brown to greenish. **Male** Similar to female, but with white v on abdomen reduced or absent. Both sexes with black spots on sternum.

Habitat Marshes. **Season** Spring to early summer. **Distribution** Common and widespread throughout.

Pirata tenuitarsus Simon

Size female 6 mm; male 5 mm

Closely resembles *P. piraticus*.

Carapace Lateral bands are wider, although often obscured by white hairs. **Abdomen** No white v. Cardiac mark less distinct, but lighter patches which follow it are clearer. White spots usually very clear.

Habitat and Season As *P. piraticus*. **Distribution** In southern Britain, possibly more abundant on heathland than *P. piraticus* although, because of confusion with *P. piraticus*, it was not recorded until 1980. Very widespread and common throughout Europe.

Pirata piccolo Dahl

Size male and female 3 mm

Smallest European lycosid. In its markings has family resemblance to *P. tennuitarsus*. Sternum has lighter median area with light spots near coxae. Size of adults should identify species.

Habitat Damp, open places. **Season** Spring to midsummer. **Distribution** Germany, Sweden.

Pirata hygrophilus Thorell

Size female 6·5 mm; male 5·5 mm

Dark species with markings similar to *P. tenuitarsus* but more obscure.

Abdomen White spots usually clear. **Sternum** Dark brown with light-yellow median band, about three-quarters sternum length. **Legs** Faint annulations on femora.

Habitat Often in shaded parts of damp woods. **Season** Spring to summer. **Distribution** Very common and widespread throughout.

Pirata uliginosus Thorell

Similar to *P. hygrophilus* but male and female 1·5 mm smaller.

Habitat and Season Drier places than *P. hygrophilus* at same season. **Distribution** As *P. hygrophilus*.

♀
Pirata piraticus

♀
Pirata tenuitarsus

♀
Pirata hygrophilus

Pirata knorri (Scopoli)

Size female 8 mm; male 6 mm
Large, dark species. Resembles *P. hygrophilus*.
Sternum Has short light median band, less than half sternum length
Habitat At sides of fast-flowing streams with gravelly banks, especially where there is some shade. **Season** Spring to midsummer
Distribution France, Germany, Holland, Belgium.

Pirata latitans (Blackwall)

Size female 5 mm; male 4 mm
Female Carapace Dark brown with scarcely any markings. Sides clothed in fine white hairs. **Abdomen** Dark brown without any discernible dorsal markings apart from two rows of white spots. Sides clothed with white hairs. **Legs** Rather dark brown. **Male Carapace and Abdomen** Similar to female but black. **Legs** Femora to tibiae of first pair black or dark brown, other segments lighter. Legs II also dark; III, IV lighter with faint annulations from femora to tibiae.
Habitat Damp places. **Season** Spring to summer. **Distribution** Uncommon in Britain. Recorded from France, Germany, Holland, Belgium.

Genus *Aulonia*

There is one uncommon species which is a small, dark spider with pale legs. The palpal tibiae are white. The spider makes a tube and small sheet web, upon which it catches its prey.

Aulonia albimana (Walckenaer)

Size female 4·5 mm; male 4 mm
Female Carapace Black with fine lateral bands composed of white hairs. Sometimes with white pubescence spreading from lateral bands. Short median band of golden hairs posteriorly. Head is thrust forward, making eyes of median row prominent. **Abdomen** Black with covering of golden hairs, which sometimes form blotches. Sometimes with short line of white hairs over cardiac area. Two lines of small white dots occur at rear in some specimens. **Legs** Brown, with femora I black. **Palp** Patellae conspicuously covered in white hairs (hence specific name). All other segments black. **Male** Identical to female, except that legs are lighter making black femora I more readily seen.
Habitat Various; grassy or stony places which are warm and sunny. **Season** Late spring to early or midsummer. **Distribution** In Britain recorded from gravel pit in Somerset where habitat has now been destroyed. Widespread in Europe, but uncommon in north.

♀
Pirata latitans

♂
Pirata latitans

♀
Aulonia albimana
with egg sac

Family Pisauridae

Three species in two genera represent this family in the region. They are large spiders with long legs; the two pairs of forelegs are held close together. The eye pattern is very similar to the Lycosidae, but the shape of the adults, and their abdominal and carapace markings make the two genera easily identified. The female makes large spherical egg sacs which she holds in the chelicerae and below her sternum. When the young are about to emerge, in midsummer, the female hangs the sac on low vegetation and weaves a 'nursery' tent of fine silk strands around it. The mother stays on guard on the outside of the tent, but is easily frightened away, only to return later. The young emerge from the sac and form a nursery cluster in the same manner as the araneids, but within the safety of the tent. After a second moult they disperse.

Genus *Pisaura*

Pisaura mirabilis, a hunter of the ground layer and the only member of the genus in northern Europe, is also the only spider where the male presents the female with a courtship 'gift'; the male catches a fly or other suitable prey item and wraps it thickly in silk. He carries this in his chelicerae until he finds a female and then presents it to her. If the male does not encounter a mate within about twenty-four hours, then he will eat the prey himself. Mating lasts an hour or more while the female feeds on the fly. In June and July the large pale sac may be seen below the wandering female.

Pisaura mirabilis (Clerck)
Size female 12–15 mm; male 10–12 mm
Overall coloration varies from grey to brown.
Carapace Broad darker median band bisected by thin white or yellow line, usually ending in tuft of hairs between posterior median eyes. Conspicuous 'tear marks' at sides of lateral eyes. **Abdomen** Pale at sides with highly variable folium dorsally. Has irregular outline and tapers to spinners. Within folium there may be paler band or chevrons; usually clearer in male. **Legs** Coloured as lighter parts of carapace.
Habitat Woods, heaths, etc. **Season** Early summer. **Distribution** Very common and widespread in Europe.

Genus *Dolomedes*

The two species of this genus are very similar and are only found in or near damp places. Both are large and robust spiders with a strong

♀
Pisaura mirabilis
and egg sac

♀
Pisaura mirabilis

and imposing appearance. The adults will take large prey, including bluebottle flies, damselflies, and even small fishes which the spiders attract to the surface by vibrating the water with their front legs. The males do not share the courting habits of *Pisaura*, and merely wave their front legs alternately at the female in a prolonged display which culminates in a very brief mating in which each palp is used once only. The females will lay more than 1000 eggs in two or more greenish sacs. The spiderlings are pale brown at first, getting darker as they grow. The earlier instars have greenish legs and light-brown abdomens. The immatures are not always found in the same habitat as the adults, but climb up into trees and bushes, where they can sometimes be found in some abundance. The adults are scarcer.

Dolomedes fimbriatus (Clerck)
Size female up to 22 mm; male 10–13 mm
Males more clearly marked than females.
Carapace Dark brown with yellowish submarginal bands. **Abdomen** Dark brown with white or yellow sides. Sometimes with faint, lighter cardiac mark and white spots. **Legs** Brown (femora greenish in immatures) with dense pubescence on patellae, tibiae, metatarsi, and tarsi.
Habitat Swamps etc with permanent water. **Season** Early summer.
Distribution Fairly common locally in southern England; scattered and very local up to northern Scotland. Widespread in Europe.

Dolomedes plantarius (Clerck)
Rather variably marked, but very similar to *D. fimbriatus*.
Distribution Much rarer in Britain, recorded only from Suffolk and Norfolk; on Endangered Species List in Britain. Widespread in Europe but less frequent than *D. fimbriatus*.

Families Agelenidae, Hahniidae

The spiders of these two families make sheet webs usually with tubular retreats at one side. All the species run down their prey on the upper side of the web.

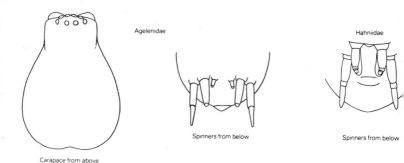

Agelenidae

Hahniidae

Spinners from below

Spinners from below

Carapace from above

There is some dispute over the membership of the Agelenidae; *Argyroneta* (the water spider) is sometimes placed in its own family. Some of the agelenids have the posterior spinners very long and clearly with two segments, but in *Coelotes, Cicurina*, and *Tetrilus*, the spinners are all short. The spiders of the Hahniidae were included in the Agelenidae, although they differ from that family by having the spinners set in a longitudinal row.

♂
Dolomedes
fimbriatus

The family characteristics are based on the genus *Tegenaria*, to which the common European house spider belongs.
Carapace The thorax is rather flat and slightly elongated; the head is raised and narrow, projecting in front. **Eyes** These are arranged in two short rows; they are pearly and subequal in size. **Abdomen** It is oval. When a pattern is present, this consists of pairs of dots or bars. **Legs** The legs are subequal in length, long, and fairly thickly covered in long hairs. Spines are few and rather thin. **Spinners** The posterior spinners are very long and slim, with two distinct segments

Genus *Argyroneta*

The single species of this genus is widespread in the palaearctic region, and is the only spider known to live permanently below water. The spider can swim with ease and constructs an inverted retreat which it fills with air. This is accomplished by trapping air on the abdomen. The air is collected at the surface with a flick from one of the rear legs. At the retreat, the air is brushed off and several journeys are required to fill the 'bell'. Prey is taken to the retreat for consumption, although rarely it may be taken to the surface. Moulting also takes place at the water's surface or, at least, in the vegetation above it. This would seem to be necessary for the new cuticle to harden although moulting has also been observed within the bell.

Courtship by the larger male is rudimentary but, as in other genera of this family, the couple spend a considerable time together. The eggs are laid in late spring and summer; they are surrounded by a thick white silk which is placed in the top of the cell. In the late autumn the spider thickens the silk of its retreat (possibly to stop the air escaping) and seals itself up in the bell for the winter.

Argyroneta aquatica (Clerck)
Size female 8–15 mm; male 9–12 mm
Males often larger than females.
Carapace Pale to dark yellow-brown, with darker striations covered by rows of very short dark hairs. **Abdomen** With grey pubescence. Under water this is covered dorsally and ventrally by air bubble, giving silvery appearance. **Legs** Coloured as carapace. I and II with few spines and short hairs; III and IV with many long spines and long hairs (latter absent from rear sides of these legs).
Habitat Bell attached to underwater plants in ponds and streams where there is little water movement. **Season** Adults at all times of year. **Distribution** Local but often numerous. Widespread throughout.

Genus *Agelena*

The two European species are attractively marked spiders which make their large sheet webs in bushes. *A. labyrinthica* makes an extensive web, in area and height, but the conspicuous tubular retreat is never far from the ground. The spiders are difficult to see because they dash into their retreats on sensing footsteps. The aerial strands of the web arrest the motion of flying and jumping insects which then fall on to the extensive sheet. Large prey is bitten a number of times on the extremities, the spider making fast attacks from all sides. It is taken to the mouth of the tube to be eaten.

Courtship consists of the male tapping on the sheet with his palps, and roughly dragging the passive female to a suitable site to copulate. The pair spend some weeks together.

Agelena labyrinthica (Clerck)
Size female up to 12 mm; male 9 mm
Carapace Dark reddish brown with broad median and lateral bands of light grey-brown pubescence. **Abdomen** Black dorsal area encloses thin pale median stripe, flanked by spots anteriorly and sinuous bars towards spinners. Sides pale. **Legs** Pubescent and coloured as carapace, with some darker mottlings.
Habitat Low vegetation and bushes. Web is of large volume with tubular retreat open at both ends. Egg sac built at greater height and consists of inner sac suspended by thin supports in larger bag. Both are white. Female remains on guard in 'labyrinth' and dies there. **Season** Midsummer. Male and female can be found together. **Distribution** Absent from Scotland. Common and widespread elsewhere.

♀
*Argyroneta
aquatica*

♀
*Agelena
labyrinthica*

Agelena gracilens C. L. Koch

Size female 7–10 mm; male 5–8 mm.
Similar to *A. labyrinthica*.

Carapace Darker areas larger than *A. labyrinthica*. **Abdomen** Fore spots more elongated; rear bars reduced to spots. Ventrally much darker. **Sternum** Darker. **Legs** Pale with grey annulations.

Habitat Bushes etc but web is higher. **Season** Late summer to autumn. **Distribution** Absent from Britain. Widespread in Europe but less common than *A. labyrinthica*.

Genus *Textrix*

Textrix is a small, but prettily marked spider that lives in dry habitats. The head is conspicuously narrowed and the eyes are not unlike those of the Lycosidae, the posterior medians being largest. Because of the agility and speed of the spider, and its habitat, it is difficult to catch. The web is often rather small. A second species, *T. caudata*, occurs in Belgium.

Textrix denticulata (Olivier)
Size female 6–8 mm; male 6–7 mm
Carapace Dark brown with pale median band. Head very narrow and high. **Abdomen** Dark grey with cream-coloured markings; u-shaped mark followed by pairs of white spots with chevrons between them on reddish median band posteriorly. Sides mottled. **Legs** Brown, annulated with black and with rings of light hairs.
Habitat Among stones, dry-stone walls, or on low bushes. **Season** Early summer. Females throughout year. **Distribution** Widespread and generally common throughout Britain, especially in the north and on hills. Throughout Europe.

Genus *Tegenaria*

Eleven species are found in the region. The sternum pattern is very characteristic for the genus, and is often helpful in determining the species. The domestic species are relatively easy to identify although there has been considerable confusion in the names, especially *T. gigantea*, which has been known as *T. atrica* and *T. saeva*.

The webs are typical of the family but are often rather small and with the tubes absent in some species. Males and females live together for some weeks until the male dies, when his remains will be eaten by the female. The egg sac is spherical and covered with a thin layer of soil or wood chips (according to the spider's habitat) or, if these materials are not available, then with the remains of prey, and so on. This layer is often covered with an additional layer of silk. The sac is placed in the web structure.

The females of the larger species are known to be able to live for a number of years as adults. They are capable of surviving for many months without food or water, often in very dry habitats, such as houses.

Tegenaria gigantea Chamberlin and Ivie.
Size female up to 18 mm; male c. 14 mm
Carapace Brown with two rows of darker radiating marks and dark margin. **Abdomen** Yellow-brown to reddish brown with black areas. Lighter areas clearest on small or immature spiders and males; pat- *

♀
*Textrix
denticulata*

♂
*Tegenaria
gigantea*

tern composed of two rows of dots connected by chevrons in rear half. In larger specimens posterior pattern is more like light circles broken in mid-line. **Sternum** With broad median band, tapering posteriorly, flanked by three light spots. **Legs** Brown, femora slightly darker, twice body length in females, three times body length in males.

Habitat Houses and gardens but also under logs and holes in banks etc, at least in southern England. Web often quite small. **Season** Autumn. Females long lived and can be found throughout year. **Distribution** Owing to confusion between this species and *T. saeva* (west of England and Wales) unclear. Probably found throughout Britain and Europe. Certainly common in southern England.

Tegenaria parietina (Fourcroy)

Size female 11–20 mm; male 11–17 mm
Carapace Similar to *T. gigantea* but with smaller inner bands and three patches on margin. **Abdomen** Yellow to brown median band flanked by spots; those at mid-line largest. **Legs** Nearly three times body length in females and five times in males. Brown with faint, darker marks, amounting to annulations on tibiae IV. **Sternum** Sometimes uniform, otherwise with thin median stripe and spots.
Habitat Houses. **Season** Late summer and autumn. Also recorded in spring. **Distribution** Absent from Wales or Scotland. Less common than *T. gigantea* but widespread elsewhere in England and Europe.

Tegenaria ferruginea (Panzer)

Size female 11–14 mm; male 9–11 mm
Resembles *T. parietina* but has more reddish appearance.
Legs Clearly marked. **Sternum** Clearer pattern.
Season Males adult in May.

Tegenaria domestica (Clerck)

Size female 10 mm; male 6–9 mm
Carapace Yellow-brown, sometimes with faint markings, otherwise unmarked. **Abdomen** With faint markings like *T. gigantea* or uniformly pale brown to grey. Appears more hairy than other species. **Legs** Coloured as carapace, sometimes annulated on femora. Male has darker femora. **Sternum** Pattern very faint. Like *T. gigantea.* Median light band is constricted about middle. Dots vary in size.
Habitat Houses. **Season** Males in early summer, probably adult at all times of year. Females known to be capable of surviving four years.
Distribution Cosmopolitan. Occurs in houses in all climates.

Tegenaria agrestis (Walckenaer)

Size female 11–15 mm; male 8–10 mm
Carapace Greyish brown with two darker-brown broad bands, edged posteriorly with little black. These extend length of carapace. **Abdomen** Often with dark-grey colour. Pattern resembles median row of triangles on mottled background. **Legs** Brown. **Sternum** With broad median band, strongly constricted posteriorly. Three pairs of dots very faint.
Habitat Waste ground and other places in low vegetation. Usually away from houses. **Season** Autumn. **Distribution** Fairly common locally in England and Scotland. Widespread in Europe.

♂
*Tegenaria
parietina*

♂
*Tegenaria
domestica*

♀
*Tegenaria
agrestis*

Tegenaria silvestris L. Koch
Size female 7 mm; male 6 mm
Carapace Light greyish brown with distinct darker markings. **Abdomen** Dark grey with light yellow-brown dots. Cardiac mark sometimes brown. **Legs** Clearly annulated. **Sternum** With thin median line, sometimes only in anterior half with posterior dot. Three lateral dots small but clear.
Habitat Under stones and logs etc, often in woods. **Season** All year. **Distribution** Fairly common in England and Wales. Widespread in Europe.

Tegenaria campestris C. L. Koch
Size female 7 mm; male 5 mm
Resembles *T. silvestris*.
Carapace Dark marks consist of three pairs of spots, separated from one another. **Sternum** With broad median band, tapering posteriorly. Lateral spots large and joined. **Distribution** Holland, Belgium.

Tegenaria picta Simon
Size female 7–9 mm; male 6–8 mm
Carapace Rather dark brown without any markings. **Abdomen** Dark greyish brown, sometimes with pattern like *T. agrestis*. **Legs** Coloured as carapace, without markings. **Sternum** With very faint parallel median band, or unmarked.
Habitat Recent addition to British fauna has been found under lumps of chalk. European specimens found under stones and among low vegetation. **Season** Late spring. In Europe adults also found in autumn. **Distribution** Sussex. Very widespread but uncommon in Europe.

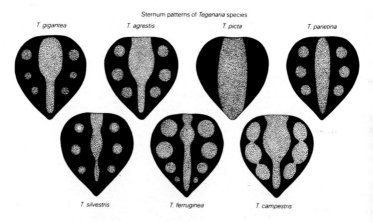

Sternum patterns of *Tegenaria* species

T. gigantea   T. agrestis   T. picta   T. parietina

T. silvestris   T. ferruginea   T. campestris

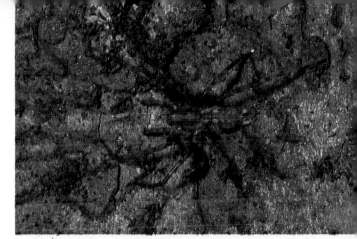

♀
*Tegenaria
silvestris*

♀
Tegenaria picta
with egg sac

Histopona torpida (C. L. Koch)

Size female 6 mm; male 5 mm
Sometimes referred to genus *Tegenaria*. Pale reddish-brown spider.
Carapace Head lighter than thorax. **Abdomen** Light with median band bordered by broad dark spots which coalesce and become curved lines posteriorly. Sides have dark lines. Ventrally with U-shaped mark in front of spinners, otherwise light and unmarked. **Legs** Femora to mid-tibiae light (mottled in female), the remaining segments darker. **Sternum** With oval, light median band.
Habitat Similar to *T. silvestris*. **Season** All year. **Distribution** Absent from Britain. Frequent in Germany. Also Holland, Belgium, France.

Genus *Coelotes*

The carapace is much broader anteriorly with robust chelicerae which are clearly visible from above. The legs are of moderate length and stout. The spinners are relatively short. The spider makes an extensive tube under stones or in banks and it is often divided into two at the nether end. At the opening, a collar of silk surrounds the tube. The eggs are laid in early summer and the pale youngsters share the tube and prey with the mother, remaining in the tube with her until they become quite large; initially they are fed by regurgitation. In the autumn the female dies and is eaten by her offspring, before they disperse to make their own individual webs. Occasionally it is possible to see the remains of the female with the fat spiderlings still occupying the tube.

C. inermis L. Koch, is absent from Britain but widespread in Europe. The abdomen lacks the dark median mark but has three or four light broken chevrons.

Coelotes atropos (Walckenaer)

Size female 9–12 mm; male 7–9 mm
Carapace Dark brown, shiny. **Abdomen** With black wedge-shaped median band, tapering to spinners. Sides lighter, greyish brown with variable amounts of dark spots. In posterior half are several lighter chevrons broken by median band. **Legs** Dark brown but lighter than carapace.
Habitat Under stones, logs, etc. **Season** Spring and early summer.
Distribution Very common on high ground in northern England, Devon, and Wales; less common elsewhere in Britain. Records in Europe confuse it with *C. terrestris* but probably widespread.

Coelotes terrestris (Wider)

Very similar and some specimens may be impossible to assign to definite species in field. Chief difference lies in abdomen: anterior part is darker, especially at sides. Broken chevrons sometimes clearer, but there is no obvious dark wedge.
Habitat and Season As *C. atropos*. **Distribution** Widespread in England and Wales and more common in south. Probably widespread in Europe.

Genus *Cicurina*

The single, uncommon species of this genus bears a close resemblance to the clubionids except that the carapace is glossy and not covered with fine hairs. The web is very small with a very vague retreat. The spider rests on the underside of the web but hunts in the normal fashion. Males are less frequently found than females.

♀
Coelotes atropos
with egg sac

♀
Cicurina cicur

Cicurina cicur (Fabricius)

Size female 7 mm; male 6 mm

Carapace Yellow-brown. Shiny. **Abdomen** Pinkish brown with greyish pubescence, dorsally and ventrally. **Legs** Femora coloured as carapace; remaining segments slightly darker. **Spinners** Short and stubby.

Habitat Dark, damp places, cellars, under stones, etc. **Season** Females at most seasons, males probably as well. **Distribution** South and east England; and from Yorkshire to Scottish border. Rare. Widespread in Europe.

Genus *Cryphoeca*

Only one species represents the genus in northern Europe. The adults are very small but with fairly typical markings and form. The web is small but typical.

Cryphoeca silvicola (C. L. Koch)
Size female 3 mm; male 2·5 mm
Carapace Head dark; thorax lighter, especially towards margins. **Abdomen** Black or grey with lighter broken chevrons reinforced by pale bristles. Darker areas covered in greyish hairs. **Legs** Pale, annulated in black.
Habitat Woods; in leaf litter or on lichen- and moss-covered bark. **Season** Autumn. **Distribution** Widespread in Britain but absent or very local in south-east. Widespread in Europe.

Genus *Tetrilus*

There are two rare species in the region. They are distinguished from each other by the size of the eyes. The males have extraordinary and unique palps. These spiders are often found with ants.

Tetrilus macrophthalmus (Kulczynski)
Size female 3·5 mm; male 3 mm
Carapace Pale brown. Shiny. **Abdomen** Pale pinkish brown with very faint grey chevrons. Sides pale grey with gap midway. **Legs** Coloured as carapace. **Male palps** Notable for extraordinary length of lamellae which sweep backwards over carapace. Unlike any other European spider.
Habitat Under dead bark and stones, in association with ants. **Season** Probably all year. **Distribution** Very rare in one Welsh and five English counties. Other records from France and Hungary only.

Tetrilus arietinus (Thorell)
Slightly smaller and differs from *T. macrophthalmus* mainly in smaller eyes, particularly lateral triads. **Distribution** Known from only three English counties. Widespread in Europe and Scandinavia.

Family Hahniidae

Genera *Antistea* and *Hahnia*

The spiders of this family are small with the spinners arranged in a transverse row. The outermost pair are long and two-segmented as in the Agelenidae. The spiders make small sheet webs and hunt on the upper side of the sheet.

♀
Cryphoeca
silvicola

♂
Tetrilus
macrophthalmus

Antistea elegans (Blackwall)
Size female 3 mm; male 2·5 mm
Carapace Reddish brown, very glossy. Fovea and sometimes midline black. **Abdomen** Dark grey with brownish chevrons in posterior half. **Legs** Reddish brown with apical ends of femora to mid-tibiae darkened. Metatarsi and tarsi also darker. **Spinners** In transverse row.
Habitat Among vegetation in wet places. **Season** Mid-summer. **Distribution** Widespread in Britain but local. Widespread in Europe.

Hahnia montana (Blackwall)
Size female c. 2 mm; male 1·5 mm
Carapace Light grey with darker markings. Shiny. **Abdomen** Black or dark brown. **Legs** Light to dark brown. **Spinners** Coloured as legs; in transverse row.
Habitat Leaf litter, fallen pine needles, etc. in woods. **Season** All year. **Distribution** Common and widespread throughout.

Hahnia nava (Blackwall)
Same size and colour as *H. montana*.
Habitat Moss and grass in exposed sites, not in woods. **Season** Adult in summer and autumn. **Distribution** Widespread but local in Britain. Widespread in Europe.

Hahnia helveola Simon
Size female 3 mm; male 2·25 mm
Carapace Pale, sometimes with darker fovea and striae. **Abdomen** Darker dorsally with pale bars posteriorly, sometimes absent. **Legs** Coloured as carapace, sometimes with vague, darker markings.
Habitat Detritus in woods. **Season** Autumn and winter. **Distribution** Locally common throughout Britain. Widespread in Europe.

Hahnia pusilla C. L. Koch
Size female and male c. 1·5 mm
Pale like *H. helveola* but lacking any darker marks.
Habitat Stones and detritus. **Distribution** Rare but widespread throughout.

Hahnia candida Simon
Size female and male 1·4 mm
Resembles *H. helveola* and *H. pusilla* but with darker legs.
Distribution Only recorded from Dorset, England. Widespread but rare in Europe.

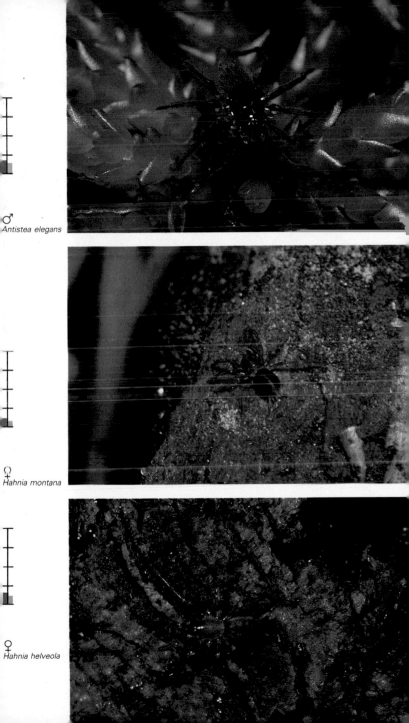

♂
Antistea elegans

♀
Hahnia montana

♀
Hahnia helveola

Family Mimetidae

This is a small family, with the single genus *Ero* represented within the region. Both the larger, southern European *Mimetus* and *Ero* are predatory on other spiders, and are known as pirate spiders.

Genus *Ero*

Ero species are distinguished by the abdomen which is higher than long with dorsal tubercles. The legs are fairly long, especially legs I. They are usually clearly annulated, and the tibiae and metatarsi of I and II are furnished with a row of alternately long and short spines on their inner sides. Metatarsi I and II are slightly curved.

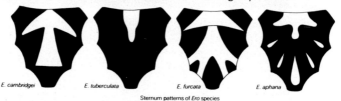

E. cambridgei   E. tuberculata   E. furcata   E. aphana

Sternum patterns of *Ero* species

Ero cambridgei Kulczynski
Size female c. 3 mm; male c. 2·5 mm
Carapace With dark bands. **Abdomen** With two small tubercles dorsally. In front of these is lighter area with dark cardiac mark. Posteriorly with reddish tinge in some specimens. **Sternum** Brown with arrow-shaped median band.
Habitat Fairly common in damp places, near or in webs of other spiders of comparable size. **Season** Late summer and autumn. Females throughout year. **Distribution** Widespread in Britain. France, Holland, Belgium.

Ero furcata (Villers)
Very similar to *E. cambridgei* in size, shape, and markings. Sternum pattern consists of dark radiating bars.
Habitat Various. **Season** As *E. cambridgei*. **Distribution** Fairly common throughout.

Ero tuberculata (Degeer)
Size female c. 4 mm; male 3 mm
Abdomen With two large tubercles at apex and smaller one on each side; four tubercles distributed on edge of posterior flat region. Often with reddish colour but sometimes dark brown anteriorly, whitish posteriorly.
Habitat Bushes and lower foliage of trees, eg pines. **Season** Late

summer and autumn in England. Earlier in Germany. **Distribution** Uncommon and local in southern England. Absent from Scandinavia. Widespread elsewhere.

Ero aphana (Walckenaer)

Size female 3 mm; male c. 2·5 mm

Abdomen With four conspicuous tubercles either of equal size or with posteriors larger. Latter tubercles behind, rather than at the sides of median pair. Same variations in colour as in *E. tuberculata*. **Sternum** With light radiating bars.

Habitat and Season Similar to *E. tuberculata*. **Distribution** In Britain, only recorded from Dorset. Absent from Scandinavia. Widespread elsewhere.

Family Theridiidae

Theridiids are medium to small, glossy spiders with thin legs bearing few spines. They weave tangled, three-dimensional webs.

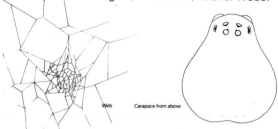

Web   Carapace from above

Carapace Usually glossy but it may be pitted in some genera. It has few hairs or spines. In shape, the carapace may be flattish, bulbous, or high in different genera. **Eyes** These are relatively large and protuberant. The anterior medians are smaller and dark while the remaining eyes are pearly. They are set in two short rows. **Abdomen** In the majority of species, the abdomen is globular but can be pointed or broader posteriorly, or oval. It has a covering of bristles but it is usually glossy to some degree. Stridulating organs, where present, consist of a row of teeth on the abdomen (in close proximity to the pedicel) which are rubbed against ridges on the back of the carapace. Usually the abdomen has a dorsal and ventral pattern. **Legs** Typically, theridiid legs are short and slender, with a short pubescence but very few spines. Tarsi IV have a ventral row of serrated bristles which give rise to the name comb-footed spiders, but this is not a field character.

The webs of theridiid spiders consist of short, interconnected threads at all angles and without any apparent design. As exemplified by the genus *Theridion*, they are designed to catch flying insects, and are furnished with outer threads coated with adhesive. In the webs of *Dipoena* and *Steatoda* species, the tangle is thickened into a sheet at its midst, with lower holding lines which reach the substrate; these lines are coated with a few millimetres of viscid drops at their extremities. When crawling insects, such as ants and beetles, become stuck to these threads, the threads rupture and lift the prey into the air. This effectively prevents the animal from exerting any force on the thread to escape. Characteristically, all the spiders of this family throw viscid silk over the prey before biting it. Although the chelicerae are of moderate size (except in the males of *Enoplognatha*), the poison acts rapidly on the prey. It is worth noting that the infamous black widow spider, *Latrodectus mactans*, is a theridiid.

In general the males bear a close resemblance to the females. The male courts the female by vibrating her web, either with his legs and palps or with the stridulating apparatus.

♀
Achaearanea lunata on web

Genus *Episinus*

There are three similar species with abdomens broadened posteriorly and with legs I and IV long, II and III almost equal and short. The web consists of half-a-dozen strands or less, with 'viscid feet'. The egg sac is white, pear shaped, and has a short stalk.

Episinus angulatus (Blackwall)
Size female and male 4 mm
Carapace Dark brown to black with lighter border, very variable in width. **Abdomen** Mottled brown with lighter sides. Ventrally with large light region. **Legs** Clearly annulated. **Sternum** Uniformly brown. **Habitat** Low vegetation, etc. Specimen shown found under piece of detached bark. Very reduced web, consisting of several strands of silk, sometimes in the form of H. **Season** Early summer. **Distribution** Uncommon but widespread throughout.

♀
Episinus angulatus

Episinus maculipes Cavanna
Slightly larger than *E. angulatus.*
Sternum Has light, tapered median band.
Habitat Foliage of trees. **Season** As *E. angulatus.* **Distribution** Essex, Isle of Wight. Other records from Mediterranean.

Episinus truncatus Latreille
Similar to *E. angulatus*
Carapace Uniformly dark. **Abdomen** Ventrally uniformly dark with lighter median line or dots. **Legs** I, II, IV dark from apical end of femora to basal part of metatarsi which is also darkened apically.

Genus *Dipoena*

Eight uncommon species occur in the region. *D. melanogaster* is unique in having a light abdomen with a faint pattern; the other species are black but distinguished from linyphiids by the carapace which is high anteriorly in both sexes. The legs have markings unique to this genus. Most of the species appear to eat ants.

Dipoena inornata (O.P.-Cambridge)
Size female c. 2 mm; male 1·5 mm
Carapace Dark brown. **Abdomen** Globular; black with many fine recumbent hairs. **Legs** Reddish brown with tarsi I and II black. Tibiae IV darkened in apical half.
Habitat Under stones, pieces of wood, low vegetation, etc. **Season** Summer. **Distribution** Uncommon but most widespread *Dipoena* in Britain. France, Germany, Norway, Holland.

Dipoena tristis (Hahn)
Size female 3–4 mm; male c. 2·5 mm
Carapace Almost black. **Abdomen** Black and glossy, with short hairs. **Legs** I, II, III uniformly black; IV black with basal two-thirds of femora reddish, less clearly reddish on basal halves of tibiae and metatarsi.
Habitat Bushes or lower foliage of trees. **Season** Early summer. **Distribution** Very local in southern England. Absent from Scandinavia. Most frequent *Dipoena* in Germany. Throughout Europe.

Dipoena melanogaster (C. L. Koch)
Size female 3 mm; male 2·5 mm
Differs from other *Dipoena* species in the following:
Abdomen Pale, mottled, and indented anteriorly.
Habitat Bushes. **Season** Summer. **Distribution** Absent from Scandinavia. Rare elsewhere.

♀
Dipoena inornata

♀
Dipoena tristis

♀
Dipoena melanogaster

Genus *Euryopis*

The abdomen is pointed posteriorly and rather metallic in the light areas. Little is known of their biology but it is thought that none of the species makes a web, but are hunters of ants or other small arthropods.

Euryopis flavomaculata (C. L. Koch)
Size female 4 mm; male c. 3 mm
Carapace Brown, head darker. **Abdomen** Dark brown with yellow-brown spots. Covered with long bristles. **Legs** Brown, getting progressively darker at extremities.
Habitat Moss etc. Does not make web. **Season** Early to midsummer.
Distribution Widespread but rare in Britain. Widespread in Europe.

Euryopis laeta (Westring)
Size female 2·5 mm; male 2 mm
Carapace Black. **Abdomen** Black across anterior portion with broad irregular median patch extending to spinners. Sides are light with metallic appearance. **Legs** Light-yellow femora, IV has dark ring apically. Tibiae darkened, with remaining segments reddish brown.
Habitat Under heather and stones in dry, sandy places. **Season** Midsummer. **Distribution** Absent from Britain. Germany, France, Sweden.

Genus *Crustulina*

There are two small species with pitted carapaces and abdominal patterns which make them easily identified. Both make small webs almost at ground-level.

Crustulina guttata (Wider)
Size female and male c. 2 mm
Carapace Dark brown to black. With warty texture. **Abdomen** Black with clear white spots in median line and laterally. Rather granular with short hairs. **Legs** Reddish brown with darker annulations on apices of femora and tibiae I and II. Less clearly annulated on other legs and segments.
Habitat Among grass or detritus. **Season** Early summer. **Distribution** Widespread but uncommon in Britain. Widespread in Europe.

♀
Euryopis
flavomaculata

♀
Crustulina guttata

Crustulina sticta (O.P.-Cambridge)
Size female c. 2·5 mm; male c. 2·5 mm
Carapace Dark brown, with fewer warts than *C. guttata*. **Abdomen**
Pale brown with broken white line around anterior margin and down
median line. Two dark-brown patches at junction of these lines. Below
white lines at sides, irregular dark-brown patches. Abdomen almost
totally black in some specimens. **Legs** Pale yellow-brown in females;
reddish brown in males. No annulations.
Habitat Damper situations than *C. guttata*. Fens, swamps, sandhills.
Season Early summer. **Distribution** Very local in southern England.
Apparently no other records for region.

Genus *Steatoda*

These are larger spiders with oval abdomens carrying a light band on
the front margin, with various patterns of spots and bars that identify
the individual species. Older females have a tendency to become
very dark, but the males have the clearest patterns and are usually
more easily identified. Some of the females are known to live a
number of years as adults. The webs sometimes have an irregular
sheet in the middle and 'viscid feet'; there is also a tendency for
small patches of fluffy silk to be attached to various parts of the web.

Steatoda phalerata (Panzer)
Size female c. 5 mm; male 4 mm
Carapace Black with fine punctuations. **Abdomen** Black with yellow
marks. Broken anterior line and short transverse lines at mid-point.
Sometimes with median dot anteriorly and pair of dots or irregular
line above spinners. Females frequently lack abdominal marks. **Legs**
Reddish brown with darker annulations on tibiae. Tibiae I black.
Habitat Low vegetation or detritus in sandy places, and chalk downs.
Season Early summer. **Distribution** Widespread but infrequent
throughout.

Steatoda albomaculata (Degeer)
Size female up to 6 mm; male c. 5 mm
Carapace Dark brown to black. No punctuations. **Abdomen** Black
with broad lighter edge, dentate posteriorly, and with double row of
spots down median line. Lighter areas white or pink. Ventrally with
lighter T-shaped mark. **Legs** Almost black with faint lighter-brown
annulations on III and IV at bases of segments.
Habitat Under stones and low vegetation in sandy places exposed to
sun. Predators of beetles and ants. **Season** Males in spring, autumn.
Females at most seasons. **Distribution** Very local in south-east England. Absent from Scandinavia. Widespread elsewhere.

♀
Crustulina sticta

♂
*Steatoda
phalerata*

♂
*Steatoda
albomaculata*

Steatoda bipunctata (Linnaeus)

Size female up to 7 mm; male 5 mm
Carapace Brown with sparse punctuations. Darker in male. **Abdomen** Light brown to almost black. With thin anterior and median white line. Latter often missing in females. Glossy but with many fine hairs. Ventrally pale brown with two divergent dark lines from spinners. Legs Brown with segments darkened apically, sometimes with additional annulations.
Habitat Common in and around houses. Less frequent on trunks of pines etc. Season Autumn. Females can live for up to four years. Distribution Common throughout.

Steatoda castanea (Olivier)

Size female 7 mm; male 6 mm
Carapace More punctuations than *S. bipunctata*. Abdomen White median line edged in dark brown, or at least much clearer in female. Posteriorly there are number of lateral 'spikes'. Ventrally with white median line edged in dark brown.
Habitat As *S. bipunctata*. Season Early to midsummer. Distribution Germany, Holland, Sweden.

Steatoda grossa (C. L. Koch)

Size female up to 10 mm; male 6 mm
Carapace Brown to dark brown with few punctuations. Abdomen Dark purplish brown (female) or black (male). With broad anterior line and row of broad or triangular patches down centre, with one at each side of front patch. Lighter marks can be absent on large females. Legs Coloured as carapace without annulations.
Habitat Houses. Season Autumn. Females probably long lived. Distribution Isolated in habitat in southern half of Britain. Absent from Scandinavia. Widespread in Europe. This spider occurs in North America and has been reported as preying on black widows.

Steatoda triangulosa (Walckenaer)

Size female 5 mm; male 4 mm
Carapace Dark brown to black. Smooth. Abdomen White, reticulated with grey lines; with two thick, black dentate bands on dorsum. Ventrally with median white patch with thin, darker borders. Legs Pale brown (female) or orange-brown (male) with very faint, darker annulations on mid-region of femora and tibiae, sometimes on other segments as well.
Habitat Houses. Season Autumn. Distribution France, Germany, Belgium.

♀
*Steatoda
bipunctata*

♂
Steatoda grossa

♀
*Steatoda
triangulosa*

Steatoda paykulliana (Walckenaer)

Size female up to 13 mm; male 6 mm
Could be poisonous to humans. Two males were found in Britain in 1980 but males considered harmless.
Carapace Dark brown to black, with slight punctuations. **Abdomen** Black with orange line anteriorly. Sometimes with broken chevrons diminishing in size towards spinners. Male as illustrated. **Legs** Dark brown in female. Yellow-brown in male with each end of all segments black.
Habitat Under stones. **Season** Early summer? **Distribution** France and more rarely Germany.

Anelosimus vittatus (C. L. Koch)

Size female 3·5 mm; male 3 mm
Carapace With dark median stripe and very fine black border. **Abdomen** With broad dark median band, often clearest anteriorly and wider posteriorly. **Legs** Annulations rather faint; tibiae and sometimes femora darkened apically. **Sternum** Brown with yellowish triangle in middle third. **Male Palp** Elongated (cf *A. aulicus*).
Habitat Typically on foliage of trees, especially oak. Also on tall plants. **Season** Spring. Egg sac white, subcircular, and found in summer. **Distribution** Widespread and common in England and Europe.

Anelosimus pulchellus (Walckenaer)

Greatly resembles *A. vittatus.*
Legs Femora light brown with no marks. Patellae with dark, apical ring; tibiae, metatarsi I, II annulated apically and in middle, III, IV with apical marks only.
Distribution Single record from Berkshire. Uncommon but widespread in Europe.

Anelosimus aulicus (C. L. Koch)

Size female 3 mm; male 2·5 mm.
Similar to *A. vittatus.*
Carapace Dark border quite distinct. **Abdomen** Median band more uniform in width and with sharper edges. **Sternum** Yellow triangle much broader, at least half the width. **Legs** All segments have thin, dark apical rings. Annulations also occur at mid-points of femora and tibiae. **Male Palp** Subcircular.
Habitat Trees, bushes, low plants. **Season** Early summer. Subcircular egg sac is light brown with three points. **Distribution** Rare in southern England and Germany. More commonly found in Mediterranean region.

♂
*Steatoda
paykulliana*

♀
*Anelosimus
vittatus* with egg
sac

♀
*Anelosimus
aulicus* with egg
sac

Genus *Achaearanea*

Previously included in the genus *Theridion*, the four species are characterized by the high abdomen, much higher than long and with the spinners placed ventrally, not terminally. They are variable in markings but may be identified by the habitat and form of the retreat.

Achaearanea lunata (Clerck)
Size female 3 mm; male 2·5 mm
Very variable in colour.
Carapace Light brown to black. **Abdomen** Grey to black anteriorly. Posteriorly with two white dots on apex of abdomen, with several lines curving over sides. **Legs** Practically unmarked in lighter specimens, usually with apical end of femora to end of tibiae darkened on I and II. Much clearer marks on III and especially IV, on apical ends of last three segments.
Habitat In web of large volume adhering to tree trunks or bushes 1·5–2 m above ground. Retreat made of fallen leaves etc in upper part of web. Egg sacs brown, papery, and wrinkled. Sometimes in dark places in woods. **Season** Early summer. **Distribution** Uncommon in southern Britain. Widespread in Europe.

Achaearanea riparia (Blackwall)
Size female 3·5 mm; male 3 mm
Carapace Dark brown to black. **Abdomen** Greyish to reddish brown. Markings less clear than *A. lunata* but similar. **Legs** Annulated apically on all segments and in middle of tibiae I, II. Less clear in males.
Habitat Low vegetation, overhanging banks, and base of walls. Web lower than 0·5 m. Retreat c. 4 mm in diameter and c. 30 mm long placed vertically near top of web; covered in sand, twigs, etc. Silk lines with 'viscid feet' touch ground. Feeds mainly on ants and young are fed by mother. **Season** Early summer. **Distribution** Rare, but widespread in Britain; absent from Scotland. Widespread in Europe.

Achaearanea tepidariorum (C. L. Koch)
Size female up to 7 mm; male 4 mm
Carapace Mid- to dark brown. **Abdomen** Greyish brown with darker median band in front half. **Legs** Usually clearly annulated. **Male** Often with more reddish coloration, especially on legs which are not as clearly marked as female.
Habitat Heated greenhouses, sometimes found in open. **Season** Adults found at most seasons indoors. Egg sac brown and pear shaped. **Distribution** Cosmopolitan.

♀
*Achaearanea lun-
ata* with egg sac

♀
*Achaearanea
riparia* with prey

♀
*Achaearanea
tepidariorum*

Achaearanea simulans (Thorell)

Size female 4 mm; male 3 mm
Very similar to *A. tepidariorum* but smaller.
Habitat Bushes and trees, never indoors. **Season** Early to midsummer, females to autumn. **Distribution** In England, Dorset, Hampshire, Berkshire, Surrey. Not recorded from Belgium. Probably widespread elsewhere.

Achaearanea veruculata (Urquhart)

Size female up to 5 mm; male c. 3 mm
Australasian species introduced to Scilly Isles.
Abdomen With large black median band, flanked by pair of white spots anteriorly, and surrounded on sides and rear by large, reddish to purplish-brown area. Ventrally with large white area flanked by black bars.
Habitat Bushes. **Season** Summer. **Distribution** Scilly Isles.

Genus *Theridion*

Seventeen species occur in the region, of which fifteen are described. The majority make typical webs with retreats in the form of inverted cups of silk. Prey remnants may be attached to the retreats, and it is here that the egg sac is located and guarded by the female. Males of some species have epigastric region swollen.

Theridion sisyphium (Clerck)

Size female 4 mm; male 3 mm
Carapace Light brown with darker median stripe and thin border.
Abdomen Two broad black bands, divided by three thin white lines surround reddish-brown median band. Ventrally with black patch in front of spinners. **Epigyne** Circular. **Legs** All segments darkened apically.
Habitat Bushes and low vegetation. Egg sac spherical and green, fussed over constantly by female. Young fed by mother. **Season** Early summer. **Distribution** Common and widespread throughout.

Theridion impressum L. Koch

Size female 4·5 mm; male 3·5 mm
Carapace Border thicker than *T. sisyphium*. **Abdomen** Ventrally with dark subtriangular region between black patch and epigastric fold.
Epigyne Broadly oval.
Habitat Similar to *T. sisyphium*. **Season** Adults in July. **Distribution** Widespread but less common in Britain. Widespread and common in Europe.

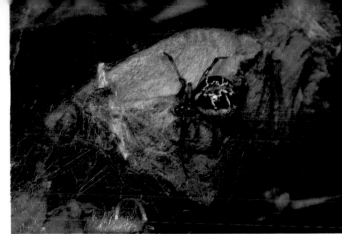

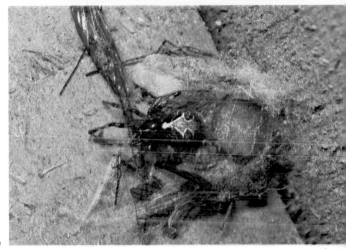

♀
Theridion pictum

Theridion pictum (Walckenaer)

Size female up to 5 mm; male 3·5 mm

Carapace Brown with dark median band and margins. **Abdomen** Median band very dentate, with inner white outline and reddish centre. First two triangles very conspicuous. **Legs** Light brown with dark annulations. Femora with dark spots near middle, ventrally and dorsally.

Habitat Bushes, low plants, etc in damp places. **Season** Early summer. **Distribution** Common locally and widespread in Britain. Widespread in Europe.

Theridion simile C. L. Koch

Size female 2 mm; male 2 mm
Carapace Uniformly brown. **Abdomen** With single conspicuous triangle, white or pale yellow. Posteriorly with thin dentate band to spinners. **Legs** Brown, with variable annulations on apical ends of segments.
Habitat Heather and other low plants; occasionally trees. **Season** Early summer. **Distribution** Abundant on heathland in southern England; as far north as Yorkshire with one record for northern Scotland. Widespread in Europe.

Theridion varians Hahn

Size female up to 3·5 mm; male 2·5 mm
Immensely variable in colour and pattern of abdomen.
Carapace Pale with black median band and margins. **Abdomen** Sometimes with very vague markings. Otherwise with two median triangles and thin dentate band reaching spinners. Inside this region white to reddish. Ventrally with varied marks, but epigyne dark and oval. **Legs** Pale, annulated with black.
Habitat Trees, bushes, fences, etc. **Season** Early summer. Females until autumn. **Distribution** Common and widespread throughout.

Theridion melanurum Hahn

Size female up to 4 mm; male c. 3 mm
Carapace Dark brown. **Abdomen** Brown to grey. Dentate band of uniform width throughout its length. Ventrally with large pale triangular patch. **Legs** Light brown with many small annulations.
Habitat Buildings. **Season** Early summer. **Distribution** Common in southern Britain and Europe.

♀
Theridion simile

♀
Theridion varians

♀
*Theridion
melanurum*

Theridion mystaceum L. Koch
Size female and male up to 2·5 mm
Very similar to *T. melanurum* in pattern and colour.
Habitat More typically on tree trunks and bushes, but sometimes on buildings.

Theridion pinastri L. Koch
Size female 4 mm; male 3 mm
Similar pattern to *T. melanurum*.
Abdomen Median band brownish red.
Distribution In England male found once in Surrey. Recorded from Holland, Belgium. More common to south.

Theridion familiare O.P.-Cambridge
Size female 2 mm; male 1·5 mm.
Abdomen Has median band like *T. melanurum* but with a more reddish colour overall.
Habitat Houses. **Distribution** Widespread but rare in southern England and Europe.

Theridion blackwalli O.P.-Cambridge
Size female c. 3 mm; male c. 2 mm
Some specimens black with faint annulations on pale legs making them difficult to distinguish from linyphiids in field.
Carapace Brown with head black. **Abdomen** With large black patch anteriorly, followed by widely spaced pairs of black spots. Lighter areas reticulated and sometimes with reddish spots. **Legs** Pale with faint annulations. Ventrally with spots on femora, tibiae, and metatarsi.
Habitat Among low plants, on tree trunks, and in houses. **Season** Early summer. **Distribution** Rare and scattered in England. Rare but widespread in Europe.

Theridion tinctum (Walckenaer)
Size female c. 3 mm; male c. 2·5 mm
Carapace Pale, with triangular black mark on head. Black spots along margin. **Abdomen** With two black patches anteriorly followed by grey or reddish-brown mottlings, sometimes amounting to median band. **Legs** Pale, sometimes with many black rings of varying width, or with ventral blotches. **Palps** Also with dark ring. **Sternum** Pale with dark borders and black median mark, sometimes divided.
Habitat Bushes and trees. Frequently seen in webs of other spiders (theridiids and small araneids) which it preys upon. **Season** Early summer principally, but extended to autumn. **Distribution** Common in southern half of Britain. Widespread in Europe.

♀
*Theridion
mystaceum*

♂ and ♀
*Theridion
blackwalli*

♀
Theridion tinctum

Theridion instabile O.P.-Cambridge
Size female 2·5 mm; male 2 mm
Carapace Pale yellow with darker median band. Abdomen Variable:
light median region bordered by reddish-brown dots, yellow at sides;
or with dots joined to give large grey patch of variable extent. Legs
Uniformly pale yellow-brown. Male has elongated chelicerae.
Habitat Low vegetation in wet places. Female drags pinkish-brown
egg sac with her. Season Early summer to autumn. Females through
winter. Distribution Very local but widespread in England. Uncommon in France, Belgium, Germany?

Theridion bellicosum Simon
Size female 2 mm; male less than 2 mm
Very similar to *T. instabile*.
Habitat Among stones on high ground. Distribution Rare in Wales,
northern England, Scotland. France, Germany, Holland, Belgium.

Theridion bimaculatum (Linnaeus)
Size female c. 3 mm; male 2·5 mm
Female Carapace Brown with head darker, or black. Abdomen
Brown to black with broad yellow to white median band; in darker
specimens sometimes reddish. Legs Uniform pale brown. Epigyne
Triangular and points upwards and forwards. Male Abdomen Pattern
reduced or absent. Palps Dark and held away from head when running. Legs Bases of femora IV have tooth. Sternum With median
keel.
Habitat Low vegetation on sandhills, meadows, etc. Sometimes on
trees. Season Early to mid-summer. Females persist until autumn.
Distribution Common and widespread throughout.

Theridion pallens Blackwall
Size female under 2 mm; male smaller
Very variable in markings.
Carapace Pale with head pale grey to black. Abdomen Pale with
white or yellow transverse line, sometimes with four dark patches
forming cross. Often dorsally black in male. Legs Very pale, unmarked
or with broad annulations on tibiae and metatarsi.
Habitat Typically foliage of trees, but also among low plants. Egg sac
very distinctive – white and with sharp projections pointing in one
direction. Fastened to underside of leaf which shelters web. Season
Early summer but females can be found throughout winter. Distribution Common and widespread throughout.

♀
Theridion instabile
with egg sac

♀
Theridion
bimaculatum

♂ and ♀
Theridion pallens
courting

Genus *Robertus*

The spiders of this genus are superficially like those of the Linyphi
idae, at least in coloration. The carapace is broader and the legs are
stouter and less spiny; the fine structure of the spiders, especially o
the male genitalia, gives them a clear relationship to the Theridiidae
Of the five species in the region, only *R. lividus* is common.

Robertus lividus (Blackwall)
Size female up to 4 mm; male 3 mm
Carapace Dark brown, glossy. **Abdomen** Greyish to dark brown with
network of paler lines. **Legs** Reddish brown, darkest towards
extremities.
Habitat Detritus, moss, etc. **Season** Adults at all seasons. **Distri
bution** More common in north of Britain, but recorded from nearly
every county. Widespread in Europe.

Genus *Pholcomma*

There is one species in the region. It is a very small, but character
istically shaped theridiid, found in the ground-layer.

Pholcomma gibbum (Westring)
Size female and male c. 1·5 mm
Carapace Reddish brown; wide and high. **Abdomen** Globular; grey
ish brown in female; reddish brown in male and with dorsal and
ventral scuta. **Legs** Yellow-brown to reddish brown.
Habitat Detritus, moss, etc in wide variety of habitats. **Season** Au
tumn to spring. **Distribution** Common and widespread throughout.

Genus *Theonoë*

Theonoë minutissima is similar in size and shape to *Pholcomma*, but
the male lacks a scutum; it is much rarer in the same habitat. The
eyes of the lateral triads are considerably smaller in this species but
because of the small size of the spider, difficult to see in the field.

Theonoë minutissima (O.P.-Cambridge)
Size female and male 1·25 mm
Similar to *Pholcomma* but more greyish brown.
Eyes Laterals smaller than those of *Pholcomma*.
Distribution Rare but widespread throughout.

2
obertus lividus

♀
Pholcomma
gibbum

♂
Pholcomma
gibbum

Genus *Enoplognatha*

The most common member of this genus, *E. ovata*, was formerly known as *Theridion ovatum*. The next most common is *E. thoracica* a small dark spider not unlike a linyphiid, except for the stouter legs. The males have large, divergent chelicerae with long teeth.

Enoplognatha ovata (Clerck)
Size female c. 5 mm; male 4 mm
Carapace Pale with vague, grey median band and fine grey line around margin. **Abdomen** With three distinct patterns, in order of frequency: yellowish white, with two rows of widely spaced dots; with two broad red bands, sometimes with black dots; single broad red band over dorsum, sometimes with black dots or with pale centre band. Ventrally with dark stripe flanked by white bars. Around spinners are two pairs of black and white spots. **Legs** Pale, usually with tibiae I darkened apically.
Habitat Bushes and plants. Egg sac greyish turquoise. **Season** Summer. **Distribution** Very common and widespread throughout.

Enoplognatha thoracica (Hahn)
Size female up to 5 mm; male 3 mm
Carapace Brown to dark brown. **Abdomen** Black. European specimens sometimes have white spots – four in square anteriorly, with four more in curved line posteriorly. **Legs** Brown; rather stout.
Habitat Under stones etc in woods, sandy heaths; often with two or three egg sacs in late summer. **Season** Summer. **Distribution** Common and widespread throughout.

Enoplognatha oelandica (Thorell)
Size female 3·5 mm; male 3 mm
Carapace Mid- to dark brown. **Abdomen** Brown with numerous white spots. Ring of black blotches encircles dorsum. With median black stripe, sometimes divided into two spots. **Legs** Brown, annulated with black at apices of all segments.
Habitat Sandy heathland or dunes, under stones, etc. **Season** Early summer. **Distribution** Rare and scattered in south-east England. Rare in north and central Europe. Absent from Holland.

Enoplognatha crucifera (Thorell)
Size female up to 4·5 mm; male 3·5 mm
Similar to *E. oelandica* but dorsum surrounded by a black line. Ventrally with two parallel white lines in the female.
Habitat Coastal in Britain. **Season** Early Summer. **Distribution** Rare but probably widespread in Europe.

♀ *Enoplognatha ovata* with egg sac

♀ *Enoplognatha thoracica* with egg sac

♀ *Enoplognatha zelandica* with egg sac

Family Nesticidae

The single species in the region has a strong resemblance to the larger members of the Theridiidae, but with longer legs, particularly the first pair. The legs are thickly set with longish bristles, longer than in any theridiid. The most obvious difference between the two families is seen in the form of the male palp. Theridiid male palps have a rather smooth outline, with a row of parallel bristles arising from the tibia and covering the palpal organs. In *Nesticus cellulanus* the palp has a conspicuous paracymbium and a 'spiky' appearance ventrally.

The spider makes a fine web, similar in design to those of *Steatoda*. The courting male jerks the female's web briefly and is accepted without petulance. Mating lasts up to ten minutes, after which the spiders part. The sac is spherical and as broad as the length of the mother; it is carried by her attached to the spinners. The sac is pale brown (white or pale yellow according to other authorities).

Nesticus cellulanus (Clerck)
Size female 4–6 mm; male 3–5 mm
Carapace Very pale brown with irregular dark median band and black margins. Shiny. **Abdomen** Same colour as carapace, with dark rings. Posteriorly with median row of black bars. Ventrally with dark mark in front of spinners and pair of convergent lines, widest anteriorly. In paler specimens, these markings are difficult to make out. **Legs** Coloured as carapace. Sometimes with clear, dark annulations; when absent, tibiae and metatarsi usually have dark apical rings.
Habitat Dark, damp places – cellars, low vegetation in marshes, and in woods. **Season** Midsummer, possibly at other times of year. **Distribution** Infrequent but sometimes several found in small area. Widespread throughout Europe.

♀
Nesticus cellulanus

Families Theridiosomatidae, Tetragnathidae, Metidae, Araneidae: orb weavers

The spiders of these four families construct orb webs, during at least some stage in their development. (The cribellate orb weavers of the family Uloboridae are described on page 58.)

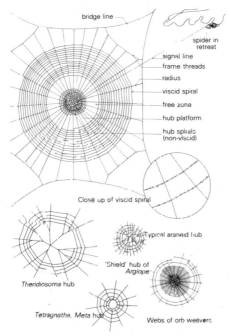

The geometric orb web is a complex structure in its construction and use. A detailed account of it would occupy a book as large as this guide, and it is dealt with in many of the titles in the reading list. In outline, however, the building of the web is described below.

1 A *bridge line* is established using a strand of wind-borne silk or trailed by the spider as it walks. When the wind-borne line is used, the spider tests the strength of the strand by tugging on it. It is reinforced by repeated journeys along the strand.

2 A Y-shaped structure is formed, which becomes the basis for all the radii.

3 *Frame lines* are added at the sides, together with more radii.

4 The remaining radii are placed, using the first radii as means of access. The frame lines may be modified, and existing radii may be moved to give constant angles between them.

237

5 The *strengthening spiral* is woven, uniting the radii at the hub. Due to the tightness of this, the radii are displaced, giving a 'notched' appearance. This spiral is continued, with a much wider spacing, to form the *temporary spiral* which reaches the periphery of the web.

6 After a pause, the spider retraces its steps, using the temporary spiral as 'stepping stones' to traverse the wide gaps between the outer parts of the radii and as a guide for placing the *viscid spiral*. This silk is coated with gum which forms beads on the spiral lines; this probably delays the adhesive drying, and provides better stopping power to prey hitting the web.

7 The viscid spiral is continued, with occasional reverses of direction to within a short distance of the hub, where it is stopped abruptly leaving a *free zone*. The spider then goes to the hub and removes the conspicuous knot of white silk (the inner ends of the radii). *Tetragnatha*, *Meta*, and *Cercidia* leave their hubs 'open', but the other araneids fill the void with random strands of silk.

8 *Cyclosa* and *Argiope* species add a *stabilmentum* to their webs. This probably has little effect on its stability and is more likely to serve as camouflage because it is made only by spiders which continuously occupy the hub.

Many species of orb weaver find some secluded place (the underside of a branch or leaf) where they spend the daylight hours with one of the first pair of legs on the *signal line*. This runs from the *retreat* to the hub of the web and relays the struggles of prey to the spider in its retreat. (Sometimes a radius is used as a signal line.) Some species merely fasten a few leaves together, while others make a thick silk bag for this protective structure. The retreat is usually higher than the hub of the web.

An average orb web consists of over 1000 junctions uniting about 20 metres of silk with a total weight of less than half a milligram. Paradoxically, some of the orb weavers are among our largest and heaviest spiders. A female *Araneus quadratus*, weighing 2·25 grams, was still able to make a web capable of supporting her considerable bulk.

The orb weavers prefer to construct their webs at night, but stormy weather prevents this, and web making is frequently seen at all hours of the day. The web must constantly be renewed as it becomes damaged by prey; the adhesive properties of the viscid spiral are reduced after a couple of days. Prey is first wrapped in silk and then bitten. It is cut free from the web and taken to the hub or retreat to be eaten. The finished meal is reduced to a small black pellet which the spider casts out of the web. *Cyclosa* attaches these remains to the stabilmentum but *Argiope* does not.

Immatures and females make their characteristic snares but, once the males become mature, they abandon this practice and probably do not eat in the ensuing weeks when they are roaming free in their search for females. *Tetragnatha* males do not court but leap upon the female while she is on the hub, quickly engaging their long chelicerae with those of the female. Male *Meta* species wait patiently at the side of the female's web until a fly gets entangled when they rush to the female and copulate while her predatory habits are directed towards the prey.

To the frame of the female's web *Araneus* males attach a courting thread which they strum with the strong spurs on the inner sides of tibiae II. This courtship can take up to an hour and brings the female to the edge of her web where the brief mating (10 to 20 seconds) takes place. One palp is used, and the courtship is repeated if the other is to be used. *Argiope* males invade the webs of their mates, briefly courting and mating on the hub. They are frequently wrapped and eaten after copulation has started.

The egg sacs of *Araneus* spiders are composed of fluffy silk and guarded by the mother until her death although, occasionally, she will resume web making and subsequently lay more eggs. In the spring- and summer-maturing species, the eggs develop quickly and, by autumn, the spiders are large enough to be identified in many cases. The eggs of the larger autumn species do not start to develop until the spring of the following year and, in the early summer, little nursery clusters of species like *A. diadematus* and *A. quadratus* are common sights. Exceptionally, *Argiope* eggs are further wrapped in a papery enclosure; the young spiders hatch within a few weeks and remain in the sac throughout the winter, to emerge in spring.

The spiderlings are just as capable of web making as their parents were but they catch smaller prey. Moulting usually takes place from a thread attached to the bridge line or the retreat although *Argiope* moults at the hub. The spring species appear to take one year to become adult but females can be found until the autumn in some cases. In contrast, the autumnal orb weavers appear to require a second season to mature but whether this applies to all species or to all individuals of a particular species is not clear. If the individuals varied in the time needed to attain maturity, then this would explain the large variation in size of the females of some species.

Family Theridiosomatidae

The single European species makes a small orb web without a hub. The radii are joined at various places near the middle of the web and converge at the centre where a signal line pulls the entire web into a conical form, like an inverted umbrella. The spider sits at the centre of the web holding the signal line, but with its back to the web (*Araneus*). The spider, which looks like a small theridiid, makes small, stalked egg sac, 2 to 3 millimetres in diameter, which attached to very high vegetation.

Theridiosoma gemmosum (L. Koch)
Size female c. 2 mm; male c. 1·5 mm
Carapace Pale brown to black. **Abdomen** Globular and greatly over-hanging carapace. Dorsally with silvery blotches. Anterior U-shaped mark sometimes absent. Large dark patch on each side and dark triangular mark posteriorly. **Legs** Femora and tibiae I thickened and darkened, apart from basal half of femora. These markings also on leg II.
Habitat Among low plants in wet places. **Season** Summer. **Distribution** Rare in southern Britain, France, Germany, Holland.

Family Tetragnathidae

The family includes two genera which make orb webs with open hubs. *Pachygnatha* immatures also do this but the adults run about in low vegetation.

Genus *Tetragnatha*

These are elongated spiders with long legs and chelicerae. The abdomen has a metallic appearance. Their inclined webs have few radii and spirals (about fifteen of each); there is no signal line and no retreat. The egg sacs vary in colour but often have a 'mouldy' appearance; they are fastened to a leaf. Some species are common near water. All the European species are described.

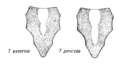
T. extensa *T. pinicola*

Tetragnatha extensa (Linnaeus)
Size female 8–11 mm; male 6–9 mm
Carapace Yellow-brown; head slightly darker. **Abdomen** Silvery white with pair of undulating stripes, varying from pale yellow to reddish brown. **Legs** Coloured as carapace, sometimes with one or two dark spots on femora. **Sternum** Dark brown with distinct yellow triangle anteriorly.
Habitat Low vegetation in damp places. **Season** Summer. **Distribution** Probably the most common *Tetragnatha* in Europe.

Tetragnatha striata L. Koch
lso known as *Eugnatha* and *Arundognatha*. Similar to *T. extensa*.
es Laterals more widely spaced than medians. **Sternum** Brown.
itat Reeds in or very near water. **Season** Summer. **Distribution**
and rare. Widespread in Britain (not Scotland) and northern
e.

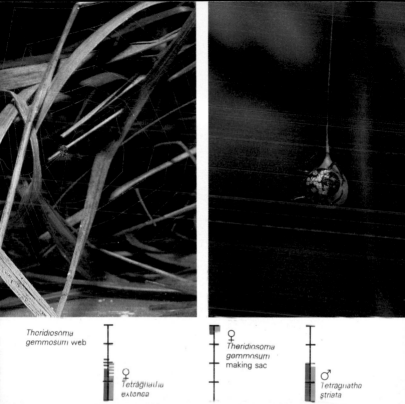

*Theridiosoma
gemmosum* web

♀
*Tetragnatha
extensa*

♀
*Theridiosoma
gemmosum*
making sac

♂
*Tetragnatha
striata*

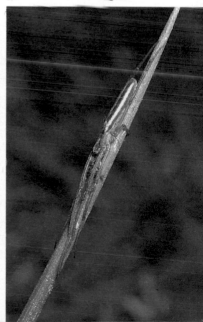

Tetragnatha pinicola L. Koch
Size female 6 mm; male 5 mm
Carapace Brown with paler striae. Abdomen Very silvery dorsally. Dark ventral band often contains silvery blotches. Legs Uniformly coloured as carapace. Sternum Dark brown with thin lighter median line extending almost entire length.
Habitat Trees and low vegetation. Not always near water. Season Summer. Distribution Infrequent but widespread throughout.

Tetragnatha montana Simon
Size female 7–10 mm; male 8 mm
Abdomen With network of black lines. Black sides have wavy edges. Sternum Uniformly brown.
Habitat Trees, bushes, etc, not always near water. Often in shade. Season Early summer. Distribution Locally common throughout.

Tetragnatha obtusa C. L. Koch
Size female 5–7 mm; male 4–6 mm
Carapace Dark triangle covering head. Abdomen Distinct folium has broken black edges. Two pairs of black spots extend to sides. Legs Variable in colour. Sometimes annulated (especially in immatures) but not in males. Sternum Brown with slightly darker edges.
Habitat Trees, especially common on pines on heathland or in damp woods. Season Early summer. Distribution Locally abundant in England. Widespread throughout.

Tetragnatha nigrita Lendl
Size female 7–10 mm; male 5–8 mm
Carapace Dark brown; head black. Abdomen More elongated than *T. obtusa*. Folium broad in front, tapered behind with three or four lobes on each side. Some specimens have white areas reduced. Legs and Sternum Like *T. obtusa* but darker.
Habitat Trees. Season Summer. Distribution Rare in southern Britain. France, Germany, Sweden.

Tetragnatha dearmata Thorell
Size female 8–10 mm; male 6–8 mm
Carapace Brown with clear striae. With dark border and dark streaks outlining head, which is lighter (cf *T. obtusa*). Abdomen Pattern not unlike *T. nigrita* but much lighter with black areas considerably reduced. More elongated posteriorly than *T. nigrita*. Similar in shape to *T. extensa*. Legs Brown with conspicuous dark spots at base of spines. All segments darkened apically. Sternum Dark brown with narrow dark border.
Habitat Pine trees. Season Summer. Distribution Not recorded from Britain. Widespread in Europe.

242

♀ *Tetragnatha pinicola*

♀ *Tetragnatha obtusa*

♀ *Tetragnatha montana*

♀ *Tetragnatha nigrita*

Genus *Pachygnatha*

These spiders have enlarged, divergent chelicerae. The abdomen is not so metallic as *Tetragnatha*. Both sexes are adult at most times of the year. The spiders of this genus are found in low vegetation or running on the ground beneath it. Three species are found in Europe.

Pachygnatha clercki Sundevall
Size female 6 mm; male 5–6 mm
Female Carapace Brown with dark median band, fainter submarginal bands, and dark line on junction of head and thorax. Glossy, with very faint punctuations. **Abdomen** With reticulated appearance. Yellow to greyish brown. Folium has light median band with dark spot or line at mid-point. **Legs** Lighter than carapace; unmarked. **Male** Very similar to female. **Abdomen** Pattern clearer. Folium dark brown with white median stripe and sides.
Habitat Among low vegetation in damp places. **Season** All year. **Distribution** Fairly common and widespread throughout.

Pachygnatha listeri Sundevall
Size female c. 5 mm; male 4 mm
Similar to *P. clercki*.
Carapace Dark marks less consistent. Distinctly pitted. **Abdomen** Variable in colour, the folium with more irregular edges than *P. clercki*. Median region with pairs of lighter spots in place of stripe. **Male** Similar to female, but with clearer pattern.
Habitat As *P. clercki*, particularly in damp woods. **Season** Probably all year. **Distribution** Rare but widespread throughout.

Pachygnatha degeeri Sundevall
Size female 3–4 mm; male 3 mm
Female Carapace Dark brown to black. Heavily pitted. **Abdomen** Folium dark brown with light spots in median line. Edges very irregular. Sides whitish to red. **Legs** Pale brown. **Male** Similar to female. **Abdomen** Clearer markings.
Habitat Low vegetation. **Season** All year. **Distribution** Very common throughout.

Family Metidae

The spiders of this family are intermediate in form between the Tetragnathidae and Araneidae. They have legs of moderate length and rather shiny bodies, but they are not noticeably metallic. The males of *M. segmentata* and *M. mengei* wait at the side of the female's web and mate only when the female catches prey. The web has an open hub and is often small compared to the spider.

♀
Pachygnatha
clercki

♀
Pachygnatha
listeri

♂ Pachygnatha
degeeri

Meta segmentata (Clerck)
Size female 5–8 mm; male 5–6 mm
Extremely variable in markings and colour.
Carapace With fork-shaped mark. Abdomen Characteristic shape
Usually with pair of triangular marks anteriorly, with folium extending
from apices of each triangle. Ventral median band does not exten
beyond epigastric furrow. Legs Pale brown, sometimes with ver
clear annulations; often without any markings. Few long ventral hair
on tibiae and metatarsi of I, II in male.
Habitat Woods, gardens, wasteland. Web at ground-level up t
1·5 m, and is frequently rather small. Season Late summer to au
tumn. Occasionally in spring. Distribution Abundant throughout.

Meta mengei (Blackwall)
Size female 4–5 mm; male 4 mm
Abdomen Pattern more rounded anteriorly and less clear. Ventrall
median band extends beyond epigastric furrow. Male Legs I, II hav
many long ventral hairs on tibiae and metatarsi.
Habitat As M. segmentata. Season Spring to early summer. Distr
bution Common throughout.

Meta merianae (Scopoli)
Size female 6–9 mm; male 5–8 mm
Carapace Pale brown with black triangle covering head. Margin
black, and black streaks on thorax. Abdomen Broader than M. seg
mentata. With dark pattern like M. mengei, lighter areas sometime
reddish or quite dark. Legs Femora I, II with large black spots. Othe
segments usually annulated with dark brown.
Habitat Damp, shaded sites such as caves, cellars, disused rabbi
holes; occasionally on trees. Season Late spring and early summe
Distribution Fairly common and widespread throughout.

Meta merianae var celata (Blackwall)
Very similar to M. merianae. Abdomen Broad golden median band
slightly dentate and running whole length.
Distribution Less common than normal form.

Meta menardi (Latreille)
Size female c. 13 mm; male c. 11 mm
Carapace Brown to reddish brown. With black median band. Sides
broadly darkened. Abdomen With pair of dark blotches anteriorly
often followed by golden area, becoming reddish midway. Dark bars
at rear. Legs With longer and more abundant spines than M. seg
mentata. Dark reddish brown with black annulations.
Habitat Cellars, caves, especially when deep and dark. Season A
year. Distribution Uncommon but widespread throughout.

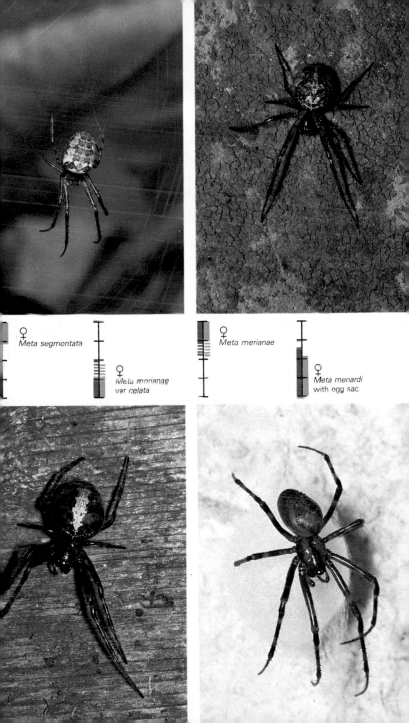

♀ *Meta segmentata*

♀ *Meta merianae var. celata*

♀ *Meta merianae*

♀ *Meta menardi* with egg sac

Family Araneidae

All the spiders make orb webs which are large in comparison to th
spider. Except for *Cercidia*, the webs have closed hubs. Stabilment
are present in the webs of *Cyclosa* and *Argiope* spiders. They a
distinguished by the rather short, stout legs which are very spiny i
most genera.

Many of these spiders have been placed in the genus *Araneus*
the present arrangement is based on the genitalia, and broadly re
flects the difference in appearance of spiders which were previousl
grouped together.

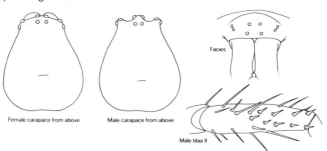

Female carapace from above   Male carapace from above   Facies   Male tibia II

Gibbaranea gibbosa (Walckenaer)
Size female 7 mm; male 5 mm
Carapace Dark brown with lighter hairs. **Abdomen** With dark-brow
folium and greenish sides, and anterior spots. With prominent humps
Legs Brown with darker annulations.
Habitat Trees and bushes, especially evergreens. **Season** Early t
midsummer. **Distribution** Common in southern half of England, les
common to north. Widespread but infrequent in Europe.

Gibbaranea omoeda (Thorell)
Size female 10 mm; male 8 mm
Darker than *A. gibbosus*.
Abdomen Folium outlined in white.
Habitat High on pine trees. **Season** Summer. **Distribution** Absen
from Britain. Widespread in Europe.

Gibbaranea bituberculata (Walckenaer)
Size female 9 mm; male 7 mm
Similar to *A. gibbosus* but brown, never green.
Abdomen Dark brown. Ventrally, light patch behind epigastric regior
distinguishes spider. Humps very prominent.
Habitat In Europe on low vegetation in open areas. **Season** Adult
early summer. **Distribution** In England only in Buckinghamshire
More common in Europe.

♀
Gibbaranea
gibbosa

♀
Araneus angula-tus with prey

Araneus angulatus Clerck
Size female 15 mm; male 12 mm
Largest British angulate spider.
Abdomen Folium usually has clearly defined dentate edges; occasionally lighter triangle occurs in front of humps. **Sternum** With broad, irregular, yellow-brown median band.
Habitat Evergreen trees and bushes. **Season** Midsummer to early autumn. **Distribution** Rare in England or very local along south coast from Devon to Kent. Uncommon but widespread in Europe.

Araneus zimmermanni (Thorell)
Size female 20 mm; male 12 mm
Similar to *A. angulatus*.
Abdomen Larger humps; line of dots down middle. **Sternum** Uniformly coloured.
Habitat Walls of houses. **Distribution** Rare in Europe only.

Araneus nordmanni (Thorell)

Size female 9 mm
Abdomen Folium has very broad white borders which almost mee
anteriorly; sometimes a white line extends down folium.
Habitat Mountains. **Distribution** Rare in Scandinavia and Germany

Araneus diadematus Clerck

Size female c. 12 mm; male c. 8 mm
Varied in colour (black to ginger) and depth of pattern.
Abdomen Shoulders have faint tubercles, and abdomen widest here
Folium contains alternate lighter and darker transverse bars. Row c
white spots medially, with transverse white blotches, forming cros
anteriorly.
Habitat Woods, heaths, gardens. Web reaches 40 cm in diameter a
heights of between 1·5 and 2·5 m. **Season** Late summer to autumn
Distribution Widespread and common throughout Europe.

Araneus quadratus Clerck

Size female 9–20 mm; male c. 8 mm
Carapace With broad irregular median band (cf *A. marmoreus*). **Abdo
men** Varies in colour from greenish grey to orange, brown, or red
Larger females have circular abdomens with four large white spot
in anterior half with white median line on fore margin.
Habitat Low bushes, heather, grass, etc. Web diameter up to 40 cm
but not usually over 1·5 m above ground. **Season** Late summer t
autumn. **Distribution** Widespread and common throughout Europe

Araneus marmoreus Clerck

Size female 5–15 mm; male 5–9 mm
Greatly resembles *A. quadratus* and is almost as variable in colour.
Carapace With *thin* median line, sometimes with dark patches behind
eyes. **Abdomen** Sides marbled with dark lines.
Habitat Trees and tall plants in damp woods. Web usually highe
than *A. quadratus*. **Season** Late summer to autumn. **Distribution**
Very local in eastern England. Widespread throughout Europe.

Araneus marmoreus **var** *pyramidatus* Clerck

Very distinct variety differs from *A. marmoreus* only in pattern o
dorsum.
Habitat Trees and bushes in woods. **Season** As *A. marmoreus*
Distribution Uncommon but widespread throughout.

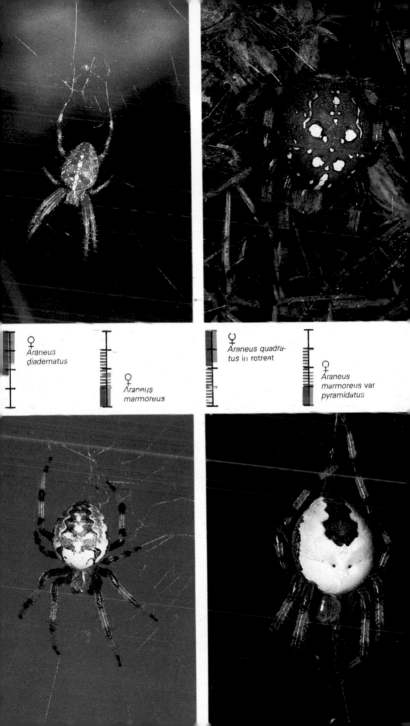

♀ *Araneus diadematus*

♀ *Araneus marmoreus*

⚥ *Araneus quadratus* in retreat

♀ *Araneus marmoreus* var *pyramidatus*

Araneus alsine (Walckenaer)

Size female 8 mm; male 6 mm
Carapace Pinkish brown, sparsely covered with white hairs. **Abdomen** Red to purple. Glossy, but covered in short white hairs. Speckling of many small light spots does not form any definite pattern. Outlines of folium only visible in posterior half of abdomen, and become very faint in larger specimens. **Legs** Pinkish brown; thickly covered with white hairs. Spines all dark. In darker specimens legs are annulated, especially III, IV.
Habitat Low vegetation in damp, sheltered places (woods etc). Retreat consists of one or two leaves, shaped into cone, open below and suspended in top of web. Spirals often reduced in area of signal line, like *Zygiella*. **Season** Midsummer to autumn. **Distribution** Rare and local in England, Wales. Widespread in Europe.

Nuctenea umbratica Clerck

Size female up to 14 mm; male 9 mm
Dark flattened species. Little variation in colour.
Abdomen Heart shaped, indented anteriorly, and with broad dentate folium which extends full length; several light spots within folium and sides of abdomen usually lighter.
Habitat Concealed under bark, particularly of dead trees. Common on fences. **Season** Females all year, males summer. **Distribution** Common throughout.

Nuctenea cornuta (Clerck)

Size female 6–12 mm; male 5–8 mm
Abdomen Ground colour varies from white, cream, or brown to bright red. Folium composed of two broad divergent black bars, with strongly dentate edges. Frequently thin white transverse lines give appearance that bars are composed of small squares. After gap, lines converge on fore part of abdomen, and enclose dark cardiac mark.
Habitat Very common near water. Low plants and reeds. Sometimes on buildings. Hub of web sometimes almost open. **Season** Early summer to late autumn. **Distribution** Widespread and common in habitat throughout.

Nuctenea patagiata (Clerck)

Size female 6–10 mm; male c. 6 mm
Abdomen Usually lacking white lateral lines on folium, and sometimes with anterior part of folium lacking. Not so variable in colour as *N. cornuta*. **Genitalia** May be distinguished in field; give best distinction of species in both sexes.
Habitat Sometimes mixed with *N. cornuta* near water, but also on trees and bushes in drier habitats. **Season** As *N. cornuta*. **Distribution** Uncommon and local throughout.

♀ Araneus alsine in retreat

♀ Nuctenea ornata

♀ Nuctenea umbratica

♀ Nuctenea patagiata

Nuctenea sclopetaria (Clerck)

Size female up to 14 mm; male 8 mm
Resembles *N. cornuta* and *N. patagiata* except that it is usually larger and with more velvety appearance.
Carapace Distinct v of white hairs which continues around front margin. **Abdomen** Folium has distinct white outline.
Habitat Bridges and buildings near water but not vegetation. **Season** As *N. cornuta*. **Distribution** Very local in England and Wales. Absent from Finland. Widespread elsewhere.

Aculepeira ceropegia (Walckenaer)

Size female up to 14 mm; male up to 8 mm
Abdomen From above and side shape is distinctive. In plan rather pointed in front and behind, where it extends so that spinners are not terminal. Pattern resembles that of *N. adiantum*, except that white lobes of folium are linear, not curved. Sparsely covered with long silky hairs.
Habitat Web in bushes etc and has shield-like hub. Retreat similar to *N. adiantum* – saucer of silk on which spider crouches, not below.
Season Early to midsummer. **Distribution** Chepstow 1853, but never rediscovered in Britain. Widespread in Europe; rather rare in north.

Neoscona adiantum (Walckenaer)

Size female 7 mm; male c. 4 mm
Rather slim. Some similarities to *A. ceropegia* but female half length.
Abdomen Colour varies from reddish to greyish brown but pattern remarkably constant. Two pairs of large white patches occur on anterior, followed by three pairs of much smaller streaks outlined in black to varying extent. Abdomen rounds off smoothly to spinners. (cf *A. ceropegia*).
Habitat Low vegetation, especially heather, sometimes grass. Makes silk saucer upon which it sits. Hub has unfinished look similar to *A redii*. **Season** Midsummer to early autumn. **Distribution** Locally common in southern England; recently found in Yorkshire. Absent from Finland. Locally common elsewhere.

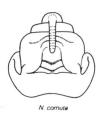

Female epigynes of *Nuctenea* species

N. cornuta   *N. sclopetaria*   *N. patagiata*

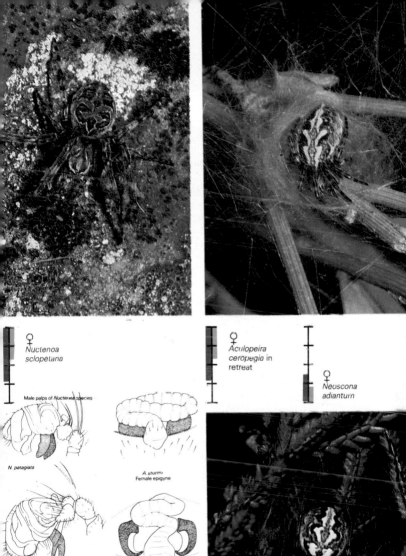

♀
*Nuctenea
sclopetaria*

Male palps of *Nuctenea* species

N. patagiata

N. sclopetaria

N. cornuta

A. sturmi
Female epigyne

A. triguttata
Female epigyne

♀
*Aculepeira
ceropegia* in
retreat

♀
*Neoscona
adiantum*

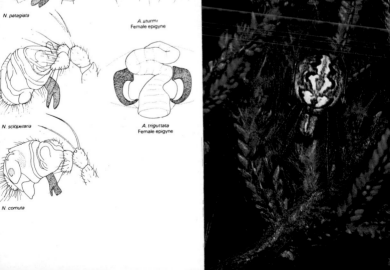

Agalenatea redii (Scopoli)
Size female 7 mm; male 4 mm
Broad-bodied species with variable markings. Several varieties are recognized, following found in Britain.
Abdomen Common form subcircular with dark broken line in middle; flanked by several dark bars which reach edges of folium; outside this is mottled darker area. Colour varies from grey to brown.

Agalenatea redii **var** δ
Similar in shape and size to *A. redii*.
Abdomen Fore part of folium has pair of white spots.

Agalenatea redii **var** ζ
Rarest form in Britain. Smaller.
Abdomen More triangular. In rear half is triangular brown patch with light border.
Habitat Bushes and low plants. Web usually below 1 m above ground and characterized by hub containing much white silk. Spider sits uppermost on nearby vegetation or in silk saucer. **Season** Spring.
Distribution Not recorded from Scotland; more common in south, especially on heathland. Absent from Finland. Widespread elsewhere.

Atea sturmi (Hahn)
Size female c. 5 mm; male 3·5 mm
Difficult to separate from *A. triguttata* in the field. Female may be identified by scape of epigyne, which is folded and much broader than long covering the epigyne.
Abdomen Subtriangular, with shoulders often darkened, and edged posteriorly with white. Folium, when present, consists of outline composed of dark curved lines with white outer edges. Colour varies from yellow to reddish brown.
Habitat Evergreen trees and bushes. **Season** Spring. **Distribution** Widespread throughout but uncommon, except locally.

Atea triguttata (Fabricius)
Size female 6 mm; male c. 4 mm
Usually larger than *A. sturmi*.
Abdomen More triangular than *A. sturmi*. Colour is often pink. Scape of epigyne much narrower than long, dark curved edges of epigyne being visible.
Habitat Usually deciduous bushes and trees. **Season** As *A. sturmi*.
Distribution Rarer than *A. sturmi*. Mainly southern England. Absent from Denmark and more northern countries. Widespread elsewhere.

♀ *Agalenata redii*

♀ *Agalenatea rodii* var ζ

♀ *Agalenatea rodii* var δ

♀ *Atea sturmi*

Zilla diodia (Walckenaer)

Size female c. 4 mm; male c. 2·5 mm

Abdomen Triangular; overhangs carapace so much that spider appears headless as it occupies the web. Rather shiny with white patch anteriorly. Behind this is pair of transverse lines followed by irregular triangular patch containing two pairs of lighter spots, or sometimes divided longitudinally. Coloration varies little.

Habitat Web, with its large hub, always vertical. No retreat, spider always on web. Bushes and lower branches of trees. Season Early to midsummer. Distribution Fairly frequent but not normally numerous in southern England. Absent from Scandinavia and Finland. Common elsewhere.

Cercidia prominens (Westring)

Size female c. 5 mm; male c. 4 mm

Carapace Covered in white bristles, and is darker than abdomen. Abdomen Rather pointed in front and bears three or four small, black spines on each side of the front edge. Darker females and males have light median stripe dorsally. Legs With few spines.

Habitat Web just above ground-level among low vegetation; spirals rather widely spaced but, in hub, they are few and close, with large opening that spider straddles. Web is vertical and there is no retreat. Season Adult at most seasons. Distribution Uncommon but widespread throughout.

Araniella cucurbitina (Clerck)

Size female 6 mm; male 4 mm

Female Carapace Brown and glossy, with few hairs confined to head. Abdomen Yellow to yellow-green with four dorsal depressions. Posteriorly two divergent rows of four black spots. Scarlet patch above spinners. Ventrally green patch extends from spinners to epigastric region. Legs Usually more greenish brown than carapace.

Male Carapace Very glossy, with two broad black lateral bands posteriorly. Abdomen Yellow with long hairs. Legs Coloured as carapace, with many long black spines. With black annulations.

Habitat Bushes and trees. Small web frequently very eccentric; usually above 1·5 m above ground. Season Late spring and summer. Distribution Common and widespread throughout.

Araniella inconspicua (Simon)

Size female 5 mm; male 4 mm

Abdomen Posterior black spots usually absent. In some specimens sides have red bands.

Habitat Trees, oak, pine, etc. Season Spring. Distribution Rare in southern Britain. Rare in France, Germany. Probably more common in southern Europe.

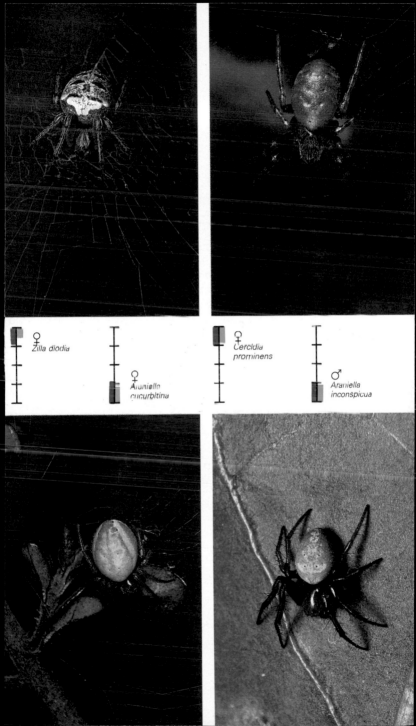

♀ *Zilla diodia*

♀ *Araniella cucurbitina*

♀ *Cercidia prominens*

♂ *Araniella inconspicua*

Araniella alpica (L. Koch)

Size female 6 mm; male 4 mm
Similar to *A. inconspicua*.
Abdomen Usually with two pairs of black spots posteriorly. English specimens have broad, dark-green median band ventrally which has two pairs of yellow spots contained within it; front spots sometimes fused together. **Male** Similar to *A. cucurbitina*. **Carapace** No lateral bands on thorax.
Habitat Trees. **Season** Late spring and summer. **Distribution** Very rare in central southern England. Belgium, Sweden. Not uncommon in Germany.

Araniella displicata (Hentz)

Size female 6–11 mm; male c. 5 mm
Abdomen With dorsal pattern; colours vary from red to green but design usually very clear, with white border around dorsal marks. Ventrally there is orange band with dots disposed as in *A. alpicus* or these may be fused into one large yellow-green area with orange edges. **Legs** Darker specimens may have faint annulations especially III, IV. **Male Abdomen** With dorsal pattern, but ventral light dots replaced by median band.
Habitat Typically on pines. **Season** Spring. **Distribution** Rare and very local in south-east England. Absent from France. Widespread but rare elsewhere. Apparently more common in North America.

Hypsosinga albovittata (Westring)

Size female c. 3 mm; male c. 2·5 mm
Female Carapace Dark brown with white median stripe. **Abdomen** Ventrally with broad dark area flanked by white u-shaped line surrounding whole area including spinners. **Male** Similar to female. **Legs** Femora I, II, IV darkened.
Habitat Low vegetation. Web has widely spaced spirals and occurs under 20 cm from ground. **Season** Early summer. **Distribution** Local and scattered in Britain. Generally more common in Europe.

Hypsosinga pygmaea (Sundevall)

Size female c. 4 mm; male c. 3 mm
Female Carapace Black. **Abdomen** Black with three lighter stripes. Median yellow, laterals white. Some specimens totally black. **Legs** Brown. **Male Abdomen** Always black. **Legs** Femora I darkened apically. Somewhat ant-like in movements.
Habitat Low vegetation in damp places. **Season** Early summer. **Distribution** Infrequent but widespread throughout.

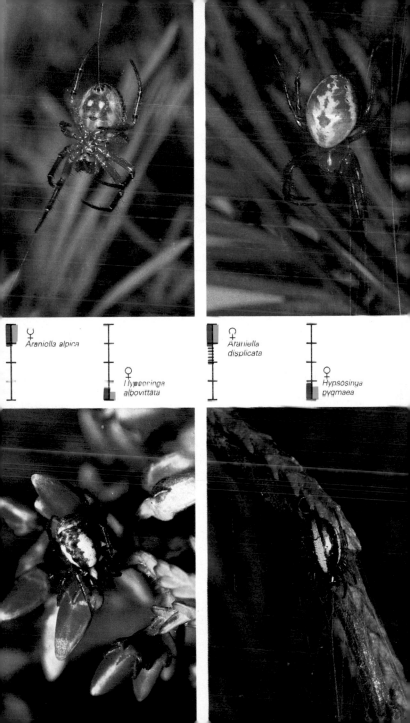

♀ Araniolla alpica

♀ Hypsosinga albovittata

♀ Araniella displicata

♀ Hypsosinga pygmaea

Hypsosinga sanguinea (C. L. Koch)
Size female c. 3·5 mm; male c. 3 mm
Similar to *H. pygmaea*.
Abdomen Stripes, when present, all white. Darker areas vary from black to brown; in lighter specimens brown areas have black spot posteriorly. **Male Legs** Femora I darkened entirely or only ventrally.
Habitat, Season, Distribution As *H. pygmaea*.

Hypsosinga heri (Hahn)
Size female c. 4 mm; male c. 3 mm
Female and Male Carapace Orange with head darker.
Habitat Low vegetation near standing water. **Season** As *H. pygmaea*.
Distribution Very rare in England. Widespread but rare in Europe.

Singa hamata (Clerck)
Size female c. 6 mm; male c. 4 mm
Abdomen Two darker areas of dorsum broken into three transverse lines in mid-region; ventrally light lateral lines very short. **Legs** Segments sometimes darkened apically.
Habitat Damp places. Web slightly higher *H. sanguinea*. Retreat is pale pink-brown and contains egg sacs. **Season** Spring to mid summer. **Distribution** Very local but widespread in Britain. Widespread but uncommon in Europe.

Singa nitidula C. L. Koch
Size female c. 6 mm; male c. 4 mm
Abdomen Narrow, almost cylindrical; the dorsal pattern similar to *S. hamata* but darker areas more entire with several white lines encroaching in mid-region.
Habitat Among low vegetation on the banks of fast-flowing streams.
Season as *S. hamata*. **Distribution** Absent from Britain, Norway, Sweden. Locally common elsewhere.

Zygiella x-notata (Clerck)
Size female c. 6 mm; male c. 5 mm
Female Carapace Pale brown with head much darker. **Abdomen** Oval with large grey-brown folium; within this there is silvery lustre. Sides vary in colour from pale brown to reddish brown. **Legs** Pale brown with vague markings. Few spines. **Sternum** Yellowish with darker edges. **Male Palps** Segments moderate size (cf *Z. atrica*).
Habitat Nearly always in vicinity of houses, typically on window frames etc. **Season** Late summer to autumn. Female is only orb weaver to continue web building through winter. Some females live on until early summer of following year. **Distribution** Abundant throughout Britain. Absent from Finland. Less common in east. Generally common elsewhere.

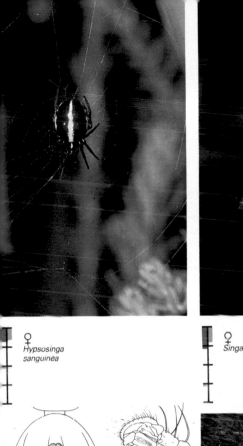

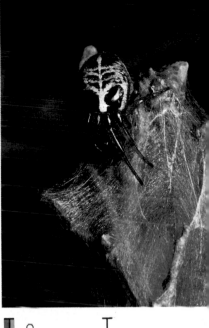

♀ *Hypsosinga sanguinea*

♀ *Singa hamata*

♀ *Zygiella x-notata*

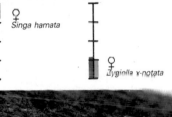

Venter of female
Z. stroemi

Male palps of *Zygiella* species

Z. x-notata

Z. atrica

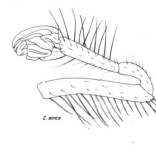

Zygiella atrica (C. L. Koch)

Size female c. 6 mm; male c. 5 mm
Female Similar to *Z. x-notata*. **Abdomen** Edges of folium fainter and area within more uniform, often golden. Fore patches characteristically reddish brown. **Male Palps** Femur almost as long as carapace, with long patella and tarsus.
Habitat Common on heathland in bushes and on pine trunks. Not normally on buildings. **Season** As *Z. x-notata* but long season of female perhaps not so extended. **Distribution** Throughout Europe.

Zygiella stroemi (Thorell)

Size female c. 4 mm; male c. 3 mm
Smallest *Zygiella* in Europe resembles *Z. atrica*.
Female Abdomen Relatively broader than *Z. atrica*. Outline of folium more even and thicker. Background pinkish brown with white spots.
Legs With very vague markings. **Epigyne** With long dark scape about quarter length of abdomen. All other species described have small, lateral epigynes. **Male Palps** Segments all rather short but copulatory organs relatively larger than other species.
Habitat Trunks of deeply fissured pine trees etc. Web small (10 cm diameter) and very delicate. **Season** In southern England females throughout year; males from June to September. **Distribution** Very local in Britain but common locally in south-east England. Rare in France, Belgium, Denmark. More common in Scandinavia, Finland.

Zygiella montana C. L. Koch

Size female c. 7 mm; male c. 5 mm
Montane species resembles *Z. x-notata*.
Abdomen Folium mottled, with characteristic dark spot near middle.
Sternum Uniformly blackish, unlike other *Zygiella* species.
Habitat Tree trunks, walls, under boulders etc, above 350 m. **Season** May take up to three years to reach maturity; adults at most times of year. **Distribution** Harz and Eifel regions of Germany.

Mangora acalypha (Walckenaer)

Size female c. 4 mm; male 2·5 mm
Carapace Yellow-brown with black border and thin median band.
Abdomen White with black folium confined to medial region, broader posteriorly with thin line reaching front margin. Reminiscent of long-necked bottle or cricket bat. Lighter spots occur in rear section and yellow or brown v-shaped line occurs in front half. Sides streaked with black and sometimes have reddish colour. **Legs** Colour as carapace, and spotted.
Habitat Low vegetation. **Season** Early summer. **Distribution** Abundant in heather in southern England, also in grasses, etc. Common throughout Europe. Absent from Finland.

♀ *Zygiella atrica*

♀ *Zygiella möbliana*

♀ *Zygiella stroemi*

♀ *Mangora acalypha*

Cyclosa conica (Pallas)
Size female up to 7 mm; male c. 4 mm
Extremely variable in markings and colour.
Female Carapace Black, but normally covered by legs. **Abdomen** With single tubercle posteriorly. Pattern and colour variable and of little diagnostic value, except that some specimens are very pretty, especially when sides and ventral side of prominence are orange. **Legs** Pale brown. Distal half of femora, patellae, and base of tibiae usually dark brown to orange. Remaining segments sometimes very sharply annulated. **Sternum** Black. **Male** Similar to female but usually more sombre in colour. **Carapace** Very attenuated anteriorly. **Abdomen** Tubercle smaller than in female.
Habitat Foliage of evergreens. Stabilmentum often absent. **Season** Spring and early summer. **Distribution** Widespread and common throughout.

Cyclosa oculata (Walckenaer)
Size female c. 5 mm; male 4 mm
Similar to *C. conica*.
Abdomen With number of small tubercles, a pair dorsally in fore part and further pair at side of posterior tubercle making three in all at rear end. **Sternum** Black with red-brown spots opposite coxae.
Habitat Low bushes, etc. Hub usually about 25 cm above ground. **Season** Summer. **Distribution** Absent from Britain. Recorded from Belgium? France, Germany but rare.

Argiope bruennichi (Scopoli)
Size female 15 mm; male c. 4 mm
Female Carapace Thickly covered in short, grey, silky hairs. **Abdomen** With sinuous black bars, alternately white and yellow areas between. Small anterior tubercles give flat-fronted appearance. Pair of bright-yellow lines ventrally. **Legs** Pale brown annulated with black. Femora I (and to lesser extent II, III, IV) black with pale ring distally. **Sternum** Bright yellow with black borders. **Male Carapace** Brown with some silky hairs. Darker lateral bands. **Abdomen** Elongated, with two vague longitudinal brown stripes. **Legs** Pale brown with black spots on femora; other segments obscurely annulated.
Habitat Large web (30 cm diameter) at ground-level in grass and other low vegetation. **Season** Adult at end of May in some parts of Europe, but male and female adult in mid-August in England. Females until October. **Distribution** In Britain south coast from Dorset to Kent; sometimes abundant locally. Local in France, Germany, Holland, Belgium.

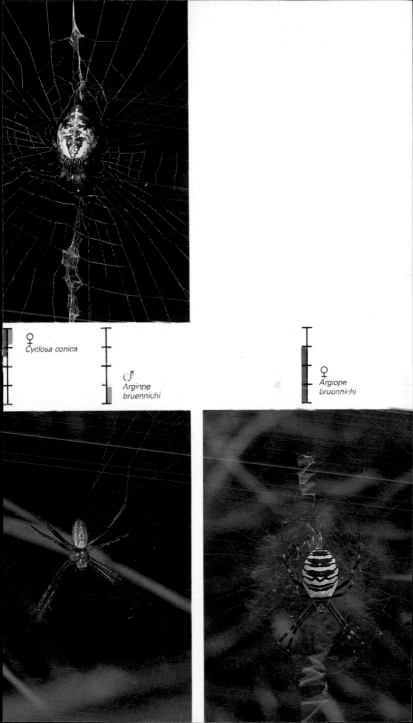

♀ Cyclosa conica

♂ Argiope bruennichi

♀ Argiope bruennichi

Family Linyphiidae

This is a large family and the majority of the spiders are known a. money spiders. Most of them make small sheet webs with no retrea The spiders hang, inverted, below the sheet. They constitute the major proportion of those spiders which 'balloon'.

Of 620 British species, over two-fifths are linyphiids. For the mos part they are about 2 millimetres in length although one or two are just half that size. Most have uniformly black bodies and brownist legs. They cannot be seen in sufficient detail using a times-ten len: to determine to species level in every case so that only the larger o more distinctive species are described here.

The family is split into two subfamilies although these are raisec to family status by some authorities. The subfamily Erigoninae is characterized by the dark pigmentation of the body, small size (none larger than 3·5 millimetres), and the extraordinary shapes which the male head takes in many genera. There are sixty-eight genera founc in Britain.

The Linyphiinae contains thirty-three British genera; none of the males has lobes or other accoutrements on the carapace and, while some of the genera are very small, some are quite large (up to 6 millimetres) and more than a third have patterns on the abdomen o carapace.

SUBFAMILY ERIGONINAE

Of the selected species from this group, the first genus, *Walckenaera* contains the largest spiders of the subfamily and with males whict have the most highly developed heads. The remaining genera, ending with *Lophomma*, are mostly dark spiders but *Trematocephalus, Os tearius, Hypomma*, and *Gonatium* are distinctive in their orange o red colouring. *Peponocranium, Evansia*, and *Lessertia* are not the only pale species in the subfamily, but they are readily identifiable by the features mentioned in the descriptions, whereas the omitted species are either rare, very small, or both. *Lessertia* is the largest pale species found in Britain.

Because of the difficulties of identifying these species, relatively little work has been done on their biology, other than their distribution and habitats. It is not clear whether all of them make webs, in the

Walckenaera acuminata

♂ Walckenaera antica

Tromatocephalus cristatus

♂ Hypomma bituberculatum

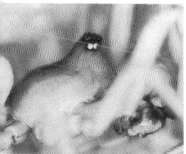

Gonatium rubens

♂ Peponocranium ludicrum

Oedothorax apicatus

♂ Floronia bucculenta

sense of a sheet which is much larger than they are and used to catch food, as a courting platform for the male, and so on. It is known that the odd shape of the male head and the small pits which occur at the sides in many genera are used by the female to grip her mate during copulation. In one species, *Baryphyma pratensis* (Blackwall) and possibly another, *Acanthophyma gowerensis* (Locket), the female's fangs actually draw blood from the male's carapace, and she drinks it during copulation.

The egg sacs are of various types; some, like araneids', are composed of white fluffy silk while others, like those of *Erigone arctica* are similar in shape and colour to those of *Zelotes*. The life expectancy for probably all of these spiders is between nine months and one year.

Walckenaera acuminata Blackwall
Size female 3·5 mm; male c. 3 mm
Carapace Extraordinary development of head in male, with parallel but lesser elevation in female, makes it easy to identify. **Eyes** In male distributed in two groups of four, one group at thickening of 'stalk' about midway, remaining eyes situated at tip.
Habitat Leaf litter and moss in sheltered places, woods, etc. **Season** Males from autumn to spring; females all year, but most frequent in colder seasons. **Distribution** Rather uncommon but widespread throughout.

Walckenaera antica (Wider) and *Walckenaera alticeps*
Size female c. 2·5 mm; male c. 2 mm
Carapace Uniformly dark. Heads of males developed into two lobes (*see* page 00), smaller front lobe having pair of small horns formed of fused hairs projecting forwards. **Legs** Tibiae I, II darkened anteriorly.
Habitat *W. antica* typically in sites exposed to sun, such as rubbish or vegetable detritus in open places. *W. alticeps* prefers damp sites such as shaded *Sphagnum* bogs. **Season** Autumn to spring. **Distribution** *W. antica* common and widespread throughout. *W. alticeps* confused with *W. antica* in past; probably equally widespread but much less common.

Walckenaera melanocephala (O.P.-Cambridge)
Size female 2·5 mm male 2 mm
Carapace Orange-brown with head dark brown. **Legs** Tibiae I, II marked as *W. antica* but more clearly.
Habitat Grass and heather. **Season** Summer. **Distribution** Widespread in Britain but very local. Recorded from France, Belgium, Holland, Germany.

270

♂
Walckenaera
acuminata

♀
Walckenaera
antica

♀
Walckenaera
melanocephala

Trematocephalus cristatus (Wider)
Size female 2·5 mm; male 2 mm
Carapace Orange-red. Head with three thin, black lines. **Abdomen** Dark brown, sometimes with faint, lighter median band. **Legs** Reddish to yellowish brown with dark brown or black on apical segments. Joints of these lighter. **Male Head** With horizontal protuberance which touches ocular region. From side, distinct hole can be seen; aperture is developed at last moult and is only found in mature male. **Habitat** Trees and bushes often above 1·5 m. **Season** Spring and early summer. **Distribution** In England very local in Surrey, Sussex. Widespread in Europe.

Gongylidium rufipes (Sundevall)
Size female 3·5 mm; male 3 mm
Carapace Orange-brown. Head dark brown, usually in both sexes, but sometimes less developed in female.
Habitat Trees, bushes, and tall plants in woods. **Season** Males in spring and autumn; females throughout summer. **Distribution** Widespread in Britain, often found in large numbers. Widespread in Europe.

Hypomma bituberculatum (Wider)
Size female c. 3 mm; male c. 2·5 mm
Orange prosoma, legs, and black abdomen characteristic of *H. bituberculatum* and much rarer *H. fulvum*.
Carapace, Sternum, Legs Orange-brown. **Abdomen** Black. Darker head of male is produced into two large lobes.
Habitat Wet places, often in low vegetation at side of water. **Season** Spring, summer, autumn. **Distribution** Common and widespread throughout.

♀ *Trematocephalus*
cristatus

♀ *Gonglydium*
rufipes with egg
sac

♀ *Hypomma*
bituberculatum
with egg sac

Gonatium rubens (Blackwall)
Size female 3 mm; male 2·5 mm
Whole spider orange-brown. Both sexes similarly coloured.
Abdomen Sometimes slightly darker. **Male Carapace** Ocular region
prominent. **Legs** Tibiae I, II somewhat curved and thickened apically
Palps Femur and patella enlarged to same diameter as legs; femur
has patch of short, black teeth near apex, culminating in long, single
tooth.
Habitat Low vegetation or bushes, often in shaded places. **Season**
All year. **Distribution** Common and widespread in Europe and North
America.

Gonatium rubellum (Blackwall)
Similar to *G. rubens* in size and coloration.
Female Epigyne Larger than *G. rubens*. **Male Palp** Lacks teeth of *G.
rubens* but has patella greatly enlarged (wider than femur)
Distribution Less common than *G. rubens*, but widespread in
Europe.

Ostearius melanopygius (O.P.-Cambridge)
Size female 2·5 mm; male 2–2·5 mm
Unique coloration makes it easily identified.
Carapace Dark brown to black. **Abdomen** Reddish brown with spin-
ners and surrounding area black. **Legs** Yellow-brown.
Habitat Almost anywhere. **Season** Spring to autumn. **Distribution**
Probably most widely found species in the world. In remote places
in every continent – the Azores, Hawaii, a cave in Australia, mountain
tops of East Africa, an ants' nest in Brazil, under burnt wood in Surrey,
England, and as a ballooner on nature reserves in Hampshire and
Dorset. Widespread in Britain (up to Highlands of Scotland). Widespread in Europe.

Peponocranium ludicrum (O.P.-Cambridge)
Size female c. 2 mm; male 1·8 mm
Pale species with distinctive male. 'Ludicrous' shape of male's head
and darkening of lobe make this spider recognizable in spite of small
size.
Habitat Low vegetation and bushes. **Season** Males in early summer;
females all year. **Distribution** Locally very common and widespread
in Britain. Throughout Europe.

♀
Gonatium rubens

♀
*Ostearius
melanopygius*

♂
*Peponocranium
ludicrum*

Evansia merens O.P.-Cambridge
Size female c. 2·5 mm; male c. 2 mm
Some specimens rather pale but habitat is characteristic.
Habitat Under stones frequented by ants. **Season** Mainly autumn, but female and male can be found at other times. **Distribution** Northern Britain but also found in north and south Wales, Devon, Cornwall. Southern France.

Lessertia denticimelis (Simon)
Size female c. 3 mm; male c. 3 mm
Rather variably marked spider but usually pale.
Carapace Varies from pale yellow-brown to brown. **Abdomen** Varies from greenish to pinkish brown.
Habitat Damp subterranean places, such as caves, mines, and sewers, and on sandhills. **Season** Probably all year, but males in autumn only. **Distribution** Local but widespread in Britain. Uncommon but widespread in Europe.

Erigone arctica (White)
Size female c. 2·5 mm; male 2·5 mm
Eleven species in Britain of which two, *E. atra* and *E. dentipalpis*, are commonly found ballooning. All species appear similar in field.
Carapace Black. Head smoothly raised, slightly in female, distinctly in male. Males with prominent teeth on margins and on palp. **Abdomen** Black. **Legs** Yellow-brown in female, reddish brown in male.
Habitat Under stones and seaweed at coasts or under stones by freshwater pools. Other *Erigone* sp make small webs in holes in ground, moss, and other low vegetation. **Season** Adults at all times of year. Commonly found aeronaut in midsummer and autumn. **Distribution** Common locally around British coasts. This and other species widespread in northern hemisphere.

♂
Erigone atra
ballooning

♀
Evansia merens

♀
*Lessertia
dentichelis*

♀
Erigone arctica

Lophomma punctatum (Blackwall)
Size female 2·5 mm; male 2·25 mm
Dark species.
Carapace and sternum Covered in punctuations. **Legs** Reddish brown; rather long and thin.
Habitat Low vegetation in marshes. **Season** All year. **Distribution** Locally common and widespread throughout.

SUBFAMILY LINYPHIINAE

Unless otherwise stated, there is just a single species in each genus that is found in the region. The spiders have been grouped into species which are similar in appearance so that direct comparisons of form and pattern can be made.

Bathyphantes gracilis (Blackwall)
Size female c. 2·5 mm; male c. 1·5 mm
Eight species occur in Britain, but this is most common and usually has clearest markings.
Carapace Black. **Abdomen** Variable. Light to mid- yellow-brown. Well-marked specimens have black median band with three to four thin lateral bands, like fish bone. Parts of pattern sometimes absent, leaving row of triangles in centre line. **Legs** Coloured as lighter parts of abdomen.
Habitat Among low vegetation. **Season** Spring, summer, autumn. **Distribution** Very common throughout. A common aeronaut.

Poeciloneta globosa (Wider)
Size female 2 mm; male 1·75 mm
Resembles members of genus *Lepthyphantes* but has different and distinctive carapace and abdomen patterns.
Carapace Brown, with head black and with radiating streaks opposite legs. **Abdomen** With pale shining patches. Cardiac mark very dentate and followed by three pairs of black irregular patches. Immediately above spinners are three or four short black lines. **Legs** Yellow-brown, sometimes with clear annulations or with apices of segments darkened.
Habitat Low vegetation, moss, under stones, or on bushes and trees. **Season** Spring, summer, autumn. **Distribution** Locally common throughout.

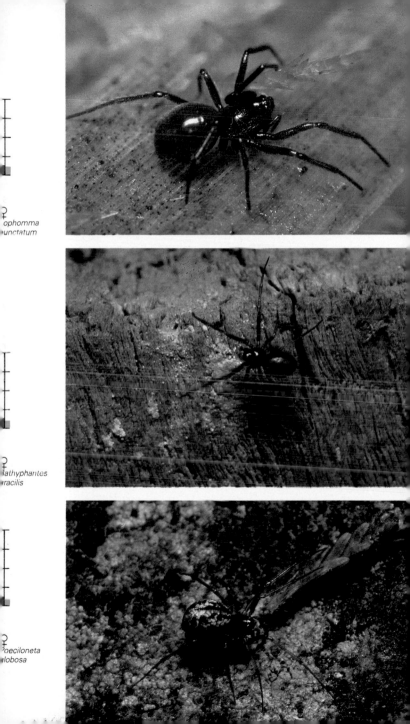

♀
Lophomma
punctatum

♀
Bathyphantes
gracilis

♀
Poeciloneta
globosa

Genus *Drapetisca*

The single European species, and its two counterparts in North America, are peculiar because they make extremely fine webs on the vertical bark of trees. This web is extremely difficult to see and web making in these spiders has been a subject of some controversy. It is known that the web measures about 60 by 40 millimetres and that the spider catches small insects, such as aphids, which move on the bark. The male uses the web to communicate with the female by pulling and drumming on it with the palps; this method is similar in outline to that adopted by many weaving spiders. The coloration of the lighter parts of the abdomen is variable in *D. socialis*, a pinkish hue being common, as well as a darkening of the whole dorsal surface in industrial areas.

Drapetisca socialis (Sundevall)
Size female 4 mm; male 3·5 mm
Carapace Yellow-brown with black marks. Median band with fork on head. Margins black with three or four streaks opposite legs. **Abdomen** Sometimes with black band on sides and front. Dorsally with white area anteriorly and with dark irregular folium containing number of lighter chevrons posteriorly. **Legs** Pale with clear black annulations. **Female Palps** With long, stout spines ventrally.
Habitat Trunks of trees (pines and beech, for example) or at their bases. Sometimes on fences in woods. **Season** Late summer to autumn. **Distribution** Locally very common and widespread throughout.

Tapinopa longidens (Wider)
Size female 4 mm; male 4 mm
Carapace Rather long, but broad anteriorly. Yellow-brown with broad grey submarginal bands. **Abdomen** Pale to dark yellow-brown with few small white spots. Dorsally with three to four pairs of large diffuse grey patches. **Legs** Coloured as carapace, sometimes with faint, dark annulations on femora and tibiae. **Female** Epigyne Large and protuberant. **Male Palp** Has long 'spike' on base of tarsus.
Habitat Highly characteristic web consists of thick and often patched sheet over hollow in ground or in low vegetation. **Season** Males in late summer, females throughout colder months of year. **Distribution** Common and widespread throughout.

♀
Drapetisca socialis

♀
Tapinopa longidens

Tapinopa longidens web

Labulla thoracica (Wider)

Size female c. 5 mm; male 4·5 mm
Carapace Yellow-brown with thick black marginal band and dark patch at rear of head which extends backwards. **Abdomen** Rather variable in colour – reddish, yellowish brown, to almost white; with variable amount of small white patches and dark blotches. Shiny but covered in long pale hairs. Ventrally with one large and two smaller white spots near spinners. **Legs** Yellow-brown with clear annulations usually. **Male Palps** Disc shaped with long, coiled embolus.
Habitat Typically at base of trees, with sheet web slung between exposed roots. **Season** Autumn. **Distribution** Common and widespread throughout.

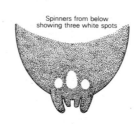

Spinners from below
showing three white spots

Stemonyphantes lineatus (Linnaeus)

Size female 5 mm; male 4 mm
Carapace Yellow-brown with black marginal and median bands, both rather thin. Broadly oval in male. **Abdomen** With whitish or pink spots. Three longitudinal rows of black spots. **Legs** Coloured as carapace and annulated.
Habitat Very small web in spite of spider's relatively large size. Wide range of habitats – seashore, chalk downs, and sandy heathland; under stones or in low vegetation. **Season** Late summer and autumn. **Distribution** Widespread and locally common throughout. Also North America.

Taracnucnus setosus (O.P.-Cambridge)

Size female 3 mm; male 2·5 mm
Carapace Brown, slightly darker towards edges. **Abdomen** Reddish brown with black marks dorsally. **Legs** Almost same colour as abdomen. Young specimens have greyish legs which are darker than body.
Habitat Among vegetation in swamps. **Season** Autumn to early spring. **Distribution** Absent from Scotland; widespread elsewhere in Britain but local. Western and northern Europe.

♀
Labulla thoracica

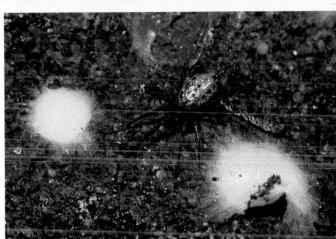

♀
*Stemonyphantes
lineatus* with egg
sacs

♀
*Taracnucnus
setosus*

Helophora insignis (Blackwall)
Size female 4 mm; male 3·5 mm
Reddish-brown appearance.
Carapace Brown with thin dark marginal line. **Abdomen** Orange-brown, usually with two or three thin black chevrons posteriorly, and black patches at sides. **Legs** Orange-brown, paler than abdomen.
Female Epigyne With long broad scape.
Habitat Among low vegetation in woods, especially in damp places.
Season Autumn and winter. **Distribution** Widely distributed in Britain but rather local in south. Widespread in Europe.

Genus *Lepthyphantes*

This is the largest genus in the subfamily, with species occurring worldwide, but with more described from the northern hemisphere than elsewhere. The European species may be divided into two groups: larger spiders with an abdominal pattern of paired spots; and smaller species which are uniformly coloured and often rather pale. They share the following characteristics: **Carapace** This is narrowed anteriorly and glabrous. **Eyes** The eyes are prominent and on black spots. **Abdomen** It is somewhat pointed posteriorly. **Legs** The legs are rather slender and have long spines. The webs of this genus are simple sheets, mostly of moderate size, although *L. leprosus* will make an extensive sheet given the space.

Lepthyphantes nebulosus (Sundevall)
Size female 4 mm; male 3·5 mm
Carapace Yellow-brown with darker median line which forks on head. Dark irregular margins. **Abdomen** Brownish with white spots. Darker marks consist of large spots joined by sinuous lines, fairly consistent in different specimens. **Legs** Coloured as abdomen with dark annulations. With more spines than other members of genus.
Habitat Houses and gardens. **Season** All year. **Distribution** Widespread and common in Britain, especially south; as well as Europe and North America.

Lepthyphantes leprosus (Ohlert)
Size female 3 mm; male 2·5 mm
Similar to *L. nebulosus.*
Carapace Median line not forked. **Abdomen** Usually light yellow-brown with grey marks. **Legs** Pale and uniformly coloured.
Habitat As *L. nebulosus*, but also found away from houses. **Distribution** Widespread and common throughout.

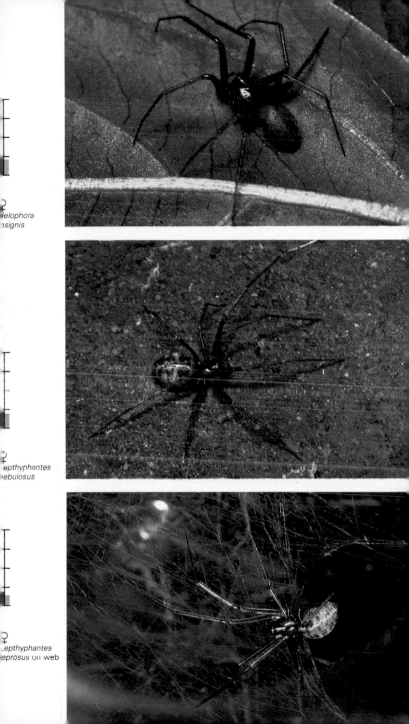

♀
*Melophora
insignis*

♀
*Lepthyphantes
nebulosus*

♀
*Lepthyphantes
leprosus* on web

Lepthyphantes minutus (Blackwall)
Size female 4 mm; male 3·5 mm
Carapace Dark brown. **Abdomen** Characteristically with golden spots. Background colour sometimes reddish. Black marks as in *L. nebulosus*. **Legs** Yellow to reddish brown with dark annulations.
Habitat Tree trunks or under logs. Sometimes in houses. **Season** Autumn. **Distribution** Widespread throughout.

Lepthyphantes alacris (Blackwall)
Size female 3 mm; male 2·5 mm
Carapace Dark brown. **Abdomen** Reddish to greyish brown with pale-yellow spots. Cardiac mark is characteristic as is absence of dark spots, their place being taken by lateral bars. **Legs** Pale brown without annulations.
Habitat Low vegetation in woods. **Season** Autumn to spring. **Distribution** Widespread throughout.

Lepthyphantes obscurus (Blackwall)
Size female 2·25 mm; male 2 mm
Carapace Very dark brown or black. **Abdomen** With dark band anteriorly joined to irregular cardiac mark, followed by several pairs of large spots sometimes joined by lines. **Legs** Yellow-brown. **Female Epigyne** Extremely protuberant.
Habitat Low plants and bushes. **Season** Spring to autumn but mainly in summer. **Distribution** Widespread throughout.

Lepthyphantes tenuis (Blackwall)
Size female 2·5 mm; male 2 mm
Carapace Dark brown. **Abdomen** Light to mid-brown with clear black spots usually joined by sinuous lines. **Legs** Brown.
Habitat Low vegetation. **Season** Throughout year. **Distribution** Almost every county of Britain. Widespread in Europe.

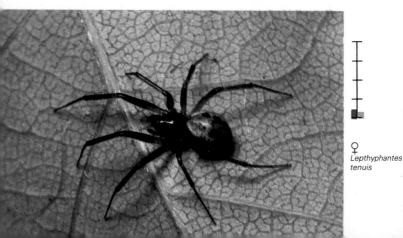

♀
Lepthyphantes tenuis

♀
*Lepthyphantes
minutus*

♀
*Lepthyphantes
alacris*

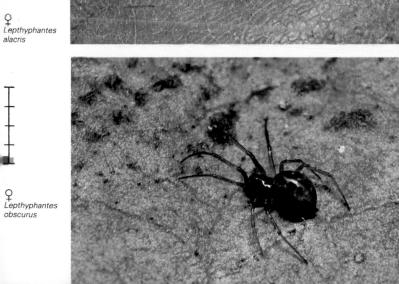

♀
*Lepthyphantes
obscurus*

Lepthyphantes zimmermanni Bertkau
Very similar to L. *tenuis* and almost equally common. Not possible to distinguish in the field.

Lepthyphantes cristatus (Menge)
Similar pattern to L. *tenuis* but rather protuberant epigyne. Much less common.

Lepthyphantes mengei Kulczynski and Lepthyphantes flavipes (Blackwall)
Overall appearance approaches that of L. *tenuis* but palps of males are dark, a feature found in some females of both species.
Distribution Common throughout.

Lepthyphantes ericaeus (Blackwall)
Size female 1·5 mm; male 1·5 mm
Tiny, pale species.
Eyes On dark spots. Legs have the long spines characteristic of the genus. Also found in France, Germany, Holland and Belgium.

Lepthyphantes expunctus (O.P.-Cambridge)
Size female 2·5 mm; male 2·2 mm
Carapace Brown with darker mark behind head and dark margins.
Abdomen Pale brown with distinctive dark-brown cardiac mark, usually followed by several flattened chevrons. Small dark mark on sides anteriorly.
Habitat On trunks and lower foliage of conifers. Occurs at greater height above ground than most *Lepthyphantes* sp. **Season** Early autumn. **Distribution** In Britain common locally in Scotland, Yorkshire, Cumbria, Northumberland. Widespread in Europe.

Pityohyphantes phrygianus (C. L. Koch)
Size female c. 5 mm; male 4·5 mm
Carapace Pale with darker border posteriorly and black median band divided by thin light stripe on head. **Abdomen** Superficially like *Linyphia (Neriene) peltata* but median band has many deep cuts which meet darker midline. **Legs** Coloured as carapace with some annulations and ventral spots on all femora. With many long spines.
Habitat Lower foliage of conifers. **Season** In Europe adults in early summer. In Britain in early spring and other times of year. **Distribution** In Britain recently found in Roxburgh, Peebles, Northumberland, and Yorkshire. Widespread in Europe and North America.

♂
epthyphantes
ricaeus

♀
epthyphantes
xpunctus

♀
ityohyphantes
hrygianus

Floronia bucculenta (Clerck)

Size female 4 mm; male 4 mm

In field, slightly resembles _Linyphia triangularis_, except that body is much shorter.

Female Carapace Pale grey with darker submarginal bands. **Abdomen** Very high in profile, pointed at spinners. Dorsally dull reddish brown with numerous white spots; these contract and almost disappear if spider is knocked off web. Posteriorly with some black blotches. Sides with black loops. **Legs** Long and rather thin. Greyish brown with many spines. Faintly darkened at apex of each segment. **Male** Like female. **Carapace** Head is raised broadly in front with many long forward-directed hairs in ocular region. **Abdomen** Flatter than female.

Habitat Bushes and low vegetation in damp places. Sheet web has no superstructure, can be quite large. **Season** Late summer and autumn. **Distribution** Widespread but very local in Britain. Widespread in Europe.

Genus _Linyphia (Neriene, Microlinyphia, Frontinellina)_

All the members of this genus make similar webs, except for _L. marginata_ which makes a web with some features of a _Theridion_ design. The typical web consists of a horizontal sheet under which the spider runs. Above there are numerous strands which support the web to nearby vegetation, and below a rough barrier sheet is often made, giving the spider some protection from attack from below. Flying prey is stopped by the barrage lines and then drops to the sheet where it is bitten by the spider and pulled through the web to be eaten. It is not wrapped in silk as in other families. If the spiders are disturbed, they run to the edge of their webs, sometimes dropping down to the ground. It is probable that the more aerial species descend to lower vegetation to deposit their eggs in a sac, because the young are often found at lower levels than the adults.

Carapace This is oval and glabrous with the head protruding. **Eyes** These occur on black spots and are rather widely set. The disposition and relative sizes of the eyes are similar to the Araneidae. **Abdomen** It is oval with a dorsal and mesal pattern. The male often has a rather tubular abdomen with a constriction at the mid-point. The males of _Linyphia peltata, L. marginata,_ and _L. emphana_ have a similar pattern to the females; _L. triangularis, L. clathrata,_ and _L. montana_ males are darker than the females, and the last two have white blotches at the sides. The remaining species have very dark males, with the pattern totally absent and two anterior white marks. In general, the females can be easily identified by the abdominal pattern while the males can best be identified when they share the female's web.

The biology of the Linyphiinae resembles that of the Erigoninae.

♀
Floronia
bucculenta

Linyphia triangularis (Clerck)
Size female 6 mm; male 5 mm
Carapace Pale brown with darker submarginal bands and forked median band. **Abdomen** White with speckled brown median band with darker, deeply dentate edges. Sides are dark with several light oblique streaks. Ventrally dark. **Legs** Greyish brown with many long spines.
Habitat Truly ubiquitous. Web at almost any height up to 6 m or more on trees, or at more comfortable heights on plants and bushes. **Season** Late summer and autumn. **Distribution** Very abundant and widespread throughout.

♀
Linyphia
triangularis

Linyphia (Neriene) montana (Clerck)

Size female 6 mm; male 4 mm
Carapace Dark brown with darker margins and midline. **Abdomen** With broad brown folium having small indentations, surrounded by small light region. Anteriorly with black line on sides. **Legs** Yellow-brown with many narrow annulations.
Habitat Strong web, somewhat like *Tegenaria* (but lacking tubular retreat) under logs, in bushes, etc. **Season** Early summer. **Distribution** Widespread in Britain, and common if rather local. Widespread in Europe.

Linyphia hortensis Sundevall

Size female c. 5 mm; Male c. 4 mm
Carapace Very dark brown. **Abdomen** Dark purplish-brown folium broad with round lobes. Edged in white with black band which surrounds dorsal surface. Below this, at sides, is further white band. Ventrally dark brown. **Legs** Pale yellow-brown, unmarked.
Habitat Low vegetation in woods, etc. **Season** Early summer. **Distribution** Rather local but common throughout Britain. Widespread in Europe.

Linyphia (Neriene) clathrata Sundevall

Size female 5 mm; male 4 mm
Female Carapace Dark brown. **Abdomen** Wide brown folium has darker, slightly dentate edges; within this is number of darker chevrons, sometimes appearing as w-shaped lines. Sometimes with faint white patches outside folium. **Legs** Brown. **Male** Carapace More elongated. **Abdomen** Usually much darker than female with two white patches anteriorly. In thin or old specimens constriction occurs half-way, giving ant-like appearance.
Habitat Low vegetation often in shaded places. **Season** Adults at all times of year. **Distribution** Very common and widespread in Britain. Found throughout Europe and North America.

♀
Linyphia (Neriene)
montana with egg
sac

♀
Linyphia hortensis

♀
Linyphia (Neriene)
clathrata

Linyphia (Neriene) furtiva O.P.-Cambridge
Size female 4 mm; male 3·5 mm
Resembles closely *L. (N.) clathrata*.
Abdomen Folium broader and darker than *L. (N.) clathrata* with diffused black bars, never sinuous. Sides with clear shining blotches.
Legs General colour as *L. (N.) clathrata* but with femora I, II (to lesser extent III, IV also) darkened ventrally. **Male** Resembles male *L. (N.) clathrata*.
Habitat Heather etc in dry places exposed to sun. **Season** Summer.
Distribution Local but sometimes numerous in southern Britain. Widespread in Europe.

Linyphia (Neriene) peltata Wider
Size female 4 mm; male 2·75 mm
Carapace Reddish brown with dark-brown median band broadening to cover head. **Abdomen** Folium narrow with undulating edges. Broader and darker posteriorly. Sides have broad dark band. **Legs** Pale brown, unmarked.
Habitat Bushes and lower foliage of trees. **Season** Early summer.
Distribution Very common throughout Britain especially in south. Widespread in Europe.

Microlinyphia pusilla (Sundevall)
Size female c. 5 mm; male 3·5 mm
Carapace Black. **Abdomen** Dorsal region surrounded by thick, black line; within this is white area and black folium sometimes looking like overlapping triangles, sometimes reduced to thick line with very faint oblique lines. **Legs** Pale brown. **Male** Dark brown. **Abdomen** With two white patches on anterior.
Habitat Low vegetation, sometimes in damp places. **Season** Early summer. **Distribution** Fairly common over nearly all of Britain. Widespread in Europe and North America.

♂
Microlinyphia pusilla

♀
Linyphia (Neriene)
furtiva

♀
Linyphia (Neriene)
peltata

♀
Microlinyphia
pusilla

Frontinellina frutetorum (C. L. Koch)

Size female 5 mm; male 5 mm

Dorsally similar to *L. peltata* and *M. pusilla*.

Abdomen Rather high in profile, sharply truncated behind. Folium black, and similar in shape to *L. peltata*. Sides punctuated by two or three yellowish vertical lines, and white one on each side of black patch above spinners; this patch has several white spots within it. **Male** Resembles males of *L. peltata* and *M. pusilla*.

Habitat Bushes about 1 m above ground. **Season** Early summer. **Distribution** Absent from Britain. Absent from west and north of region. Belgium and to south and east.

Linyphia (Neriene) marginata (C. L. Koch)

Size female c. 5 mm; male c. 5 mm

Carapace Brown with very light margins; head dark brown. **Abdomen** With thin dark folium very like *F. frutetorum* but containing several pairs of white dots. Sides have dark horizontal line anteriorly, followed by three vertical white lines posteriorly. Ventrally with black almost parallel-sided median band surrounded by three bright-yellow subtriangular patches. **Legs** Long and thin. Femora colourless but darkened apically on I, II; remaining segments dark grey. **Male** Virtually identical to female but slimmer.

Habitat Bushes about 1 m above ground. Unique web has domed shape, and is not two-dimensional sheet but composed of thin three-dimensional lattice of very fine threads which reflect spectrum of pure colours in sunlight. **Season** Early summer. **Distribution** Very local in few Scottish counties, absent from rest of Britain. Widespread throughout Europe and North America.

Microlinyphia impigra (O.P.-Cambridge)

Size female 5 mm; male 4 mm

Female Carapace Greyish brown with dark median band broadening to cover head. Margins with short dark streaks. **Abdomen** White dorsally with irregular cardiac mark followed in posterior half by two rows of triangular marks. Sides white or grey, ventrally black. **Legs** Light greyish brown. **Male Carapace** Dark reddish brown. **Abdomen** Very dark brown with two white patches anteriorly. **Legs** Reddish brown.

Habitat Low vegetation in marshes, lake sides, etc. **Season** Early summer and later in some localities. **Distribution** Local and scattered in Britain. Absent from Belgium, Scandinavia. Local but widespread elsewhere.

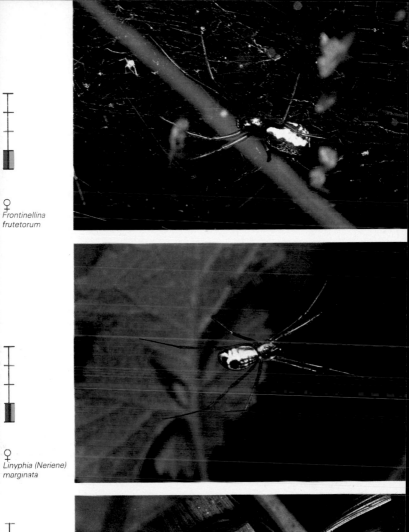

♀
Frontinellina
frutetorum

♀
Linyphia (Neriene)
marginata

♀
Microlinyphia
impigra

Linyphia (Neriene) emphana Walckenaer
Size female c. 6 mm; male 5 mm
Female Carapace Pale greyish brown with darker margins. Head light brown. **Abdomen** White with thin dark cardiac mark followed by three short, black transverse bars. Sides streaked with grey lines. Ventrally greyish. **Legs** Pale grey. **Male** Slimmer than female but with similar markings. Ventrally with swollen epigastric region like some members of genus *Theridion*. **Palps** Very dark.
Habitat Web on lower foliage of trees, 2 m and above. **Season** Summer. **Distribution** Absent from Britain, Scandinavia. Widespread elsewhere.

ORDER OPILIONES THE HARVESTMEN

This, the third largest order of the Arachnida is also known as the Phalangida. Commonly, they are known as harvestmen or harvest spiders although they are not true spiders. The order contains about 3500 species, many of which are tropical. North-west Europe has twenty-seven native species which are distinguished from the other arachnid orders by their oval bodies, the prosoma and opisthosoma being broadly joined, and the presence of a pair of odiferous glands on the sides of the prosoma but no poison glands. The legs are characteristically long with the tarsi further segmented, giving them great flexibility. In the short-legged species this feature is much reduced. There are two dark eyes, normally set facing sideways in the vertical plane on a conspicuous tubercle.

Many tropical harvestmen are armed with large, pointed tubercles on the body, chelicerae, legs, and pedipalps. A few species of harvestmen from the region under consideration have these on a much reduced scale, and the terminology is as follows: 'spines' are steeply conical tubercles arising from the surface and formed of similar cuticle – they form the trident of the subfamily Oligolophinae; 'denticles' are smaller conical tubercles, about as high as they are wide at the base – these occur in transverse rows on the abdomen of many species; 'setae' are similar to the spines as described for spiders but shorter – they cover the legs and are found arising from the apices of the denticles and the cuticular spines in some cases.

The prosoma is covered dorsally by a carapace; this has, in the mid-line, a broad, ocular tubercle, the ocularium, which carries the pair of simple eyes. In the Trogulidae, the tubercle is flattened or absent and the eyes are noticeably small. In front of the ocularium there are often a number of shallow denticles but, in the subfamily Oligolophinae, three or more of these are enlarged to form conspicuous spines. This 'trident' is just visible with a hand-lens and is useful in separating the species of the subfamily.

♀
*Linyphia (Neriene)
emphana*

The junction between the carapace and the abdomen is very difficult to see in many species, and is often covered by a dark band which runs from the head to the posterior part of the abdomen. This band is known as the 'saddle'. Its shape is a useful character for distinguishing between the species but it should be considered in conjunction with other features, because it is somewhat variable even within a species. On the rear margin of the abdomen is the single excretory pore, the anus. There are no abdominal appendages. On the ventral side of the abdomen, which is usually light in colour, small darker spots occur in some species, but these have not been used for identification purposes here.

On the ventral side of the prosoma are the elongated coxae. Between them, there is no visible sternum, but the 'genital operculum or plate'. In the immature or nymphal stages, this plate is fused to the surrounding tissue; in the adults the anterior end is separated, but visibly not to any great degree. Consequently, it is difficult to differentiate adults from subadults in the field. In many species the two sexes are remarkably similar although the males tend to be

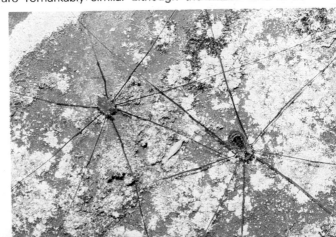

♂ and ♀
*Leiobunum
rotundum*

smaller and darker bodily, with legs of equal or greater length than in the females. Unlike most other arachnids, there is no courtship, and insemination of the female is direct and takes place with the two animals facing each other. The male has a penis which can extrude forwards from under the genital plate. It is passed between the chelicerae of the female and into the oviduct. Mating lasts from a few seconds to several minutes depending on the species and may be repeated at frequent intervals, in fact, whenever the sexes meet. The female has a corresponding extensible ovipositor, normally concealed below the genital plate. This is of great length in some species and enables the female to deposit her eggs in inaccessible and usually damp places.

The legs of harvestmen have the same segments as are found in spiders: coxa, trochanter, femur, patella, tibia, metatarsus, and tarsus. The tarsus is further subdivided, minimally in the family Trogulidae, but to a considerable extent in the other families, and this apical segment is extremely flexible. Among the spiders only the pholcids (page 68) have this feature. The coxae and trochanters have denticles and spines in some species. *Megabunus diadema* has pairs of spines on the femora and patellae, but, in the other species, the remaining segments are without much armament, although the legs are usually covered to a greater or lesser extent with setae and small denticles. Most members of the European family Phalangiidae have five-sided patellae and tibiae rather than round and the ridges usually have a row of fine setae. This 'angled' segment varies in degree and, in *Dicranopalpus ramosus*, only the patellae are at all angled, and then only very weakly.

In the Trogulidae the legs are scarcely longer than the body whereas, in *Leiobunum* species, they are ten times as long in the males. In spite of these variations, the order of length is constant in all the species described here viz II, IV, III, I. The first leg is the shortest, the second leg is the longest of all (twice as long as leg I in many species). Leg II is used to explore the substrate ahead of the harvestman in the same way that insects use the antennae. A harvestman which loses both these legs shows a marked lack of enthusiasm for eating, drinking, or mating which suggests that these legs are sensory organs as well as ambulatory ones. In spite of the ease with which harvestmen lose their legs, they are not regenerated as they are in spiders and other arachnids. Old specimens rarely have the full complement of legs.

The pedipalps, like those of spiders, are six segmented. In the Trogulidae, they are very small but, in the species *Mitostoma chrysomelas chrysomelas*, the pedipalps are considerably longer than the body, and densely covered in 'viscid setae'. These are also known as 'clubbed setae'. They consist of a normal seta, but the point is covered with a drop of viscous fluid. These viscid setae are only

*Megabunus
diadema* showing
ocularium

ound on the pedipalps and, presumably, are used for the capture or
retention of prey. On other species they occur on the inner side of
the limb and on the apophyses. The patella of the pedipalp bears the
largest apophysis and, in *Dicranopalpus*, this is almost equal to the
length of the tibia. *Rilaena* has a shorter, stouter extension on the
patella and a second smaller one on the tibia. Several other species
have small lumps in these places.

The systematics of the Opiliones are based on the relative lengths
of the tibia and tarsus of the pedipalp, whether or not a terminal claw
is present, and the presence or absence of teeth on this claw. These
features are difficult, if not impossible, to see in the field and they
have not been used here.

The remaining appendages of the prosoma are the chelicerae.
These differ from those of spiders in not containing or delivering
poison, and in their overall form. They consist of three segments: a
basal segment which lies in the plane parallel to the harvestman's
body and which is visible from above in all but the Trogulidae where
it is covered by the hood; the second segment is articulated at
right-angles to the first and, in the male *Phalangium opilio*, it has a
large pointed tubercle at its base; this second segment culminates
in a large dark tooth against which the third segment, a movable
tooth, forms a pincer. Behind the chelicerae lies the mouth.

Harvestmen are omnivorous. They will catch and eat smaller invertebrates and feed on the remains of any dead animals they find.
They will feed on bird droppings and various vegetable material such
as fungi, lepidopterists' 'sugar', and they have even been seen eating
marmalade! Trogulids are reported to feed on small snails.

In spite of their nocturnal habits, harvestmen can be found in the
same places as spiders; the smaller species occur in leaf litter and
moss. They shelter under stones, logs, and among low vegetation in
a variety of places. Several species occur on trees and can be dis-

covered by beating. To examine the majority of the species described they can be coaxed into glass tubes of between 10 and 25 millimetres diameter.

Because of the small number of species represented in the region as well as the basis for the division into families and genera, a key is impracticable for field identification. Several of the species are so distinctive that they cannot be confused with any other and, for species where confusion is likely to arise, they have been placed close together in the guide for direct comparison.

Family Trogulidae

Trogulus tricarinatus (Linnaeus)
Size female and male 7–9 mm; leg II 8 mm
Similar to *A. cambridgei* except in size, but much rarer. **Body** Flattened. **Legs** Tarsi are black; I, II with two segments, III, IV with three. **Habitat** As *A. cambridgei*. **Season** Adults all year, nymphs in early spring and autumn. **Distribution** Rare in Britain; confined to more southern counties. Very widespread elsewhere including North America.

Anelasmocephalus cambridgei (Westwood)
Size female and male 3·5 mm; leg II 3·8 mm
Body Purplish but covered with earth in adults. Eyes close to front margin, immediately behind hood which covers chelicerae and pedipalps. Abdomen is elongated and broadest about middle. **Legs** Uniformly coloured (also coated with earth), and densely covered with short curved spines and setae. Tarsi I, II with three segments, III, IV with four.
Habitat Leaf litter and other detritus. Most often on chalk. **Season** Adults all year, nymphs in autumn. **Distribution** Uncommon in Britain but most frequent in southern counties; as far north as Yorkshire. Very widespread elsewhere.

Family Nemastomatidae

Nemastoma bimaculatum (Fabricius)
Size female and male c. 2·5 mm; leg II 6 mm
Body Matt black with two rectangular patches of pale gold colour at junction of head and abdomen. Rare variety *N.b. unicolor* lacks these marks. Posterior segments glossier. Eyes widely set on low ocularium. **Legs** Of moderate length and thin. Apical two segments brownish.
Habitat Under stones, logs, etc. **Season** Adults all year, nymphs in summer and early autumn. **Distribution** Fairly common and widespread throughout.

Anelasmo-cephalus cambridgei

Nemastoma bimaculatum

Mitostoma chrysomelas (Hermann)
Size female and male c. 3 mm; leg II 7 mm
Body Broadest posteriorly; brownish with golden transverse lines, two oblique pairs at front of abdomen, one pair posteriorly. Lines of denticles follow segments. Eyes close to front margin on low ocularium. Legs Fairly long and thin with apical ends of femora and tibiae pale; femora have obscure paler rings. Pedipalps Longer than body and thickly covered with viscid setae on all longer segments.
Habitat In moss, under stones, logs, etc. Sometimes several together. Season Early spring to winter. Nymphs in late winter. Distribution Rather uncommon but widely found in Britain and Europe.

Family Phalangiidae

SUBFAMILY SCLEROSOMATINAE

Homalenotus quadridentatus (Cuvier)
Size female and male c. 5 mm; leg II 12 mm
Body Oval; pale brown with many darker blotches. Carapace semi-circular, with dark border containing light spots. Conspicuous single spine on front margin. Low ocularium lies behind this, at mid-point. Four rows of denticles lie on abdomen, medians set closely, especially anteriorly. Four longer denticles lie on posterior margin. Legs With many denticles on femora, patellae, and tibiae.
Habitat Most common on chalk; under stones etc, and in moss. Season All year. Distribution Nymphs more common than adults. In Britain recorded from southern half of England and one Scottish county. Widespread but uncommon elsewhere.

SUBFAMILY OLIGOLOPHINAE

Dicranopalpus ramosus (Simon)
Size female 4–6 mm; male 3–4 mm; leg II c. 50 mm
Body Greyish brown. Ocularium distinct, eyes set fairly widely. Abdomen has dark transverse line in front half, with pale median area edged with dark patches and lighter spots and bars. Posteriorly with large, blunt tubercle. Markings clearer in male. Legs Very long and, typically, held straight and together, covering small angle. Pale yellow-brown with darker blotches and spots. Pedipalps Equal in length to body, with long apophysis on patella; in male this is half to two-thirds length of tibiae; in female almost equalling it.
Habitat Gardens, on bushes and walls; also indoors. Season Early autumn. Distribution Mediterranean species, in Britain found rarely in Cornwall, Hampshire, Sussex, Essex.

Mitostoma chrysomelas

Homalenotus quadridentatus

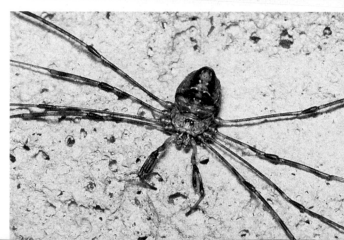

♀ *Dicranopalpus ramosus*

Mitopus morio (Fabricius)

Size female 4–8 mm; male 5–6 mm; leg II 30–40 mm
Female Body About twice as long as wide. Ocularium nearer posterior edge of carapace. No denticles under front margin, cf *Phalangium opilio*. Saddle very variable in depth of colour, dark brown on light background or whole dorsum is uniformly brown. Broadest on carapace with angular widening on front of abdomen, and smaller posterior thickening. **Legs** Long; pale brown with darker blotches; patellae and tibiae angled. **Male Body** Rather rectangular, about 50 per cent longer than wide. Saddle black, similar in shape to female but with most of abdomen dark grey with lighter spots at sides. **Legs** Similar to female but with more pronounced setae.
Habitat Among low vegetation principally, but also in bushes and on trees. **Season** Summer to late autumn. **Distribution** Very common and widespread in Europe and North America.

Mitopus ericaeus (Jennings)

Similar in pattern to *M. morio* but larger, darker, and with longer legs.
Distribution Hills in northern England.

Oligolophus tridens (C. L. Koch)

Size female c. 6 mm; male c. 5 mm; leg II 15 mm
Body About twice as long as wide. Brownish with black saddle, truncated posteriorly; triangular on carapace but with almost parallel sides on abdomen. Whole dorsal surface is matt with fine texture. **Trident** With three long, upright, subequal spines. **Legs** Moderate length. Femora, patellae, and tibiae angled. All segments with rows of small black spines.
Habitat Low vegetation in woods, occasionally on trees. **Season** Late summer to late autumn. **Distribution** Common and widespread throughout.

Oligolophus hanseni (Kraepelin)

Size female 6 mm; male 4 mm; leg II 19 mm
Body Dark greyish brown; about twice as long as wide. With rows of transverse lighter denticles on abdomen. Ocularium dark. Saddle very faint. Ventrally genital plate not notched (cf *O. agrestis*). **Trident** Three to five broad denticles set at 45 degrees, with several smaller ones behind. **Legs** Moderate length. Very dark with few lighter blotches. Patellae and tibiae lightly angled.
Habitat Mainly pines but occasionally other trees. **Season** Early to mid-autumn. **Distribution** Uncommon and local in Britain, Germany, Denmark.

♀
Mitopus morio
with mites

Oligolophus tridens

Oligolophus hanseni

Paroligolophus agrestis (Meade)

Size female c. 6 mm; male c. 4 mm; leg II 14–20 mm
Body Greyish to reddish brown with median line of light dots. Ocularium light. On posterior abdomen is pair of light transverse lines. Ventrally genital plate notched, conspicuously in female. **Trident** Three rather blunt denticles, middle one longest; one or two smaller denticles behind. **Legs** Moderately long. Patellae and tibiae angled.
Habitat Trees but also in ground-layer. **Season** Summer to autumn.
Distribution Often abundant and widespread throughout.

Paroligolophus meadii (O.P.-Cambridge)

Size female 4 mm; male 3 mm; leg II 17 mm
Body Pale yellow-brown with pairs of brown spots and transverse rows of very small denticles on abdomen. **Trident** Three denticles, central one about twice as long as outers. **Legs** Coloured as body, slightly darker towards extremities. Patellae and tibiae angled.
Habitat Sometimes in dry habitats, sandy heaths, or dunes. Also under long grass in meadows. **Season** Summer to late autumn.
Distribution Very local and scattered in England.

Odiellus spinosus (Bosc)

Size female c. 10 mm; male c. 8 mm; leg II 23 mm
Body Grey to greyish brown. Very broad. Saddle fairly thin, of uneven width, but darkest posteriorly where it is truncated sharply. With transverse rows of small denticles. Ocularium light with pale line extending forwards to trident. **Trident** Three divergent stout denticles. **Legs** Rather short and stout. Variable in markings but tending to be rather pale. Patellae and tibiae strongly angled.
Habitat In gardens, occupying walls at night. **Season** Early to late autumn. **Distribution** In Britain widespread in southern half of England with record for north Wales. Sometimes very common locally. Recorded from France, Germany.

Lacinius ephippiatus (C. L. Koch)

Size female c. 6 mm; male 4 mm; leg II 12 mm
Body Same shaped saddle as *O. spinosus* but is smaller with much shorter legs. **Legs** Femora, patellae, and tibiae darkened apically. Femora, tibiae, metatarsus strongly angled.
Habitat Low vegetation in woods and marshes. **Season** Early summer to early autumn. **Distribution** Uncommon but widespread in Britain. France, Germany, Finland.

Lacinius horridus (Panzer)

Size female 9 mm; male 7 mm; leg II 29 mm female; 16 mm male
Body With transverse rows of denticles on abdomen.
Distribution Absent from Britain. Widespread in Europe.

Paroligolophus
agrestis

Paroligolophus
headii

Odiellus spinosus

SUBFAMILY PHALANGIINAE

Lophopilio palpinalis (Herbst)
Size female 5 mm; male 3·5 mm; leg II 35 mm
Similar in general appearance to *O. spinosus* but much smaller.
Body Ocularium with two rows of four or five conspicuous denticles
Legs Longer than *O. spinosus* and pedipalps with following ventra
armature: trochanters with two robust denticles; femora with up t
seven thin denticles; tibiae with one or two. Femora have small blur
apophysis apically.
Habitat Low vegetation in open woods. **Season** Summer to autumr
Distribution Uncommon but widespread in Britain and centra
Europe.

Phalangium opilio (Linnaeus)
Size female 6–9 mm; male 4–7 mm; leg II 38 mm female; 54 mr
male
Female Body Similar in markings and with same variations as *Mitc
pus morio*. Saddle has three 'lobes' on the carapace, fore, and rea
abdomen; usually with row of elongated spots in median line. Belov
front margin of carapace are two pale denticles, a feature unique t
P. opilio. Ocularium light with two rows of small denticles leading t
front margin. **Legs** Pale with very few small dark spots. Femora wit
many black-tipped denticles. **Male** Similar to female but generall
less clearly marked. Distinguished from any other European specie
by forward-pointing 'horn' on second segment of chelicerae. In som
specimens this excrescence is as long as body.
Habitat Low vegetation in woods, dunes, heaths, etc. **Season** Sum
mer to early winter. **Distribution** Very common and widesprea
throughout.

Opilio parietinus (Degeer)
Size female 8 mm; male 7·5 mm; leg II 44 mm
Body Saddle very obscure, abdominal pattern mainly consisting c
dark sinuous, transverse bars; rows of white denticles tend to follov
these bars, and not run in straight lines. Two rows of white denticle
on rear third of carapace. Ocularium light and there is row of sma
white patches running down median line. **Legs** Pale yellow-brow
with darker marks. Femora and tibiae faintly angled.
Habitat Gardens and woods. **Season** Early to late autumn. **Distr
bution** Fairly common and widespread throughout. Also found
North America.

♀
Phalangium opilio

♂
Phalangium opilio

Opilio perietinus

Opilio saxatilis (C. L. Koch)

Size female 5 mm; male 4·5 mm; leg II 23 mm
Body Similar to *O. parietinus* but smaller. Dorsal markings more obscure except for median row of light spots which are more conspicuous; in females these often form median line. **Legs** Pale and darkened apically on femora and tibiae; these segments faintly angled.
Habitat Most frequent on sand-dunes but also found in low vegetation elsewhere. **Season** Autumn. **Distribution** Common and widespread throughout.

Rilaena triangularis (Herbst)

Size female 6 mm; male 4 mm; leg II 35 mm
Body Pale brown with darker saddle, truncated and darker posteriorly. Sometimes almost uniformly brown. Ocularium larger than in any other species in the region, and eyes more widely spaced. **Legs** Usually unmarked. **Chelicerae** With small apophysis on front side of second segment in male. **Pedipalps** With two conspicuous apophyses, one on each patella, and smaller one on tibiae. Thickly covered with short viscid setae.
Habitat Low vegetation in woods. **Season** Spring to midsummer. **Distribution** Common and widespread throughout.

Megabunus diadema (Fabricius)

Size female 4·5 mm; male 3 mm; leg II 35 mm
Body Often with speckled appearance; saddle similar in shape to *Phalangium opilio*. Lighter areas sometimes greenish. Ocularium large with enormous spines set around eyes like long lashes. Front margin of carapace carries single thin spine; sides have two further spines. **Legs** Fairly long and thin; joints lighter and apices of all but tarsi darkened; femora and patellae with pair of light spines darkened at tips. **Pedipalps** Femora with strong black-tipped spines. Patellae with large apophysis apically; tibiae with a smaller one; both thickly covered on inner side with viscid setae.
Habitat On lichen-covered tree trunks and logs, especially in damp woods. Also moss, heather, sand-dunes. **Season** Spring to late autumn. **Distribution** Rather local, but then sometimes numerous. Widespread in Britain. Coastal habitats in France, Norway, Denmark.

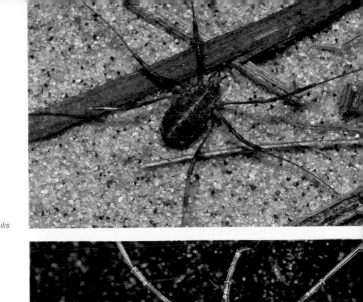

Opilio saxatilis

Rilaena triangularis

Megabunus diadema

Leiobunum rotundum (Latreille)

Size female 6 mm; male 3·5 mm; leg II 58 mm
Female Body Light brown with darker patches behind ocularium and on sides of abdomen. Dark-brown patch in front of eyes and straight-sided, dark-brown saddle, rather wider posteriorly. Eyes have dark rings surrounding them (cf *L. blackwalli*) with lighter median ring. Legs Basally and apically brown, black on middle segments. Pedipalps Darkened on patellae and tibiae. **Male** Body Reddish brown, slightly darker on abdomen. Ocularium often totally black. Legs and Pedipalps Coloured as female.
Habitat Ubiquitous. **Season** Midsummer to late autumn. **Distribution** Widespread and very common throughout.

Leiobunum blackwalli Meade

Size female 6 mm; male 3–4 mm; leg II 50 mm
Female Body Broader posteriorly than *L. rotundum*, the saddle shorter and more triangular. Ocularium golden with thin dark median ring (cf *L. rotundum*). Ocularium has dark surrounding blotches, anteriorly with lighter median patch. Legs Slightly lighter than *L. rotundum*. Pedipalps Almost uniformly pale. **Male** Body Similar to female *L. rotundum*. Ocularium as in female with light rings surrounding eyes. Ventrally, genital plate has two small dark spots about midway. Legs and Pedipalps As female.
Habitat Mainly in woods or in damp places. **Season** Midsummer to late autumn. **Distribution** Much less common than *L. rotundum* but almost equally widespread throughout.

Leiobunum rupestre (Herbst)

Size female 7 mm; male 5 mm; leg II 75 mm
Female Body With broad dark saddle with lighter edges and with dark posterior spots. Carapace dark with two small light spots on front margin. **Male** Body Dorsally very dark with lighter border. Legs Similar to *L. blackwalli* but with femora having rows of small denticles and tibiae I, III, IV with a few denticles.
Habitat Low vegetation. **Season** Early autumn. **Distribution** Absent from Britain. Mountains in France, Germany, Finland.

♀
*Leiobunum
rotundum*

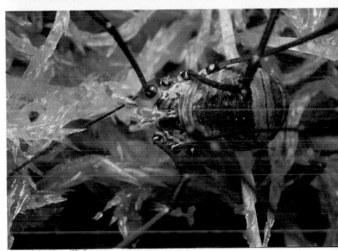

♀
*Leiobunum
blackwalli*

Nelima gothica (Simon)

Size female 3·5 mm; male 2·5 mm; leg II 50 mm
Body Pale yellow-brown with silvery patches. Abdomen has transverse lines of white spots and pairs of darker blotches. Ocularium silvery with dark rings around eyes; surrounded by darker flecks with three clear ones in front. **Legs** Light yellow. I, III, IV slightly shorter than *Leiobunum* spp; femora, patellae, tibiae brownish with lighter apical rings. **Pedipalps** Femora to tibiae brownish; other segments pale yellow.
Habitat Low vegetation and under logs, stones, etc. Also cellars and around buildings. **Season** Early autumn. **Distribution** Very local and scattered in Britain. France and Mediterranean area.

Further reading

Bristowe W.S., *Comity of Spiders*. Ray Society, London, volume I, 1939, volume II 1941.

Bristowe W.S. *The World of Spiders*. Collins New Naturalist, London, 1958.

Foelix R. F., *Biology of Spiders*. Harvard University Press, London, 1982.

Hubert M., *Les Araignées*. Boubée, Paris, 1979

Levi H.W. and Levi L.R., *Spiders and their Kin*. Golden Press, New York, 1968.

Locket G. H. and Millidge A.F., *British Spiders* Ray Society, London, volume I 1951, volume II 1953. Reprinted as one volume in 1975.

Locket G. H., Millidge A. F., and Merrett P., *British Spiders* Ray Society, London, volume III 1974.

Murphy, F., *Keeping Spiders, Insects and other Land Invertebrates in Captivity*. Bartholomew, Edinburgh, 1980.

Planet L., *Histoire Naturelle de la France 14. Araignées*, 1905. Republished by Editions Sciences Nat, Compiègne, 1978.

Sankey J. H. P. and Savory T.H., *British Harvestmen*. Linnean Society, London, 1974.

Stern H. and Kullman E., *Leben am seidenen Faden*. Bertelsmann, Munich, 1975.

Witt P.N. and Rovner J.S., *Spider Communication*, Princeton University Press, New Jersey, 1982.

Equipment suppliers and societies

Most of the equipment mentioned in this guide can be purchased from Watkins and Doncaster, The Naturalists, Four Throws, Hawkhurst, Kent, and a catalogue is available from them.

The Field Studies Council organize field courses on spiders which are led by various members of the British Arachnological Society. The BAS is well worth joining for anyone becoming seriously interested in spiders, harvestmen, pseudoscorpions, or scorpions; it publishes a *Bulletin* and the *Secretary's Newsletter* which contain up-to-date information on the distribution and ecology of arachnids. Both these publications are issued three times a year. Further details may be obtained from Dr P. Selden, Membership Secretary, British Arachnological Society, Department of Extra Mural Studies, University of Manchester, Manchester M13 9PL, England.

Line drawings by Mandy Holloway

All of the line drawings have been prepared especially for this guide. Among the reference material that has been drawn upon by the artist are the specialist and other books that have been mentioned in the 'Further reading'. The author, artist, and publishers acknowledge gratefully the invaluable assistance which these volumes have been.